Publication Design Workbook

ROCKPORT

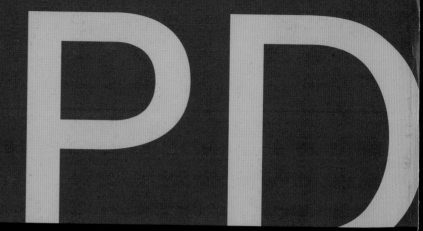

First published in the United States of America by
Rockport Publishers, a member of
Quayside Publishing Group
100 Cummings Center
Suite 406-L
Beverly, MA 01915-6101

978.282.9590 *Telephone*
978.283.2742 *Fax*
www.rockpub.com

Library of Congress Cataloging-in-Publication Data
Samara, Timothy.
    Publication design workbook : a real-world design guide / Timothy
Samara.
        p.   cm.
    Includes bibliographical references and index.
    ISBN 1-59253-170-9 (hardcover)
    1. Graphic design (Typography) 2. Layout (Printing) 3.
Newsletters   Design. 4. Magazine design. 5. Newspaper layout and
typography. I. Title.
Z246.S233 2005   2005007140
  686.2'252—dc22   CIP

ISBN-13: 978-1-59253-397-8
ISBN-10: 1-59253-397-3

10 9 8 7 6 5 4 3 2

Cover and text design: Timothy Samara
Cover Photograph: Allan Penn Photography

Printed in China

W

Publication
Design
Workbook

Magazines
Newspapers
Catalogs
Annual Reports
Newsletters
Literature
Systems—
and Everything
in Between

A Real-World Design Guide

Timothy Samara

BEVERLY MASSACHUSETTS

ROCKPORT PUBLISHERS

contents

01

Publications in Action

A Showcase of Real-World Projects

Magazines
Periodical Publications, from Glossy Consumer Rags
to Cultural and Institutional Organs

Literature Systems
Corporate and Nonprofit Branding Systems:
Brochure Families, Mailers, and Serial Literature

Newsletters
Monthly and Quarterly Small-Format News Organs
from Corporations and Cultural Institutions

Annual Reports
Image- and Message-Driven Financial Statements
and Organizational Status Reports

Catalogs
Product and Service Offerings in Print, from Hardware
and Art School Courses to Performance and Fashion

Newspapers
Dailies, Weeklies, Tabloids, and Supplements

Printing for the People
From Gutenberg to the New Millennium

As recently as 1995, a notable graphic designer declared that print was dead: the digital age! The Internet! The PDF! It seemed that the paperless vision of the future was upon us. A decade later now, in the early years of the twenty-first century, this daring forecast appears to have been a bit premature. Walk down a city street—large or small. Run through an airport or cruise down the aisle at the supermarket. At any given moment, you will encounter a rack—or ten—filled with magazines on every conceivable subject.

And not just one title in each subject, but twenty. Never mind the countless editions of daily newspapers in English, Spanish, Slovak, or Tagalog. Nor the myriad documents published by businesses and organizations—families of brochures and reports and newsletters and calendars and mailers . . . Millions of impressions of ink on paper are made every week, and public appetite for them seems insatiable. As consumers in an increasingly global community, we not only rely on a constant stream of information to tell us about the world we live in, we relish it. Subscribing to a particular cooking magazine, picking up the paper with coffee on the weekend, poring through an annual report to track our investments, looking at housewares in a slick catalog—publications draw us together as part of a larger community, even as they cater to our individual lifestyles. When we read a newspaper, we're connecting with people on the other side of town . . .

or the other side of the world. When we flip through a trendy fashion or music magazine, we're part of the in-crowd, elevated to the status of elite cultural insiders. And we understand that other people like us are reading and looking at the same things. Though we enjoy life as individuals, we are, after all, social animals—and we like to know that there are other individuals like ourselves.

Print offers other, more physical benefits. As dynamic and immediate as the Internet is, it lacks the tactile fun of flipping through pages. Images online are never as sharp as those printed on paper. The screen hurts your eyes after a while, and too much clicking leads to carpal tunnel syndrome. The technology is new and undeveloped (as ubiquitous as it is, it's been around for only twenty years) and has a ways to go. These limitations in the digital experience might change after another fifty or a hundred years, in much the same way that printed

communications did in the century after they exploded in popularity upon first being produced in the mid-1400s. But for now, the 600-year evolution of the printed page still trumps the blinking pixel any day of the week.

FORTY-TWO LINES THAT CHANGED THE WORLD

When historians talk about cultural paradigm shifts—extraordinary changes in the human condition—they usually include the development of printing among the top five (along with little things like the invention of the wheel). Today, it's difficult to imagine daily life without printed reading material. But prior to the fifteenth century, there was little to be read in the Western world, and not many people to read what little there was. Fewer than 50,000 volumes of writing existed in all of Europe, and those were accessible only to the very wealthy. Though a growing middle class of merchants and tradesmen—resulting from the collapse of feudalism and popular migration from countryside to town—were afforded the opportunity to study in universities, resources were scarce. In the thirteenth century, Cambridge University boasted only 122 manuscript books, inscribed by hand on vellum, sheets of dried sheepskin that were enormously expensive to produce. A single 200-page book had a value equal to a farm and

> Today, it's difficult to imagine daily life without printed reading material. But prior to the fifteenth century, there was little to be read in the western world, and not many people to read what little there was.

required four or five months for production. Still, demand for such books had been steadily rising, and teams of lettering specialists, illuminators (experts in decorative illustration using gold leaf and pigments), and binders tried to keep up. One factor aiding production was the introduction of papermaking to Europe from China—a 600-year process that spread from east to west through a series of invasions and migrations. The first known paper mill, in Fabriano, Italy, was established in 1276; another, in Troyes, France, appeared in 1348. Paper provided an inexpensive and rapidly produced substrate to replace vellum. Along with paper, the advent of wood-block printing also seems to have been carried from the East, although the history of its invention is cloudy.

Early manifestations of European printing—devotional images of saints and printed playing cards—demonstrated the potential for previously inaccessible things to become readily available to the mainstream, illiterate culture: card games, once the sole province of nobility, could now be enjoyed by farmers as well. In the late 1300s and early 1400s, block books printed from single wood-carvings containing both text and image became available on a wider basis. Eventually, a quest for quicker production methods was undertaken—notably in the Netherlands, Germany, Italy, and France. Woodworkers, as well as goldsmiths and other tradesmen, experimented with cutting the wood blocks apart to reuse the letters or cutting individual letters from steel or iron.

But most historical evidence credits a German inventor and goldsmith, Johann Gensfleisch zum Gutenberg, with adapting several technologies to make the leap to functional, movable type.

Punchcutting, mold making, alloying, casting, ink mixing, and press methods used for wine and cheese: by adjusting and integrating these technologies, Gutenberg was able to create a system for producing thousands of reusable, durable, and extraordinarily precise letters, and a way of transferring their image onto paper at a remarkable speed. His first project, a Bible printed in 1455—set in two columns to a page, with forty-two lines per column—was a watershed in communication technology that rivals the written word itself in its importance to modern culture. The ability to disseminate enormous quantities of information, rapidly and affordably, meant that ideas previously known only to a few could be disseminated to thousands. Printing helped standardize languages and unite regions of culturally similar people where, earlier, dialects and usage could vary wildly within even short geographical ranges.

Although Gutenberg's fortunes fell and rose—the financial burden of loans for research and development cost him custody of his first works—the effect of his discovery was profound. Within thirty years, presses had sprung up throughout Europe and publishing had become a major industry in Mainz, Ulm, Venice, London, and other cities. Along with moveable type, the invention of metal engraving added illustration to the typographic page. Broadsides—single sheets printed on one side—joined books as popular publications, initially spreading religious information but eventually evolving to include information of local interest

to communities. These sheets ultimately became the first newspapers. Publications on a wider variety of subject matter began to emerge: practical guides on art and mathematics; manuals for hunting and crafts; and stories for popular entertainment. As the middle class grew, the spread of publications increased literacy and provided comfort after the grueling workday.

Once the industrial revolution of the late 1700s mechanized the printing process, demand and supply fed each other in an endless cycle of production. The standard of living improved as a result of wage labor in factories; as wages were spent on material goods and more comfortable housing, the manufacturers of these goods employed more people to meet the demand. As early as the 1820s, catalogs for products began to appear. Journals of poetry and philosophy circulated among urban populations, the progenitors of the modern magazine.

In 1826, Joseph Niepce, a lithographer in France, sought a way to transfer images directly to a printing plate; in an experiment, he exposed an emulsified sheet of pewter to light and captured an image. Photography brought a new tonal dimension to the printed page, offering not only a means of showing

1

A sample of one of the early shop types—a printer's *textura* face derived from Sweyheim's and Pannartz's double alphabet of the 1460s—prevalent in Europe following Gutenberg's now-famous experiment of 1455.

2

How time flies! This web offset press (the *web* is the continuous stream of paper fed off the enormous roll in the foreground) pounds out up to 50,000 impressions every hour, a far cry from the weeks needed to produce twenty editions of a book in 1500.

The aspect of print that has saved it from its early death foretold is its archaic physical presence: the fact that it exists. The care that print designers take in crafting the printed object results in materials that will likely stay around for a while. Designers who work in print are making something.

products in catalogs as they really appeared, but also of recording and reproducing images from travel and other experiences. Through the end of the nineteenth century and into the early twentieth, publications of all kinds became a ubiquitous feature of everyday life.

The evolution of printing and imaging technology encouraged exploration of design ideas, just as designers influenced strategies for developing publication content and production. Lettering types became more and more rational and precise in their drawing. In the late 1460s, two German printers, Conrad Sweynheym and Arnold Pannartz, developed a double alphabet of capital and miniscule forms, basing their drawings on rediscovered Roman manuscripts written in Carolingian script. These Roman faces became the models for modern alphabet development. Further refined by designers such as John Baskerville in the 1600s and Francois Didot and Giambattista Bodoni in the 1700s, increasingly light, geometric, and brightly contrasting serif type forms became prevalent. Early modernists of the Arts and Crafts movement and Jugendstil, such as William Morris and Walter Crane of England, and Koloman Moser and Peter Behrens of Germany, began to conceive of the printed page as a space to be architecturally modeled around the information it contained.

Spatial organization, contrast, and asymmetry became hallmarks of twentieth-century design in Europe and, later, in America. In the 1930s, Paul Rand, sometimes called the grandfather of American graphic design, merged the dynamic abstract sensibility of European design with the playful promotional spirit of American advertising in publications such as *Art Direction* magazine and magazines and annual reports for IBM and Yale University. Alexey Brodovitch, a Russian émigré working in New York, revolutionized editorial layout in magazines like *Harper's Bazaar*, uniting type and photography in seamless, expressive, elegant, and aggressive combinations that leapt from the pages. In Switzerland in the 1950s, the idea of a network of related geometric spaces to organize layouts—a grid—gained momentum in the work of designers such as Joseph Muller-Brockmann and Richard Lohse, among others. Oddly, the opposing idea of composition that could be free of such organization would also gain prominence in Switzerland some years later, in the kinetic design of a young German transplant named Wolfgang Weingart. The rise of corporate branding culture in the 1970s and 1980s, and media consumption in general—commercial advertising and cable proliferation creating additional, supporting demand for print—exploded the volume of publication output to unprecedented levels.

1

No longer simply reportage or entertainment, print publications embody the aspirational aspects of our culture, seen here in this classically stylish magazine page for an upscale shopping center.

Kendall Ross
Seattle (WA), USA

1

STYLE >

the gift of glam

It's a wonderful time to be a woman — celebrate the season with ultra-feminine flair.

the dress

Good-bye girly girl, hello goddess – flirty scents over to make room for floaty and fluid. "Think of Ginger Rogers' dancing dress," muses Cambria Cox, Seattle wardrobe stylist. Fabrics have a sense of weightless movement – silk chartreuse, diaphanous chiffon, in styles that embrace a feminine silhouette. Waists are tied and beribboned, cloaked with a vintage brooch or flower pin à la Coco Chanel or "Sex in the City." Arms are uncovered and décolletage revealed, making the wrap the all-important necessity. Gilt tips with the new femininity, floral fragrances are back – try the newest from Prada or Marc Jacobs.

PRINT PUBLICATIONS IN THE PIXEL PARADIGM

It may be that the digital revolution has made the printed publication all that more relevant—and necessary. The Internet, PDAs, and cell phones offer connectivity and a network of resources for finding information quickly, but there is yet no reliable record of that information beyond print. The knowledge available online, the documents wirelessly transmitted from hand-held to phone, are only so good as the servers that retain the bytes; one big system failure, and volumes of that knowledge and experience are lost. The aspect of print that has saved it from its early death foretold is its archaic physical presence: the fact that it exists. The sharing of ideas and images in tactile form may help promote feelings of communal connection in a world that is increasingly fragmented and compartmentalized because of solitary Internet use, both at home and at work. What's more, printed material offers image resolution and clarity that far exceeds what can be reproduced on a screen.

Because print material remains fixed in time and space, the care that print designers take in resolving conceptual and formal relationships, clarifying informational hierarchies, and crafting the object results in materials that will likely stay around for a while. Designers who work in print are making something, even if it's a single-issue periodical that will be stuffed into a drawer in the near future. The fact that the printed publication is an informationally complex object that must be navigated means that designers need to address issues like concept and layout, legibility and organization, to a high degree. In competing for the attention of a highly distracted audience, everything designers can do to make the information accessible, resonate with their audiences, intrigue, engage, and, be useful—above all—becomes absolutely necessary. An audience may be sucked in with cool printing tricks and flashy photography, but if the content is poorly organized or visually difficult or tiring, they will put it down.

Gathered in this book are some of the results of Gutenberg's achievements of 1455. Newspapers, magazines, annual reports, catalogs, and literature systems—these publications are a cross section of the kinds of publicly consumed reading material available today. Their startling breadth of subject matter, informational complexity, creative effort, and visual diversity testify to the importance of printed matter in our daily lives. The democratizing effect of print is evident not only in the sheer volume of work produced but also in the kinds of work and the design approaches brought to bear in making them beautiful and worthwhile for reading.

Notes on This Book

Designers who are unfamiliar with projects involving extended or editorial texts, such as magazines, annual reports, and newsletters—as well as those who work with such publication projects but would like to reinvestigate them from another perspective—will benefit from seeing the projects shown in this book. Additionally, design students who have had some experience with typography and layout, and who are interested in pursuing independent projects or careers in publishing, will find useful information and a wide range of project types to consider.

The first section, Designing to Read, examines the considerations and processes crucial to publication, from conceptualization and organization of content, image creation and color selection, typographic composition, grid structures, and integration of type with pictures and illustrations for a cohesive, unified editorial experience. This book takes a progressive, methodical, and universal approach and looks at these ideas in a non–industry-specific way, addressing the big-picture design considerations that are germane to every editorial-based design problem.

The second section, From Cover to Cover, presents in-depth case studies of publications, including strategic and conceptual statements by their respective designers that provide insight into the common, as well as individual, approaches and experiences of each. When available, the designer's own sketches, studies, and experimentations are included in order to show the paths the designer followed to arrive at the realized solution.

The third section, Publications in Action, is a showcase of relevant publication design from around the world. The work is divided among six categories that, while by no means exhaustive, offer a range of conceptual and stylistic ideas for comparison.

Designing to Read

From Concept to Printed Piece

Publications are extended applications of text and image and, as such, bring to bear a tremendous number of considerations for a designer. Unlike single-format items, such as posters or ads, even singular multipage documents with more than eight or twelve pages require designers to focus on issues that derive from extended reading: organizing large volumes of content into related parcels of information; crafting the typography to make it comfortably readable over many pages, yet lively enough to continually engage the reader; structuring the parts of pages and sections to accommodate a variety of content, whether image or text based; and integrating images with typography to achieve a unified form that builds a communication much bigger than its parts.

Every publication begins as an idea: a subject or message with a function but no form. Art shown in an exhibition, for example, is an idea. The service an organization offers is an idea. So too are popular activities: cooking, sports, and home decor. Their function—whether delivered by a magazine, a newspaper, a family of corporate literature, or a product catalog—is always the same: to involve an audience in that message or subject matter over a period of time. The form is what changes, differentiating each idea, distilling its raw content into recognizable parts, and engaging its target audience through specific colors, imagery, and typography. The vehicle for these ideas is related to their secondary functions—the kind of audience the idea addresses, their particular need for grouped or periodical information, and the static or evolutionary nature of the message. The vehicle, thus, also changes. The idea may be best served as a newspaper, providing current information on an up-to-the minute basis, or as a system of brochures that builds awareness of different aspects of the message as they become relevant at different times. No matter what the vehicle, though, the process of designing it is the same, and it begins with developing the content that will convey the message.

Thinking

Content, Message, Organization

Concept and Content

Any idea may be given any visual form. The task before the designer, in collaboration with the publisher, is to determine which form will be best. Most often, the publisher will have conceived of the content a certain kind of publication to begin with—for example, a need for an annual report, and its specific information. At other times, publisher and designer may develop the form of the publication together. In either case, the designer's role is to examine the content and to begin thinking about how it will look and feel, related to its messages.

The initial step in thinking about how a publication becomes a reality is to focus on what the subject matter of the message may be. Conceptual messages have several levels of function. The primary function is the subject matter itself, the intrinsic idea that must be given a form so that it can be perceived. The idea of French cuisine and the idea of a company's financial performance are both examples of primary function. The secondary function of an idea is to be relevant and accessible to a particular group of people in a way that makes sense for them. Some conceptual messages are serial and evolutionary, occurring periodically with new com-

ponents that build on the previous occurrence. The most familiar forms of such "periodical" messages are newspapers, magazines, and newsletters. Other messages are "systematic," occurring at one time as a group, or at several junctures, as individual parts of an overall group. Their secondary function is to deliver a message as an interrelated set of components, each with its own specific submessage that relates to the general message. Such publications as corporate literature systems—groups of brochures—serve this function. Considering up front that a publication is to be a periodical, as opposed to a static

1

PRIMARY   SECONDARY   TERTIARY

1

Publications—indeed, all visual communications—may be "peeled apart" to reveal three distinct functions of concept at work: the primary, or intrinsic aspects of the subject matter; the secondary function of relating to a specific audience; and the tertiary function—branding and positioning—that further filters the primary message for interpretation.

A publication may emphasize any of these over the other, with varying effect on audience perception. If the primary function is emphasized, the audience finds the material reliable—almost transparent. If the secondary function is emphasized, the audience senses itself as part of a community. If the tertiary function is emphasized; the audience is more likely to consider the material as a pitch or call to some particular action.

system, is an inherent part of the message: an idea's secondary function—to relate to a particular audience—is fundamental to its primary function.

Most ideas also have a tertiary function, which is to deliver emotional, associational, or cultural interpretation to the audience, to position it relative to other forms or vehicles of the same idea. In other words, to differentiate it. This interpretive function is biased on the part of the message's author and is sometimes called its "spin" or "angle." Branding—the experience of an author's corporate or cultural identity—is an example of an interpretive, tertiary function. The interpretive function may be benign or ulterior, meaning that its function is to be transparent—a signal or identifier—or layered, providing a point of view that affects the meaning of the message—developing loyalty among the audience. The branding of a newspaper,

for the most part, is benign: its goal is to differentiate the newspaper as a source of information. The branding of an annual report, on the other hand, is ulterior: its goal is to influence the audience's perception of the information in one direction or another.

Although the core message—the subject matter—is the designer's first focus, its concept is essential in exhibiting these tertiary functions in varying degrees. The concept must have a form in order for the audience to see it. That form may include stories, photographs, illustrations, tabular data, diagrams, instructions, or other visual displays. Most concepts may be displayed in any of these ways; usually, they are displayed as a combination of these forms that, together, creates a specific type of content. The author or developer of this content usually conceives of the display method in a raw,

verbal way first—writing it out. Visual forms, such as photographs, may augment the content's written form, especially if the concept is about something experiential (such as hiking) or about a product that must be seen to be understood (such as home furnishings). Regardless of whether the secondary or tertiary functions of the concept are relevant, this raw content is the basis upon which the designer must act to build the publication. And that means understanding its subject matter, its cultural context, its intended audience, and its internal structure or parts before proceeding to the design phase.

shrunken peacoat is cut to fit and colored to flatter.

A remarkable congruence flattens the primary, secondary, and tertiary aspects of communication in this spread from a mainstream clothing retailer's catalog—that is, each aspect is more or less the same relative to each other.

The primary message is clothing. It is visually represented by a neutral photograph of clothing. The target audience is mainstream, concerned with a sense of the genuine; this retailer's customers are not interested in couture fashion.

Further, the coloration of the clothes is a branded message, as well as intrinsic to their design and to the design of the catalog.

J.Crew New York City, USA

Build a Design Brief: A Concepting Checklist

☐ What is the publication's subject matter?

☐ Into how many parts will the information be broken? What are the parts?

☐ Is the subject organic or manmade? Concrete or abstract?

☐ What colors are associated with the subject matter (literal and emotional)?

☐ Who is going to read about the subject? Who will not be reading about it?

☐ What other publications already exist about the subject?

☐ List two words about each that describe their visual qualities.

☐ List five words that describe the subject as you want to interpret it. How are these different from the words that describe existing publications on the subject?

☐ How often do readers need the information? In what context will they find the information: through subscription, as a membership benefit, at a newsstand?

Visual Sources
Building on the Primary Function of the Concept

The content is its own concept and vice versa; it is the fundamental source for all that the designer will do with it. Sometimes, designers become concerned with conceptual functions beyond the primary, secondary, and tertiary, looking to achieve a particular visual display for the content that is interesting to them. If the designer exerts his or her visual or creative conceits over the intrinsic concept of the content, the result is sometimes visually interesting but inappropriate for the message. It may seem forced or contrived rather than a natural outgrowth of the designer's objective expression of the concept. Of course, the designer's creativity and aesthetic sensibilities are demonstrated in how he or she selects or invents visual means of displaying the content—for example, the typefaces to use for text or titles, the attributes of space and color, the choice between photographic or illustrative imagery. But the designer's main goal is to act as a conduit for the concept in an objective way. In that sense, the content—the conceptual idea to be communicated, the subject matter—is really the driving force behind the design.

Why does a publication look and feel the way it does? Why is a magazine about classical music visually different from one covering hip-hop? Why does an annual report for an insurance company convey stability and reserve while one for a sporting goods company communicates energy and fun?

The simple answer is that the content of each is different, so their visual qualities must be different. The more complex answer is that each individual designer has investigated the content for clues as to its intrinsic, primary idea and, from there, distilled a set of visual qualities through a decision-making process that results from asking questions and comparing the answers that present themselves. Is the subject organic or man-made? Is it critical to the audience's life and health or is it entertainment? Does the subject exist in the world, like a dog or a cat, or is it an abstraction, like politics or philosophy? If it's based on something natural, are there forms or colors that relate to it universally, as leaves or the color green relate to the environment? Does the subject present itself as one continuous thought, or is it composed of several parts?

Based on the answers to these questions, a designer begins to examine forms for typography and images that, first and foremost, document the subject matter regardless of the subject's secondary function (audience expectation) or tertiary function (branding or interpretive positioning). In order for the subject to have power in its visual form, its intrinsic characteristics must be the source. Again, however, it is the designer's subjective sensibility that brings out these visual ideas from the subject. Even if the designer is trying to be completely objective or neutral, simple matters like choosing a typeface will reflect his or her interpretation of these intrinsic qualities. No two designers will select the same typeface, for example, to communicate "elegance" or "organic." But in comparing potential choices among typefaces, both designers are likely to come to some similar conclusions, on a big-picture level, in selecting a face for text that feels right for the subject. Though design is somewhat subjective, it is rooted in universals: its goal is to solve the problem of how to make as many people as possible experience information in a similar way.

> Although distilling intrinsic visual ideas from a subject means drawing from the source objectively, the designer's own interpretation will nonetheless be subjective. Consider the idea of "natural," in both image and typeface, and the many possibilities there may be in simply describing this subject.

1, 2

Abstract form is a powerful communicator of ideas. Here, the lateral back-and-forth movement of colored bands, photographs, and type elements visually supports the idea of "crosscurrents"—the magazine's title—and creates associations of exchange or dialogue. The designers pay careful attention to the locations of each element's beginning and endpoint to ensure that the intervals created by their staggered locations are dynamic.

Studio Blue *Chicago, USA*

1

2

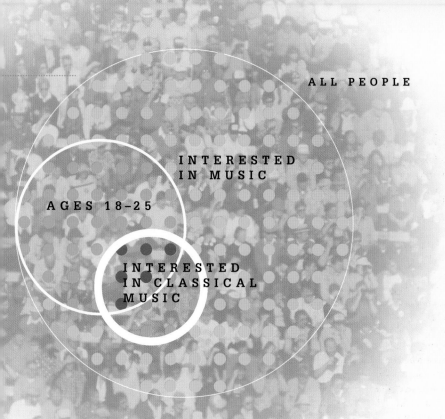

ALL PEOPLE

INTERESTED
IN MUSIC

AGES 18–25

INTERESTED
IN CLASSICAL
MUSIC

2003 SUNDANCE FILM FESTIVAL

January 16–26, 2003 • Park City, Utah

3

Targeting an audience
means defining subsets
of people from larger
sets of people. Communal
sets—subgroups composed
of people who are part
of two sets—offer an
opportunity to expand
the message beyond the
base demographic, creat-
ing a wider audience
potential that may affect
the concept.

4

A representational image—
an egg—is used as a
conceptual housing for the
program of an independent
film festival. The representational image immediately
presents a disconnect:
what is the relationship
between egg and film?
It is a conceptual one,
relying on the viewer to
make the connection and
thereby involving him
or her in completing the
message. In this sense,
the abstracted layers of
meaning are skewed once
again toward the branding
message of the festival
organizers, in that its
conceptual, generative
symbology positions the
festival as different from
other film festivals.

AdamsMorioka
Beverly Hills, USA

Resonating with the Audience
The Secondary Function of Concept

Getting a concept in front of an audience depends largely on who the audience is. This secondary function of an idea—to be relevant and accessible to a particular group of people—helps determine not only the physical form of the publication but also, to some degree, its visual style and, more important, its organization. Who an audience is derives from a variety of factors. First, the identity, or demographic makeup, of the people to be targeted is important. Are the individuals young or old? Predominantly male or female? Working class or wealthy? Do their interests reflect their ethnic or social background? How many of them are there? What joins them together as a recognizable group?

The second factor in establishing an audience is their assumed need for the information in a particular way, at particular times or through a particular delivery method. If the subject matter is complex and evolves on a continuing basis, the audience may be assumed to want the information in a periodical form—a newspaper, magazine, or newsletter. If the subject matter is finite but may be augmented from time to time—for example, a line of cosmetic products that changes seasonally, or a set of services provided by a financial institution—it might be assumed that a catalog or a system of brochures is the best delivery method.

The relationship of time to informational need is yet another factor in determining the audience. As a group, do they need to be informed on the occasion of a specific circumstance, every few months, every week, or every day? Lastly, the projected use of the material by these individuals helps define who they are. Perhaps they will count on the publication to keep them informed about ongoing events; maybe they will use the publication as a reference or record; or perhaps they will use it as a catalyst for making decisions about their lives.

Defining the audience enables the designer to make basic decisions about form and content, from basic format—kind, size, binding method—to more abstract aspects, such as the kinds of photographs or illustrations may be most interesting to them; the type- or image-to-negative space ratio; and even the selection of color and type styles. The secondary function of the content also considers how the subject resonates with the audience.

A publication that does so respects that group's demographic identity, speaking to them using visual metaphor and organization that augment the subject's core message: the audience identifies with the subject because the publication visually interprets the content for them—emotionally and intellectually. This interpretive aspect may relate to

1

The facts and the fury

1

The audience for this hip-hop magazine recognizes its message as being directed toward them because of color choice, arrangement of forms, and typographic choices. Groups of people are highly attuned to the subtleties of message in visual form; they know when the message is for them.

Eggers + Diaper
Berlin, Germany

2

3

J.Crew coats
Rich textures and colors. Cool silhouettes and clever details. J.Crew's collection of coats has a fresh, modern look with lots of flattering touches. Pick one and button up for fall.

the publication's tertiary function—branding—but most often it is simply a reflection of the designer capitalizing on the audience's shared background, giving the core message a visual and emotional context that allows the publication to speak to them rather than at them. In this sense, the audience influences many aspects of a publication's visual presentation. The audience factor also, therefore, influences the meaning of the subject content: they expect the content to have particular associations or psychological effect. As a result, the designer must consider the audience's level of taste and their assumed experience as individuals

as other sources for visual decision making, for everything from page structure to color and color integration. A home decor magazine produced for a wealthy audience, for example, may succeed with certain kinds of typography and photography but may not succeed with working-class readers because the presentation fails to resonate with them. Two home decor magazines, therefore, may have the same primary conceptual function but different secondary functions because of their different audiences; visually, they will reflect this difference in their stylistic presentation.

Branding and positioning create spin on a concept: an association or emotional response in the audience related not to the content itself but to the identity of the publisher. The diagram at right illustrates the differences between a neutral concept and a branded concept that alters both primary and secondary messages to help distinguish the concept against its competitors in the same genre.

The Influence of Brand
The Third Function of Concept

Designing to influence an audience's perception of content so that it resonates with them adds a layer of meaning to the overall content of a publication. This interpretive layer derives directly from the audience's identity and need and thus is a fundamental part of the subject concept. But a publication may also contain biased messages from the author or publisher—as well as from the designer—among which are branding and positioning messages. These messages are communicated on an abstract visual level that alters the audience's perception of the content, effectively changing the subject's meaning. The term "biased" isn't necessarily detrimental; it simply means that a point of view about the subject is being established for the audience.

This point of view can be a powerful factor in publication design: it situates the subject in the minds of the audience relative to other sources of the same information, and can be used to achieve noble ends … as well as more pragmatic or cynical ones. An annual report, for example, doesn't simply deliver information about a company's services and financial performance; it helps reinforce values

the company wants to promote, with the goal of attracting new investors or drawing investors away from competing companies. In one sense, the messaging in such a case is intrinsic to the subject, because it celebrates the achievement of its employees and the quality of its services; in another sense, the company is competing for the loyalty of a particular audience, aiming to increase its stock price and profitability.

Branding can be defined as the collective experience of a company's services, public presence, employees or representatives, and visual identity. Most often, a company's branding is wrapped up in its corporate identity—the logo and materials the company uses to identify and promote it through color, typography, image, and so on. The influence of branding on a publication is therefore visual; the publication's design, although singularly considered for its specific content and purpose, is part of a broader program of visual elements: the typography, color palette and choice of imagery reflect decisions that convey the company's image, or trade dress. A magazine is often considered its own brand because it is widely circulated, resonates deeply with its audience, and differentiates itself from others of its genre through positioning and

marketing. It is itself a message, aside from the subject matter it transmits.

A company's positioning may also have an effect on visual decisions made during the design process. Because positioning—the relationship of the company or subject matter to others in the same genre—is a direct response to audience identity, its role may be far reaching. Specific colors may be disallowed (or used exclusively) as a result of trying to avoid association with other publications or even ideas. Only certain typefaces may be permitted. A specific style of imagery may be developed to refer to some medium to which the positioning assumes the audience relates—perhaps a specific type of television program, for example, uses an out-of-focus camera technique that the target audience recognizes.

In clarifying these successive conceptual layers of content—the core subject matter, its contextual relevance to its audience, and its tertiary branding or point of view, if applicable—the designer can find relationships between them as a source for the communication's visual form. The next question, then, is how the content fits together.

2, 3
Compare the color and model presentation of these two catalogs. While each represents fashion, the message is filtered differently for their respective audiences. In the Takashimaya catalog (2), unusual model cropping in an indeterminate environment, deep jewel tone color, a nonstandard, intimate format, and staggered papers help distinguish this high-end retailer's message of exclusivity from that of the J.Crew catalog (3), whose naturalistic color and model presentation resonate with a more mainstream audience.

2 Design: MW
3 J.Crew
Both: *New York City, USA*

FASHION
PRIMARY

FASHION FASHION *fashion*
SECONDARY

FASHION
TERTIARY

FASHION

4

4
The primary source for this newsletter's visual form is not its subject matter— venture capital funding— but, rather, the authority of the publisher in its field. The details of careful typesetting, conservative color based on the client's corporate color scheme, and imagery with neutral messages are the result of communicating the company's message.

Gorska Design
San Francisco, USA

Evaluating and Organizing: Sections and Sequence

Although much of the physical content for a publication comes to a designer ready to be designed, more and more designers are actively engaged in helping develop the content from a strategic and editorial standpoint. Whatever the situation, the designer faces the task of evaluating the content's editorial form to determine what components or methods will communicate most clearly, as well as the order in which those components ought to be sequenced.

First, the content must be divided into parts relevant to the publication type—whether it's an annual report, newspaper, magazine, product catalog, newsletter, or system of brochures. Most of these publication types come with preconceived ideas about how content should be divided.

Editorial publications, including newspapers, magazines, and newsletters, organize their content as articles or stories, supported by images that are generally documentary. Articles tend to be grouped by category, especially in newspapers. A general variety of highlighted information appears on the front page, and this highlighted material continues in, or is linked to, individual sections that make a transition from more general to more specific—international events (outside the local audience's experience) segue into national and then local events, followed by different kinds of specific issues of concern to the local audience, such as dining, automotive or housing news, local employment, and the like. Magazines tend to follow a similar general-to-specific pattern in defining sections, but there are usually two major sections (rather than five or six or more, as in newspapers): a section of editorial departments and a section of features. (Departments are pages devoted to the same kind of information provided in every issue such as the dessert of the month, newly released CDs, or a question-and-answer column. The features are major articles that investigate the magazine's subject matter in depth.) Annual reports are often divided into three major sections that also become successively more focused: first, a branded positioning section, usually image driven, that describes the company's values and dramatically conveys performance highlights; then, a discussion by the company's management about its activities, which often includes a letter from a high-ranking executive; and finally, a section of financial disclosure made up

1–3
Each publication is organized so that different aspects or complexities of information come to the foreground at different times. In a newspaper, for example, the "softer" material is toward the back; in an annual report, it's up front. The annual report (1) is organized by kind; the newspaper (2) by relevance and part-to-whole; the tool catalog (3), by complexity of the information. The level and sequence of specificity for each publication change with function and target.

1 Circle K Studio *San Francisco, USA*

2 Jeff Neumann *Denver, USA*

3 Hutchinson Associates *Chicago, USA*

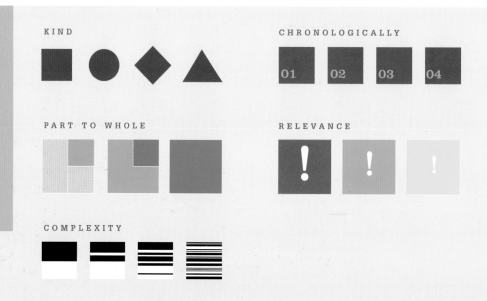

Break It Down. Strategies for organizing content involve sorting the material into manageable parts that are related to each other: by kind, by part to whole, by complexity, chronologically, by relevance. Certain strategies tend to be applied to particular kinds of publications because of convention—usually driven by the expectations of the audience. Newspapers, for example, exhibit an organizational strategy of part-to-whole based on local relevance.

KIND

PART TO WHOLE

COMPLEXITY

CHRONOLOGICALLY

01 02 03 04

RELEVANCE

! ! !

1

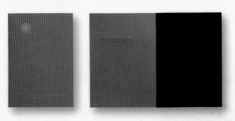

2

3

  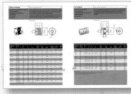

mostly of tabular data and technical descriptions of transactions, revenue, and expenses. A newsletter, meanwhile, is essentially a less-complex version of a magazine, newspaper, and report rolled into one item. It may have an actual cover or may offer content highlights on the front page like a daily newspaper; it may contain departments and features, like a magazine; and it may feature diagrams or data, like a report. Although newsletters tend to be quarterly, they may also be monthly, depending on the needs of the audience.

Convention, however, doesn't necessarily mean that the organization of the content is right for a particular publication; it's just a place to start. In analyzing the content, a designer may notice that some other structure makes more sense, or that a different sequence helps make the content more logical. For example, a designer might combine the financial discussion and positioning sections of an annual report into one, substituting some unexpected display for tables and graphs. Decisions like these are often related to the author's or publisher's branding and the way in which it wants to resonate with its audience. Presenting a financial message in an unexpected way—challenging convention—makes a statement to investors. It also signals to the investor that the company is growing and developing, as well as investigating better ways to communicate. Ultimately, dividing content and sequencing it depends on what makes it clear for the audience.

The Many Forms of Content

The content of a publication isn't limited strictly to the writing. Images, colors, and type—visual support for the writing—are also content. While this idea, as it pertains to pictures—documentary representation of experience—is immediately clear, it inlcudes not just what is shown in such images, but how the images themselves are shown.

The manipulation of images adds communication to that which is readily apparent from their subjects. On a more abstract level, color, shape, and illustrative treatment all contribute to a publication's overall message, and can be considered content in their own right. Similarly, the treatment of typography—in its typeface selection, sizing, and textural, visual qualities—will also bring additional messaging to layouts beyond what is literally conveyed through the writing itself.

1

1

A simple configuration of overlapping colored dots evokes a cluster of molecules on the cover of this annual report for a chemical company.

Ideas On Purpose
New York City, USA

2

A striking illustration leaves the literal in favor of the conceptual in this detail from an annual report for a human rights organization.

Soapbox Design *Toronto, Canada*

3

Presentation of images falls on a spectrum defined at one end by representation and at the other by abstraction. Images that lie closer to the representational end of the continuum are more literal; images that approach the abstract end are more interpretive.

3

LITERAL

ABSTRACT

The Meaning of Images
Literal and Abstract Content

Most publications rely on imagery to supplement their written content. Images provide a visual counterpoint to the texture of type, helping engage the audience. Images also offer a visceral connection to events or experiences that are described by the written language. They can also help clarify complex information—especially conceptual, abstract, or process-oriented information—by displaying it in a concise form at a glance. And they can add interpretive overlay in juxtaposition with literal text or images. A picture, as the saying goes, is worth a thousand words. A designer's choice of images, the pictorial elements they contain (or don't contain), and their treatment as photograph or illustration all have implications for meaning.

Sometimes, images are the primary content or subject of a publication. This is true of exhibition and product catalogs—in the former, the subject is the art being cataloged; in the latter, the subject is the products being sold and, therefore, the images that represent them. Product catalogs also offer imagery as a primary means of conveying concepts about lifestyle that are used to relate the products to the audience's experience—whether actual or desired. Clothing catalogs often show people wearing the products—clothes—in particular locations or situations. These images not only demonstrate the way the clothes look on real people, they also position the clothes relative to a lifestyle. These two distinct purposes highlight the potential of images to convey representational and abstract messages simultaneously.

Indeed, all images share this tension between real and abstract; the subject matter helps the designer define where the images ought to lie on the range between these two extremes. The more representational an image, the more objective or documentary the communication—in essence, the closer the content is related to the primary conceptual function. The more abstract an image, the more subjective, interpretive, or layered the communication—it is closer in relation to the secondary or tertiary conceptual functions of the subject.

6

A subdued color photograph inside the front cover of this stationery catalog displays a selected product standing upright on delicate, desiccated leaves. The simplicity of the image belies its symbolic power: a subtle shift in overall color from cool to warm alludes to change from mechanical to natural concerns, and the leaves are shown supporting the product. Even in representational images, the potential for abstract, emotional messaging is tremendous.

Studio Calavaria
Portland (OR), USA

6

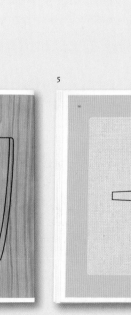

4

5

4, 5

In these product catalog illustrations, the images are stylized representations that use a mixture of abstract space and recognizable forms.

Designwork SrL *Udine, Italy*

PHOTOGRAPHY AND ILLUSTRATION An image may be mostly representational or mostly abstract, but it will always be a mixture of the two. Even images that are considered purely visual—geometric or organic forms that appear not to be of anything—communicate ideas that are grounded in the human experience of the world. A yellow circle, for instance, in the right context, becomes a sun. Regardless of this attribute, the images in a publication may be photographs, illustrations (meaning drawings or paintings), or a hybrid—manipulated photographs or drawn images in combination. The way in which a designer decides to involve image results from his or her evaluation of the content and its conceptual functions. The choice of photography, drawing, or hybrid does depend to a great degree on the documentary necessity implied by the subject matter itself, but it is the connection to the audience and any interpretive positioning that has the greatest effect on the designer's approach to image content. The images must provide informational

clarity but must do so in a way that resonates and delivers the publisher's branding or positioning message. A designer has at his or her disposal an array of methods for manipulating imagery. In photography, for example, selective focus can emphasize specific elements, the composition of the elements within the frame can indicate their relative importance, and changes in lighting can affect mood. With illustration, the choice of elements drawn, their scale relationships, and even the medium used can affect the communication. A soft charcoal drawing may feel elegant or aggressive, depending on the way the marks are made; a digital illustration may seem edgy or precise.

1

1

In this magazine spread, representational images and abstract images are juxtaposed to create conceptual, as well as visual, tension in the layout.

Flat *New York City, USA*

2, 3

Juxtapositions of relatively banal images in these spreads for a conference program ask readers to decipher their relationships in order to stimulate and provoke discussion. Simply placing two images next to each other implies a relationship in meaning. The images may be causal or not; the hand sewing is the cause of the completed quilt. They are related in meaning and form and have contrast in scale (small to large) and time (before and after). The wires and the figures both allude to connectivity and support; they are contrasted by nature (mechanical vs. human).

AdamsMorioka *Beverly Hills, USA*

2

3

4

Two representational images create an abstract illustration when they are composited together.

Jeff Neumann *Denver, USA*

5

Decisions about framing and cropping a photographic image—as well as what is included (or not)— will also affect its message. In this page spread from a furnishings catalog, the cropping enhances the diagonal, forward motion of the angles created by perspective. Along with monochromatic lighting and the shadowy presence of people, this composition creates a monolithic, progressive, almost "theoretical" message to appeal to an audience of architects and interior designers.

Designwork SrL *Udine, Italy*

Color as Communication

Few visual stimuli are as powerful as color; it is intimately connected to the natural world and, thus, is a profoundly useful communication tool. But because color results from the transmission of reflected light waves through an imperfect organ—the eye—to an imperfect interpreter—the brain—the meanings it conveys are also profoundly subjective. In other words, though the mechanism of color perception is universal among humans, what we do with it once we see it is another thing altogether. Cultural differences and individual experiences affect our interpretation of color messages. As a result, color, like text and image, is effectively content and, therefore, must be addressed when designing a publication.

1

Vivid colors are used for type as a symbol for the colored glazes used by the artists for their ceramic work. Note how the color affects the apparent spatial depth of the type—the golden type, though lighter, appears to come forward in space, while the cyan type recedes.

Faydherbe/DeVringer
Amsterdam, Netherlands

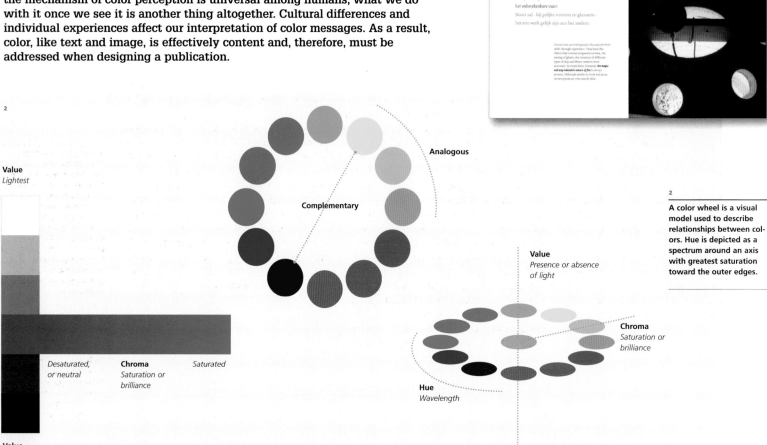

2

Value
Lightest

Desaturated, or neutral

Chroma
Saturation or brilliance

Saturated

Value
Darkest

Analogous

Complementary

Value
Presence or absence of light

Chroma
Saturation or brilliance

Hue
Wavelength

2

A color wheel is a visual model used to describe relationships between colors. Hue is depicted as a spectrum around an axis with greatest saturation toward the outer edges.

Hue
The perception of color difference resulting from wavelength

Saturation
The relative brilliance of intensity or lack of intensity

Temperature
The perception of relative warmth or coolness

Value
The relative darkness or lightness of a color

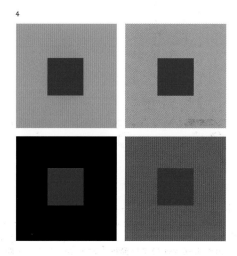

Formal Aspects of Color
Defining Chromatic Perception

A single color is defined by four qualities: hue, saturation, temperature, and value. Hue refers to the essential identity of a color—red, violet, green, yellow, and so on. The color's brilliance, or saturation, describes its intensity: a saturated color is very intense or vibrant, while a desaturated color is dull. The temperature of a color is a subjective quality that relates to experiences: a warm color, such as red or orange, reminds us of heat; a cool color, such as green or blue, reminds us of cold objects, such as plants or water. A color's value is its darkness or lightness: yellow is perceived as being light; violet is dark.

The perception of these color characteristics is relative, changing as different colors come into close contact. The perception of hue is the most absolute: a color is seen either as blue or green. However, if two similar blues are placed next to each other, one is perceived as having more red in it, and the other is perceived as having more green in it. A color's value, temperature, and saturation also appear to change when brought into context with another color. A blue may appear dark against a white field but may appear light against a black field. The same red may appear warm next to a violet but cool next to a yellow or orange. A pale violet may appear intense against a warm gray background or desaturated against a cool gray background; it may appear neutral (completely desaturated) if placed against a vibrant orange background. Two colors that are similar in value enhance each other's intensity, but their optical separation becomes less distinct. Two colors of a similar value that are complementary—opposites on a color wheel—create a severe optical buzzing when brought together: their similar values decrease their optical distinction, but their opposing hues mutually increase their intensity to the extreme.

COLOR AND SPACE Color also exhibits various spatial properties. Cool colors appear to recede, while warm colors appear to advance. Of the primary colors, blue appears to recede and yellow to advance, but red seems to sit statically at a middle depth within space. Moreover, a color appears darker the less there is of it. A large rectangle and a narrow line of the same color appear to have different values if set against a white background: the color in the rectangle appears lighter than it does in the line, because the line is surrounded by much brighter white space.

3

Altering any one of the four attributes of a color—hue, brilliance, value, and temperature—affects the color in different ways. Darkening a color tends to decrease its intensity, as does making it lighter. Changing a color's temperature affects its relative hue: as it gets cooler, it becomes more violet; as it gets warmer, it becomes more orange.

4

The same blue, situated on backgrounds of varying saturation, value, and temperature, appears to change color. This effect of color context is called simultaneous contrast.

1

1

Abstract forms take on meaning as color is applied to them. The black circle has no meaning; when it becomes yellow, it is transformed into a sun. When it is blue, it becomes the Earth.

The Psychology of Color
Perception vs. Socialization

Along with color comes a variety of psychological messages that may influence content. This emotional component of color operates at an instinctual level but also is influenced by society and culture. Many cultures equate red with feelings of hunger, anger, or energy because red is closely associated with meat, blood, and violence. Vegetarians, by contrast, may associate the color green with hunger. In Western cultures, which are predominantly Christian, black is associated with death and mourning, but Hindus associate death with the color white—the color that Christians associate with purity or cleanliness. Because of the history of Western civilization, violet conveys authority and luxury to members of that culture. Most cultures respond to blue with an association of water or life. Blue is also often perceived as deeply spiritual or

contemplative, perhaps because of this particular association.

The selection of a color for specific words in a composition, therefore, can add meaning by linking its associations to the verbal message. As a result, a headline or image in one color may take on additional, or completely different, meaning in another. Comparing color options in order to see how they affect other kinds of content helps determine which colors are most appropriate for the communication.

COLOR AS A SYSTEM Within a complex visual environment, color can help distinguish different kinds of information, as well as create relationships among components or editions of a publication. For example, a designer may develop a palette for graphic and typographic elements that helps readers distinguish between specific text components—headlines, subheads, and body—or between sections of information. Alternatively, a designer may use a

2

2

A change in color dramatically affects both words and images. Here, the feeling of the image is transformed as its color changes. Pastel coloring makes the image friendly and even childlike; sepia coloring evokes a sense of history; deep, cool color makes the image cold, but also restful; neutral tones enhance the sense of environment.

3

The color red creates an involuntary response, a mixture of arousal and hunger. For this paper promotion that uses metaphors related to things that stir the heart, the color is not just a representation but also the content.

Strichpunkt
Stuttgart, Germany

3

Make It Obvious. Color perception varies from person to person—what appears blue to one may seem violet to another. Ensure differentiation through clear color change; even if the viewer's color sense is unconventional, the amount of difference between colors in a coding system will still serve their purpose.

general palette for all elements that is based on the color or thematic content of photographs. This palette might have a consistent base, such as a selection of warm neutrals, that remains constant, while accent colors change.

Color coding—assigning colors to identify sections or components—is one option for using color as a system. To be effective, color coding must be relatively simple and easily identifiable. Coding with too many colors creates confusion, forcing the viewer to try to remember which color relates to which information. Although color coding within a related set of hues—a deep blue, an aqua blue, and a green—can help distinguish subcategories of information within an overall grouping, care must be taken to ensure that the differences between the colors are perceptible. Pushing the colors further apart from each other may help—deep blue may be skewed toward violet while yellow is added to the green, for example.

4

In this literature system, color is used to differentiate a company's product offerings. Within each set, the amount of the given color signifies the function and importance of each related document: the more color, the more promotional; the less color, the more informational.

Ruder Finn Design
New York City, USA

5

Analogous (left), complementary (middle), and triadic (right) combinations of colors, defined by their positions on a color wheel, create systems of color relationships that can be a basis for coding.

5   ANALOGOUS   COMPLEMENTARY   TRIADIC

Type as Visual Concept

When designing for a publication, one of the greatest areas of focus is the typography. On a purely functional level, a designer needs to address legibility, hierarchy, and clarity in presenting verbal information. But type also carries nonverbal messages. In selecting typefaces and integrating type with images, a designer may have a profound effect on the overall character of a publication—effectively introducing another kind of content. The choice of typeface establishes a voice for the content that positions it in a specific way through associations an audience may ascribe to the face itself.

Choosing a classical, old-style serif face, versus a contemporary sans serif, for example, may transmit a sense of credibility and reliability, or notions of tradition or historical significance. Mixing typefaces throughout a publication may create a sense of interrelated contexts, or ideas of cultural diversity, as well as help distinguish among informational components or different sections. In magazines, the use of typography as an image, related to photographs or illustrations, is especially important. A magazine's masthead, or cover title, becomes a significant image: it is clearly verbal, relates to the brand, and provides a symbolic encapsulation of the content.

TYPEFACE CLASSIFICATION The individual, distinguishing characteristics of a typeface's drawing often are related to the historical development of typefaces, and our sense of a typeface's style is sometimes colored by this historicity. From early Roman times to the fifteenth century, type was drawn by hand, either with a brush, a flat reed pen, or a chisel. In the mid-1500s, casting letters in lead allowed for a new precision in form. From that point forward, the evolution of typefaces moved away from those inspired by brush and stone carving toward a more rational aesthetic, and toward typefaces that were more finely drawn and technically demanding.

1

Archaic | Greek Lapidary

A B M O K

Archaic | Roman Capitals

A B M O K

Oldstyle | Garamond Three

A B M O K

Transitional | Baskerville

A B M O K

Neoclassical | Bodoni

A B M O K

Sans Serif | Univers 55

A B M O K

Slab Serif | Clarendon

A B M O K

Graphic | Variex

A b M o k

1

The progression from archaic to modern and then sans-serif faces shows the hand-drawn influence steadily disappear, replaced by the assertion of a precise, rational aesthetic.

2

These details from a stationery catalog evoke antique naturalist prints. The contrast of the script face coincides with that of the leaf image, while the centered all-cap serif below offers a stately counterpoint. This serif is an adaptation of an English face from the 1700s; the mixture of uppercase, letterspaced, lowercase italic, small caps, and centered-axis logic contribute to the period, archival feeling.

Studio Calavaria
Portland, USA

2

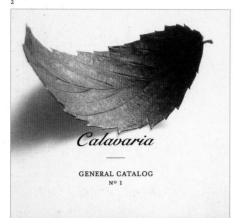

Choosing and Mixing Typefaces
Contrast and Clarity

A combination of type families increases typographic color—a variety of typographic darkness, lightness, and spatial rhythm—but mixing too many faces may become visually confusing: what do these changes signify for the viewer? As a general rule (which may, of course, be broken in the right context), the use of two type families within a project is sufficient for visual variety.

The choice of typefaces to mix must be decisive. There must be enough stylistic contrast between them that their individual qualities are evident. Mixing two similar weight oldstyle serifs, for example, will seem ambiguous: their qualities may be slightly different, but the decision to mix them will appear arbitrary. Using two radically different serif faces—a modern serif and a chunky slab serif, for instance—will make a clear visual statement. Mixing typefaces—as well as which are included in the mix—carries meaning: an archaic face and a stark, modern sans serif, for example, may communicate timelessness or the idea of continuum. Oldstyle faces mixed with newer ones, in the context of a publication about computers, may offset the coldness associated with machines, making the content friendlier. Using experimental faces, or faces that challenge legibility, may infuse the content with a sense of exclusivity or cast it as particularly hip. Additionally, the designer can use these stylistic variations to differentiate complex information within a layout by assigning certain styles or weights to captions, text, and headings.

Context Is Everything. Different audiences will make different associations about type styles, so pay attention to feedback from client meetings. Chances are the client and its audience will have similar cultural backgrounds and, therefore, respond similarly to the choice of typeface on an emotional level.

3

A wide range of type styles invigorates the text-heavy presentation of this newspaper page (detail). Although the faces have been selected for their differences, they all share some characteristics. Several condensed typefaces are used for different kinds of subheads, for example, but one is a sans serif and the others are serifs—a bracketed serif and a slab-serif wood type. The condensed sans serif corresponds to other sans-serif heads, such as is found in the Newsline column, but contrasts it in width.

Jeff Neumann *Denver, USA*

Some type families lack a full complement of weights—light, medium, bold, black—and must be supplemented by a weight selected from another family. In such cases, it's important to consider the supplement on its own merits. As it will be used to create contrast with the primary face, it may be approached from one of two directions: attempting to relate it as closely as possible to the text face, or letting it be as different as possible. The first option enables more fluid reading when the two are combined in running text, as the form difference is less noticeable; the second option implies more of a chance for fixation and, therefore, an enhanced opportunity to call out information. Each may be viable, but the designer must decide which quality best suits the needs of the text.

Comparing the overall widths, stroke weights, junctures, and stroke contrast between individual letterforms is a good way of finding similarities (and differences) between typefaces in order to mix them decisively. In this comparison, the lowercase *g* on the left shares more with the middle *g* than does the one on the right.

Swapping type styles for use as a bold weight in running text can help improve clarity when the natural bold weight isn't different enough from the medium text weight (top).

g   g   g

each **incidence** requires
each **incidence** requires
each **incidence** requires

3

Typography as Content
When Words Are Images, Too

Treating specific aspects of the content typographically, so that they become as much an image as any photograph or illustration, can be a powerful (and cost-effective) form in its own right. Unlike the treatments of section titles or the beginnings of feature articles, which are tied to an editorial function, such treatments may become additional content in their own right. The content developer and the designer, working together, may envision a supporting type component that is independent of the running texts and other type elements such as callouts, which extract portions of the running text and reproduce them as visual focal points—as opposed to being unique content.

TYPE AS IMAGE Letters and words are strong forms, able to withstand dramatic manipulation without losing their identities. When a letter or word takes on pictorial qualities beyond those that define its form, it becomes an image in its own right, and the potential for impact is enormous. A word that is also a picture fuses several kinds of understanding together: as its meaning is assimilated through each perceptual filter—visual, emotional, intellectual—it assumes the iconic stature of a symbol. Understanding on each level is immediate, and a viewer's capacity to recall images explains why corporate identity exists in the way that it does. This communicative power can be used to equal effect in designing word-pictures for content within publications such as magazines, or for cover treatments, such as titling or mastheads.

As in so many aspects of strong typographic design, making type into an image means defining a simple relationship between the intrinsic form of the letters and some other visual idea. It's easy to get lost in the endless possibilities of type manipulation and obscure the visual message or dilute it. A viewer is likely to perceive and easily remember one strong message over five weaker ones—complexity is desirable, whereas complication is not.

Words Are Pictures, Too. Type may be transformed into an image using a variety of approaches. Each provides a different avenue of exploration, and several may be appropriate both to the desired communication and to the formal aspects of the type itself.

Pictorialization When type becomes a representation of a real-world object or takes on the qualities of something from actual experience, it has been pictorialized. In illustrative pictorialization, forms are drawn to appear to be made out of a recognizable material or to form part of a recognizable object.

Pictorial Inclusion Illustrative elements brought into the type forms so that they interact with its strokes or counterforms are said to be included. The type retains its essential form, but the pictorial matter is integrated by reversing out of the type or by replacing the counterforms within or between the letters.

Syntactic Deconstruction Changing the visual relationships between the parts of a word or phrase is a deconstruction (the inherent structure of the word is called out or changed by being deformed). The cadence of the spoken word, the word's syllables, the prefix, the suffix, and individual letters are all sources for deconstruction.

Form Substitution Replacing a type form with a recognizable object or another symbol is referred to as a *substitution*. Many real-world objects share visual structure with letters. Circular objects are often substituted for a letter *O*, for example. Images aren't the only elements that may be substituted for a type form—replacing a letter with another character is also a common strategy for transforming a word into an image.

Form Alteration Changing the structural characteristics of type elements is yet another strategy for making type into an image. The alteration of the typographic forms sometimes strives to communicate a nonliteral idea. For example, altering the form of an adjective can change the quality of its description. Altering the form of type elements may have a syntactic component as well. If the word "growth" is set so that the letter *O* is larger than the other words, the scale change is syntactic—it exploits the quality of the vowel's sound by exaggerating its visual presence as it relates to the word's meaning.

Ornamentation Lastly, typographic elements may be transformed into images by adding ornamentation: borders, outlines, dingbats, dots, lines, geometric shapes, and so on. The ornament may be structurally related to the typography or may be purely decorative. If the ornaments have some kind of symbolic or representational quality, they may take on the aspect of an inclusion and, therefore, be more strongly connected to the meaning of the word. The style of the ornament may affect the viewer's sense of the historical context of the type (for example, a flourish or antique dingbat from a particular period).

Titling and supporting text are transformed into the image of aerosol spray—pictorialized—in this cover for an newspaper entertainment supplement.

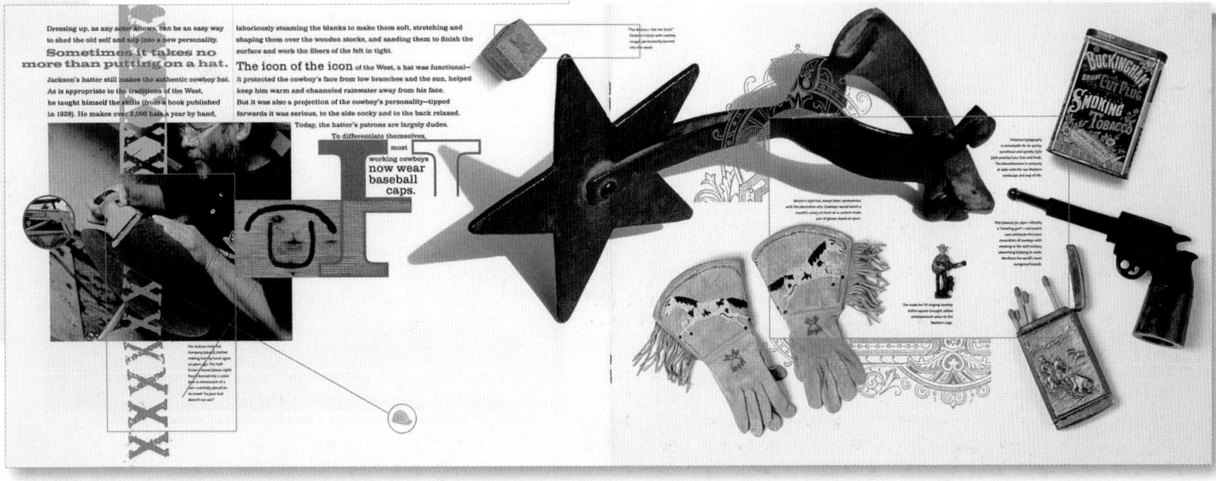

Jeff Neumann *Denver, USA*

2

Extreme scale forces even unaltered type into the realm of image. As these characters become larger, their exterior form begins to interact with the space surrounding it.

Studio Blue *Chicago, USA*

3

The type in this paper promotion, which delivers a narrative about the Wild West, evokes vernacular images such as horseshoes and brands as it becomes altered and ornamental in the layout.

Worksight
New York City, USA

The necessities of reading and comprehension inform the visual aspects of publications; their large volume of text is what fundamentally differentiates them from other kinds of typographic projects. Even publications that are driven by image—specifically, catalogs for exhibitions and product sales—require fine-tuning text typography so that readers can navigate through complex captions or listings, in addition to whatever more involved running text components there may be. Reading a long text asks a lot of an audience; in order to make the process as easy and useful as possible, the designer must focus on the text's details— sizes, spacing, and paragraph width—along with the bigger issues of layout to ensure a comfortable reading experience. Establishing clear hierarchies between text components, so that the audience is able to identify them and use them to navigate, is equally important. Last but not least, the designer must give the typography an overall character that brings the parts together and allows them to be used flexibly among system- or serial-based components, without sacrificing the fundamental continuity of reading the information.

Reading

The Typography of Publications

words   words   words

words   words   words

Ton   Ton

Tym   Tym

Wer   Wer

Ave   Ave

1–3
This comparison shows optically uniform spacing for the regular weight of a sans-serif typeface, in contrast to mathematical, overly tight, and overly loose spacing.

The normally spaced lines (2) show consistent, rhythmic alternation between dark (the strokes) and light (the counterforms) both within and between characters.

Dark spots are evident in the example spaced too tightly (3, bottom), where the strokes are closer together between letters than within them.

4
Tightening or loosening the spacing between these pairs of letters corrects for the awkward counterspaces inherent in their forms. Shifting the lowercase *y* to the right, under the right crossbar of the *T*, for example, allows the spacing between them to become optically similar to that of subsequent letters.

Crafting Extended Text

Making text comfortable for sustained reading requires more involvement by a designer than does the typography of a poster or similar, more immediate media. The complexity of information delivered in a publication assumes more complex hierarchical treatment of navigational elements such as headlines, subheads, and so on; but the core issue is the visual quality of running text, and how it relates to these elements among a publication's pages.

THE OPTICS OF SPACING The spacing of letters in words, sentences, and paragraphs is vital to create a uniform gray value for minimal reader distraction. Each typeface has a distinct rhythm of strokes and spaces. This relationship between form and counterform defines the optimal spacing of that particular typeface and, therefore, of the overall spacing between words, lines of type, and among paragraphs and columns of text.

Looking at letters set together as a word offers a clue to how they should be spaced in that particular typeface and size. Creating a consistent gray value in text depends on setting the letters so that there is even alternation of solid and void—within and between the letters. A series of letters that is set too tightly, so that the counterforms within the letters are optically bigger than those between letters, creates noticeable dark spots in the line: the exterior strokes of the letters bond to each other visually where they come together. At the other extreme, letters that are set too loosely become singular elements, divorced from the line and recognizable as individual forms, making the appraisal of words difficult. Evenly set sequences of letters show a consistent, rhythmic alternation of black and white—form and counterform repeating at the same rate from left to right.

The primary difficulty in achieving evenly spaced type is that different letters have different densities—some are lighter or darker than others. Added to this phenomenon are the directional thrusts of different strokes and the varied sizes and shapes of the counterforms. Some are open, some closed, and some decidedly uneven in relation to the distribution of strokes in a given letter. To correct for these disparities, digital typefaces are programmed to add and subtract space from between different pairs of letters depending on

Mm	Mm	5
Mm	Mm	6
Mm	Mm	9
Mm	Mm	12
Mm	Mm	14
Mm	Mm	18
Mm	Mm	24
Mm	Mm	36
Mm	Mm	48
Mm	Mm	60

The standard point measurement of type sizes, shown here in oldstyle and sans-serif specimens. Text sizes range from 9 to 12 points; sizes of 14 points and larger are called display sizes and are usually reserved for elements such as headlines. Sizes smaller than 9 points are called caption sizes. Note the apparent difference in optical size of the two styles.

1

At vero eos et accusam et justo duo.

At vero eos et accusam et justo duo.

At vero eos et accusam et justo duo.

At vero eos et accusam et justo duo.

2

Trips   Trips   Trips

1

A line specimen set here at 16 points and again at 6 points. Uncorrected, the spacing in the smaller type is inadequate for good character recognition. Adding space between letters greatly improves their legibility and their overall look.

2

Here, the same word is in three different faces at 24 points. The oldstyle serif appears smallest; its low-ercase letters have a pro-portionally small x-height. Because the sans-serif lowercase letters are larger in proportion to the cap height, they appear larger; the same is true of the modern serif to the right.

what the combinations are. These sets of letters, called kerning pairs, provide for most circumstances of letterform combination, but not all. Invariably, a designer must correct unusual spacing that the computer's software is unable to address.

TYPE SIZES AND SPACING The drawing of a typeface has an impact on the perception of its size. For example, a sentence set in an oldstyle serif and a similar-weight sans serif at the same point size will appear to be in two different sizes. The discrepancy results from the sans serif's larger x-height: its lowercase letters are larger in relation to the cap height than those of the serif. The difference in set size and apparent size can vary as much as 2 or 3 points depending on the face. A sans serif such as Univers may be perfectly comfortable to read at a size of 9 points, but an oldstyle face such as Garamond Three at that size will appear tiny and

difficult to read. Setting the Garamond at 11 or 12 points will make it more legible, as well as make it appear the same size as the Univers.

Setting type smaller or larger than the optimal reading size for text also has an impact on spacing. Comfortable and efficient reading of long texts, such as books, newspapers, or journals, is possible when the type size ranges between 10 and 14 points—the texture of the type is a uniform gray and the letterforms are small enough that their details are not perceived as distinct visual elements. Optimal spacing at reading size means that the strokes and counterforms alternate evenly. As type is decreased in size, letterspace must be increased to allow the eye to separate the letters for clarity. At the other extreme, the space between letters must be decreased as the type size increases beyond conventional reading size.

The Type Is as Big as It Looks. Judge the type size by how legible it seems at a given size, not by applying a formula: "Text should be 10 points." A 10-point sans serif may be too big; a 10-point oldstyle serif may be too small. Here's a point of reference for what readers will tolerate: the average newspaper sets its body text (usually a modern serif) at 9 points.

Paragraph Architecture
The Building Blocks of Text Type

As words and then sentences are strung together, they cluster to form a basic component of typographic design—the paragraph. Paragraphs can be set in all manner of ways: wide, narrow, aligned or nonaligned, singly or in groups. The paragraph is the archetypal building block of a text; as such, its structure, spacing, and optical qualities warrant the designer's attention. Regardless of the nature of the content in a particular paragraph, it must first be considered independently to a certain degree to find an optimal width and depth for comfortable reading. The width of a paragraph depends on a few features: type size, word space, and interline space, or leading.

SPACE BETWEEN WORDS The space between words is derived from the rhythm of strokes and counters established by the letterspacing itself. Typically, the wordspace can be defined by the width taken up by a lowercase *i* as though it has been spaced continuously with the last letter of a word and the first letter of the word that follows. The space between words is, therefore, smaller when the text is set more tightly and larger when the text is set more loosely.

The space between words should be the minimum needed to separate them. When the wordspace becomes too great, lines of type begin to fracture. If large wordspaces appear over and over again, they often align from one line to the next, creating white channels of space called rivers. Rivers are problematic because they appear to connect words between lines, interfering with sequential understanding in sentences. If the eye cannot hold the line of type, comprehension is effectively destroyed.

THE INTERLINE SPACE Leading (pronounced "ledding") is the vertical measure from the baseline of one sentence in a paragraph to the baseline of the sentence below it. Leading has a profound impact on a paragraph's legibility and changes the paragraph's visual texture. The first considerations that affect the leading of text are the height of the lowercase letters and the height and depth of their ascenders and descenders, respectively. Obviously, these strokes must not interfere with each other between lines—joined or overlapped strokes diminish character recognition and create dark spots that stop the eye. Typefaces with tall ascenders and deep descenders, therefore, need additional space between lines to avoid this problem. Likewise, typefaces with large x-height fill the line depth considerably, so more leading is required to offset the increased density created by the lowercase.

The line length of a paragraph also affects leading. A mature reader can grab a snapshot of several words simultaneously; the more advanced the reader, the more the eye grabs. Over time, a reader is able to process several snapshots together in rapid succession, but only to a point. Without a slight break in the process, the reader begins to jumble the snapshots and becomes confused. That break is the return: the end of a line and the backtrack across the paragraph in reverse to find the next line. The reader must keep track of the sequence of snapshots and locate the beginning of the next line. The designer's goal is to find the optimal relationship between these factors so that the paragraph is as easy as possible to negotiate and interferes minimally with reading comprehension. To achieve comfortable leading, therefore, the designer must also consider the paragraph width.

3

Normal, uniform wordspacing can be conceived of as the space determined by setting an invisible lowercase *i* between the words as though it is being letterspaced as continuous text. The effect of uneven wordspacing is evident in the appearance of rivers.

4

A comparison of normal (top) and loose (bottom) wordspacing, using the same lowercase *i* method.

5

Examples of leading set solid and corrected for large x-height and deep ascenders and descenders. In the example to the left, the large body of the lowercase fills the line, increasing its optical activity, as well as its density, or gray value; the ascenders and descenders begin to crash together between lines. In the example to the right, 2 points of added leading alleviates these problems, inserting "air" into the text.

3

one i hopes i the i words i are

one hopes the words are

4

one i hopes i the i words i are i spaced i evenly

o n e i h o p e s i t h e i w o r d s i a r e

5

At vero eos et accusam et justo duo dolores et ea rebum. Stet clita kasd gubergren, no sea takimata sanctus est Lorem ipsum dolor sit amet. Lorem ipsum dolor sit amet, consetetur sadipscing elitr, sed diam nonumy eirmo tempor invidunt ut labore et dolore magna aliquyam erat, sed diam voluptua. At vereos

At vero eos et accusam et justo duo dolores et ea rebum. Stet clita kasd gubergren, no sea takimata sanctus est Lorem ipsum dolor sit amet. Lorem ipsum dolor sit amet, consetetur sadipscing elitr, sed diam nonumy eirmo tempor invidunt ut labore et dolore magna

EFFECTS ON PARAGRAPH WIDTH The width of a paragraph depends heavily on the size of type being used and, therefore, the number of characters that can fit on a single line. Regardless of the type size or the reader's maturity, between fifty and eighty characters (including spaces) can be processed before a return—with words averaging between five and ten letters, that means approximately eight to twelve words per line. Achieving this character count determines the width of a paragraph. The proportions of the page format—and the amount of text that must be made to fit overall—may affect paragraph width, but character count is the best starting point for defining an optimal width for the paragraph.

Leading is somewhat dependent on the width of the paragraph, the type size, and its spacing. The space between lines should be noticeably larger than the optical height of the lines, but not so much that it becomes pronounced. Similarly, the leading must not be so tight that the reader locates the beginning of the same line after the return and begins reading it again. As paragraph width increases, so must the leading, so that the beginnings of the lines are more easily distinguished. Oddly, as the width of a paragraph narrows, the leading must also be increased: otherwise, a reader is likely to grab several lines together because the snapshots he or she takes while scanning the text encompass the full paragraph width.

1

11 points

Garamond 3 Italic
At vero eos et accusam et justo duo dolores et ea rebum veritas

Clarendon
At vero eos et accusam et justo duo

Futura Medium
At vero eos et accusam et justo duo dolores et

Impact
At vero eos et accusam et justo duo dolores et ea

Univers 45
At vero eos et accusam et justo duo dolores et

Bauer Bodoni
At vero eos et accusam et justo duo dolores et ea rebum

9 points

Garamond 3 Italic
At vero eos et accusam et justo duo dolores et ea rebum veritas in lingua fra

Clarendon
At vero eos et accusam et justo duo dolores

Futura Medium
At vero eos et accusam et justo duo dolores et ea rebum

Impact
At vero eos et accusam et justo duo dolores et ea rebum veri

Univers 45
At vero eos et accusam et justo duo dolores et ea rebum

Bauer Bodoni
At vero eos et accusam et justo duo dolores et ea rebum in lingua fr

2

In the finest book work
the pages of text are printed
in such a manner that the
lines on a recto page backup
exactly those printed on
the reverse, or verso, side.
This care in setting and
printing, nullified when extra
space is inserted between

In the finest book work
the pages of text are printed
in such a manner that the
lines on a recto page backup
exactly those printed on
the reverse, or verso, side.
This care in setting and
printing, nullified when extra
space is inserted between

1

A comparison of character count for a selection of typefaces at two text sizes on the same paragraph width. As with all typographic rules, there is a range of values that is comfortable for the average reader. Given a fifty- to eighty-character comfort range, it is easy to see that a paragraph must widen as the type size (or character width) increases and narrow as it decreases, in order to maintain optimal character count in a line.

2

A mature reader's visual snapshot of word groups may conflict with a narrow paragraph that is leaded too tight. In the first example, the snapshot takes in not just a full line of type on the narrow column but also portions of the lines below. The second example shows a reduced snapshot that aids comprehension; the reader is forced to assimilate the word groups in sequence because the lines have been leaded far enough apart to prevent subsequent lines from interfering with each other.

Text from *The Finer Points of Spacing and Arranging Type* by Geoffrey Dowding; Wace & Company, 1954

Find the Best Ratio. Wide paragraph? Add leading! Narrow paragraph? Add leading! Each kind of alteration demands extra interline space to help resolve reading problems.

The Optimal Paragraph

A desirable paragraph setting is one in which a constellation of variables achieves a harmonic balance. Since extended running text is such an important consideration for a publication, finding the optimal paragraph is one way to begin to develop overall typographic structure. A designer might first make some assumptions about the text typeface based on his or her sense of its appropriateness from a conceptual standpoint and based on its visual attributes—the relative height of the lowercase letters, the general weight of the strokes and any contrast within them, the height of the ascenders and descenders—and set a text paragraph at an arbitrary width and arbitrary text size. Judging from this first attempt, the designer may opt to adjust the size of the text, loosen or tighten its overall spacing, open or close up the leading, and change the width in successive studies.

By comparing the results of these variations, the designer will be able to determine the most comfortable text setting for extended reading. At what point is the type size too small—or uncomfortably large? Are the lines relatively even in length or do they vary a lot? Is there excessive hyphenation, indicating that the paragraph is too narrow to allow a useful character count? Is the leading creating too dense a field of text to feel comfortable? During this study, it may become clear that several options for width and leading are optimal, but the designer must choose only one as a standard for the publication. This choice has implications for the page size, the number of columns of text that may fit on it, and optimal sizes for other text groupings, such as captions, callouts, and so on.

3

A At vero eos et accusam et justo duo dolores et ea rebum. Stet clita kasd gubergren, no sea takimata sanctus est Lorem ipsum dolor sit amet. Lorem ipsum dolor sit amet, consetetur sadipscing elitr, sed diam nonumy eirmod tempor invidunt ut labore et dolore magna aliquyam erat, sed diam voluptua. At vero eos et accusam et justo duo dolores et ea rebum.

B At vero eos et accusam et justo duo dolores et ea rebum. Stet clita kasd gubergren, no sea takimata sanctus est Lorem ipsum dolor sit amet. Lorem ipsum dolor sit amet, consetetur sadipscing elitr, sed diam nonumy eirmod tempor invidunt ut labore et dolore magna aliquyam erat, sed diam voluptua. At vero eos et accusam et justo duo dolores et ea rebum.

C At vero eos et accusam et justo duo dolores et ea rebum. Stet clita kasd gubergren, no sea takimata sanctus est Lorem ipsum dolor sit amet. Lorem ipsum dolor sit amet, consetetur sadipscing elitr, sed diam nonumy eirmod tempor invidunt ut labore et dolore magna aliquyam erat, sed diam voluptua. At vero eos et accusam et justo duo dolores et ea rebum.

D At vero eos et accusam et justo duo dolores et ea rebum. Stet clita kasd gubergren, no sea takimata sanctus est Lorem ipsum dolor sit amet. Lorem ipsum dolor sit amet, consetetur sadipscing elitr, sed diam nonumy eirmod tempor invidunt ut labore et dolore magna aliquyam erat, sed diam voluptua. At vero eos et accusam et justo duo dolores et ea rebum.

E At vero eos et accusam et justo duo dolores et ea rebum. Stet clita kasd gubergren, no sea takimata sanctus est Lorem ipsum dolor sit amet. Lorem ipsum dolor sit amet, consetetur sadipscing elitr, sed diam nonumy eirmod tempor invidunt ut labore et dolore magna aliquyam erat, sed diam voluptua. At vero eos et accusam et justo duo dolores et ea rebum.

3

In this study of a paragraph, the variables of type size, spacing, leading, and paragraph width are tested to arrive at a text setting that results in the most comfortable spacing, the least hyphenation, and a decisive rag.

A Initial setting: solid leading, larger type size

B Solid leading, smaller type size: more than optimal character count for width

C Same size and leading, but substitution of a face with shallower ascents and descents

D Increased leading: more comfortable, but the paragraph is still too wide and the substituted face too small

E The paragraph width is narrowed and the type size increased by a point: optimal character count, decisive rag, and comfortable leading

Separating Paragraphs
Clarifying Sequence

As a paragraph lengthens to become deeper than it is wide, it takes on a vertical stress and becomes a column. Within a column, paragraphs that follow each other must somehow be differentiated so that the reader is aware that one has ended and another one has begun. One approach is to simply insert a hard return—a blank line of the same leading— between one paragraph and the next. In columns set with text showing a large x-height, or with a smaller x-height and tighter leading, this treatment may look fine. In other cases, though, it may seem excessive: the return may appear to separate the column, disturbing the column's vertical mass, or the return's sharp line negative space may interfere visually with other elements.

1–3

These samples show different approaches for indicating paragraph breaks. In the first, an annual report, the paragraphs run together but their breaks are indicated by an indent. The second shows an interesting approach in which the first few words of the paragraphs are shifted above the baseline and set in a style that contrasts the text. The third shows paragraphs separated by subheads after a proportional return.

1 Soapbox Design
Communications
Toronto, Canada

2 Faydherbe/DeVringer
The Hague, Netherlands

3 UNA [Amsterdam]
Designers *Amsterdam,
Netherlands*

INDENTING In traditional typesetting, columns were set without space between paragraphs, in order to save space and, thus, paper cost. Instead, the beginning of a new paragraph was indicated by an indent, in which the first line of a new paragraph starts a few character widths in from the left alignment. This treatment works particularly well in justified setting. The depth of the indent is subjective but must be noticeable. An em (set-em) indent is noticeable but often is not enough. If the leading is loose, the indent must be deeper: more interline space normalizes the perception of the column's width (this is why adding leading smooths out irregular rags), so a bigger hole must be cut into the paragraph. Sometimes, a designer may exaggerate the indent for visual effect. If the paragraphs are long and set in relatively wide columns, this treatment often helps break up the wall of text by introducing a rhythm of cuts into the columns.

Indents must be approached carefully if the text is set ragged right. Since the rag is already changing the line lengths on the right edge of the column, the indent on the left side loses some of its visual power, appearing somewhat sloppy or causing the top lines of the columns to appear as though they are changing alignment.

1

are needed for ve on any possi- the condition of g. The first of independent and against pres- econd is the gained at the ffering, which voice against rly that hidden of us who would cy for personal ng themselves st great writers he material of jouissance of gressive thrust creation. I wish on could extend dinary lives, erywhere, n we all serve,

Things fall apart; the centre cannot hold;
Mere anarchy is loosed upon the world,
The blood-dimmed tide is loosed, and everywhere
The ceremony of innocence is drowned;
The best lack all conviction, while the worst
Are full of passionate intensity

And you know the ominous augury of the last words of the poem, "the rough beast" that "slouches towards Bethlehem to be born." We are too weak to do anything about the "rough beast." This is true. But we are the archivists of every move of the rough beast. And we know from our own records that in spite of the falsification of truth that is taking place everywhere in the world, and in spite of the great advances in all spheres of life in the last hundred years, the human rights map of the world is more or less the same. The killing goes on, the torture goes on, the hidden and live burial of those who raise their voices against atrocities goes on, the suppression and the burning of books goes on, the kidnapping of journalists goes on; and the "goes on"

important step, because, someone wil been with the PEN family for so many and knew it inside out could surely do job than a person who lacked her exp

Fundraising should be the job of ev on the board, as well as the job of the tive director. And this happened in the year of my tenure as president. By av the past pitfalls, by relegating authorit right person to do the right job, we su in raising enough money not only to b sufficient, but also to have the capabi hiring a person who would work on th grams that Haroon Siddiqui, Isobel Ha myself had planned which needed im tation. With what we have done in thi tion, the Writers in Exile Committee v together all the writers living in exile i Canada, giving them hope and provid with the right apparatus for recognitic

Our job is to fight against the viola freedom of expression everywhere. T who come on board should know tha

2

tie en
s het
an de
SVB?
lemen
et de
d? Hoe

6.1   Een geoliede betaalmachine

DE SVB KAN WORDEN BETITELD als het grootste Nederland. Als uitvoeringsorganisatie van de sociale ze jaarlijks circa 36 miljoen betalingen aan ruim 4,5 miljoe gerechtigden, van wie ongeveer 200.000 mensen buiten Hiermee is per jaar *f* 53 miljard gemoeid.

DE TAKEN DIE DE SVB UITVOERT, zijn bij wet be continuïteit. Sinds hun ontstaan in de jaren vijftig en ze van drie volksverzekeringen (ouderdomspensioen, nabe kinderbijslag) tot de meest omvangrijke taak van de SV dit traditionele takenpakket aangevuld met de uitvoerin regelingen, zoals het persoonsgebonden budget in de zo voor asbestslachtoffers. Voor al deze taken geldt dat de rechtmatige, effectieve en efficiënte betaling van publie rechthebbenden.

OPGERICHT IN 1901 ONDER DE NAAM Rijksverze socialeverzekeringswet ging uitvoeren, is de SVB het o de sociale zekerheid in Nederland. Anno 2001 is het be moderne, geoliede machine, zonder toeters en bellen. zijn plaats. De SVB kent niet zozeer een genoeglijke of over als een afgemeten, gestroomlijnde organisatie; ope raderties. Ernstige storingen in de distributie van de nu

HANGING INDENTS Another alternative is to create a hanging indent for the first line of a new paragraph. This may be done whether there is additional space between paragraphs or not. A hanging indent clearly establishes the beginnings of paragraphs and may also help the reader count lines as another reference point while scanning text. On the other hand, the hanging lines require extra space between columns that appear next to each other in horizontal configurations. In addition, the use of hanging indents is so unconventional that it may be distracting.

At vero eos et accusam et justo duo era dolores et ea rebum. Stet clita kasd gubergren, no sea takimata sanc tus estorem ipsum dolor sit amet.

Lorem ipsum dolor sit amet, consete tur sadipscing elitr, sed diam non umy eirmod tempor invidunt ut labore et dolore magna aliquyamer at, sed diam voluptua. At vero eos et accusam et justo duo dolores et ea rebum. At vero eos et accusam et justo duo era dolores et ea rebum. Stet clita kasd gubergren, no sea takimata sanctus est Lorem ipsum dolor sit amet. At vero eos et accu sam et justo duo era dolores et ea rebum. Stet clita kasd gubergren, no sea takimata sanctus est Lorem ipsum dolor sit amet.

Lorem ipsum dolor sit amet, consete tur sadipscing elitr, sed diam non umy eirmod tempor invidunt ut labore et dolore magna aliquyamer at, sed diam voluptua. At vero eos et accusam et justo duo dolores et ea rebum. At vero eos et.

3

Russische troepenverplaatsingen. In 1948 rukken de Russen inderdaad een stukje verder op naar het westen, als de communistische partij in Tsjechoslowakije de macht overneemt en het land toetreedt tot het Sovjet-blok.

De paniek van drs. Lou de Jong
Meteen daarna komt drs. Lou de Jong, directeur van het Rijksinstituut voor Oorlogsdocumentatie (RIOD), in actie. Hij denkt 'dat de Derde Wereld-oorlog binnen relatief korte tijd een feit zal zijn', en stuurt een nota naar minister-president Beel, de opvolger van Schermerhorn. Hij waarschuwt voor de meedogenloosheid van de Russen en bepleit voorbereidingen: 'Geen overheidstaak is urgenter dan deze.' Bij een Russische inval moeten de bevolkingsadministraties worden vernietigd, vindt De Jong. Regering en Koninklijk Huis moeten het land verlaten, maar Koningin Wilhelmina, wier gezondheid te wensen overlaat, kan afstand doen van de troon en blijven. Een 'panische vlucht van degenen die (...) er de middelen toe hebben' moet worden voorkomen.

PARAGRAPH SPACING A designer has the option of introducing a specific amount of space between paragraphs that is different from both hard return and text leading. This option is as appropriate as any of the others already described but requires some study on the part of the designer to determine the measure of the space. A good place to start is to use a measure of 1.5 times the leading within paragraphs. With a text leading of 12 points from baseline to baseline, for instance, the measure between the baseline of one paragraph's last line and the baseline of the first sentence in the paragraph following could be 18 points. This space may be more or less than enough, or exactly the right amount, depending on the designer's sensibility.

PARAGRAPH SUBHEADS Sometimes, a paragraph may begin with a short introductory phrase, usually referred to as a subhead. The designer should first determine the space between the subhead and introductory paragraph, if any. The leading after the subhead may be the same as between the subsequent lines, or the subhead may have a distinct space following it. In any case, the space between the end of one paragraph and the subhead following must be clearly different than the space between the subhead and the text it introduces. Less space should appear between the subhead and its following paragraph than above the subhead, or the two will seem unrelated.

Typographic Detail: The Finer Points

Typically, the crafting of type beyond its big-picture aspects—getting it to fit on the page with other material and look stylish in the layout—goes unnoticed. However, the details—treatment of punctuation and symbols, alignments of subheads and text across paragraphs, leftover words—are equally, if not more, important to ensure smooth reading. It is often assumed, as with letter- and wordspacing, that font software accounts for the spacing of these characters and need never be evaluated. This is seldom true. Knowing these fundamental rules for clean text setting keeps the designer alert to potential spacing problems and helps improve the look and readability of running text.

1

AVOID A BAD CRASH The content within parentheses and brackets will usually benefit from additional space, as well as a possible baseline shift, to separate it from these marks—especially italic forms with ascenders that are likely to crash into the marks if left at the default spacing. In particular, lowercase italic *f*, *l*, *k*, and *h*, and many of the uppercase, need this adjustment.

2

QUESTION THE SPACES Exclamation and question marks often benefit from being separated from their sentences by an extra bit of space. A full wordspace is too much, as is half a wordspace; but 20/100 of an em (set-em), or +20 tracking, is usually sufficient.

say what? say yes!
say what ? say yes !

3

TAKE OUT SPACE The space before a comma or quotation mark should be reduced; these marks "carry" additional space above or below them. Similarly, the wordspace following a comma, apostrophe, or quotation mark should also be slightly reduced.

like so," he said.
like so," he said.

4

KNOW YOUR DASHES There are three horizontal punctuation lines—the hyphen, en dash, and em dash. Use the correct one for its intended function and adjust the spaces around them so that they flow optically within text. A full wordspace on either side is too much, although there are times when this may be appropriate. The default lengths and baseline orientation of each mark may need to be altered to improve their relationship to surrounding text—the hyphen often sits low and the em dash is sometimes too long.

Hyphen *Combines words or breaks them between lines*

in-depth look

En Dash *Separates ranges of figures or durations in time*

100–200 pages

Em Dash *Separates descriptive or interrupting clauses or phrases within text*

beware—it is

5 **A CLUE TO OPTIMAL SPACING** Ligatures—specially drawn characters that optically correct for spacing difficulties in particular combinations of letters—provide a clue to the optimal spacing of a given font. Since ligatures are drawn with a fixed space between the characters (for example, fi), a designer can assume that the font's creator determined this fixed space as optimal for the ligated pair based on his or her appraisal of what optimal spacing for the entire font should be. If the ligatures within running text appear more tightly, or more loosely, spaced than the nonfixed characters around them, the font either needs to be respaced accordingly, or the designer may choose to replace the ligature with the two independent characters instead.

finesse finesse
||||||||| |||||||||

6 **PUSH AND PULL** Colons and semicolons need additional space preceding them and less space following.

usually true; and just
usually true; and just

7 **FIND A FORMULA FOR SUPERS AND SUBS** The size and spacing of subscript and superscript characters, such as those used in footnotes or chemical formulae, must be determined in relation to a given font size and the leading within paragraphs. Typically, the sub- or superscript character is just shy of the x-height in size, although in an oldstyle face with a small x-height, this measure may prove too small. A subscript character should be set shifted below the baseline so that it rests on the descent line and crests just above the meanline; a superscript character should hang from the capline and rest marginally below the meanline. In terms of letterspacing, a sub- or superscript character should be set to follow the same optical rhythm of the surrounding characters.

usually CO_2 and others.[5]

8 **TAKE A LOOK AT THE FIGURES** Numerals within running text always need spacing adjustments, especially within groups of numerals. Lining numerals, which extend from baseline to cap height, usually require a bit of extra letterspace but tend to be more condensed and more varied in form than uppercase letters. Numerals in complex paragraph structures, such as tables, are generally tabulated—arranged flushing right or around a decimal point in vertical arrangements of figures.

From 1865 to 1880 there were 110 such examples, and the

125.52
3,228.00
22.65
0.2185
443.24

From 1865 to 1880 there were 110 such examples, and the

9 **UH-OH … SMALL CAPS!** Small caps within running text (used for acronyms) are smaller than full-height uppercase letters but still need additional space around them to improve their recognition. The small caps of many fonts are too small and appear lighter in weight than the upper- and even lowercase letters. A designer may elect to adjust the point size of the small caps up by as much as a point or two to achieve uniform weight and spacing, without confusing the small caps and the uppercase.

the mission of the AIGA is to bring
the mission of the AIGA is to bring
the mission of the AIGA is to bring

10 **SO IT'S NOT A LETTER** The appearance of analphabetic symbols, such as @, #, $, and %, and some linear punctuation marks, such as / (virgule), may be improved by slight spatial adjustments. The @ usually appears too high on the line; a slight shift below the baseline causes the character to center optically on the line of text. The # and % display a diagonal thrust akin to italic forms, so decreasing the space preceding them—but increasing the space following them—helps them participate in the overall rhythm of the letter- and wordspaces. The / tends to benefit from additional space on either side, although a full wordspace is far too much; +20 to +30 tracking is usually comfortable.

webmaster@info.org   hybrid serif/sans serif
webmaster@info.org   hybrid serif / sans serif

11 **MIND THE GAP** A single word space—never two—follows a period before the initial cap of the next sentence.

and thus it was. When they began to
and thus it was. When they began to

12

STYLE YOUR BULLETS The size and typeface of bullets and analphabetic symbols should be considered relative to the text surrounding them. The default bullet, for instance, is usually enormous and distracting compared to the typeface in which it appears. The bullet needs to be noticeable but not stick out—slightly heavier then the text's vertical stroke weight is enough. Don't be afraid to change the bullet's typeface—or use a dingbat or even a period, shifted off the baseline—to bring it stylistically closer to the surrounding text.

540 Evergreen Drive•London W1

540 Evergreen Drive·London W1

540 Evergreen Drive·London W1

13

A NAME IS A NAME Avoid breaking names, but if necessary, break right before the last name—never in the middle of a name, and never before an initial.

Harold Jeffer-
son

Alexandra
B. Rosenzweig

14

KEEP 'EM UPRIGHT Use upright parentheses and brackets, even if the text in which they appear is italic. In their sloped versions, these marks appear weak and usually exacerbate the spacing problems associated with them.

As he arrived (shortly before noon) there was

As he arrived (shortly before noon) there was

As he arrived (shortly before noon) there was

15

WATCH THE BREAKS! Avoid breaking words across lines (hyphenating) so that short or incomplete stubs (-ed, -or, -ing, -al, -ly, and so on) begin the line following. Likewise, make sure there are at least four letters in the word ending the line before the break.

16

TO INDENT OR NOT TO INDENT? In setting text in which paragraphs run together and are separated by indenting the first line, the first paragraph on the page should have no indent.

17

MIX AND MATCH ON PURPOSE Judge whether the difference in weight between the roman and bold within a given type family is different enough to be noticeable. If not, feel free to substitute a similarly drawn bold from a related family—or choose one that is very different to increase its contrast within the running text.

each **incidence** requires

each **incidence** requires

each **incidence** requires

18

HANG YOUR PUNCTUATION Most punctuation marks, especially quotation marks, should hang outside the aligned text if they occur at the beginning of a line. This rule sometimes applies to bullets as well; a designer may opt to maintain the alignment of the bulleted text and hang the bullets in the margin or gutter.

of listening to the sea calling
determined, and thought it h
"Think carefully," he said, agai
foremost a kind of singular wi
responds with a word in kind

· **Optional leather seats**
· **Five-speed transmission**
· **ABS braking system**
· **Power steering**

19 **TOO MUCH IS JUST TOO MUCH** In justified setting, adjusting the letterspacing to avoid rivers is inevitable, but don't adjust too much. Like rivers, overly tight—and therefore, very dark—lines of text are extremely distracting.

Lorem ipsum dolore sit amet, con sectetuerat adipiscing elit. Integer lectusi purusii, rutrumi egetii, com modorem artem, feugiat eget, erat. Pellentesque dapibus, nunc lobor tis vestibulum euismod, odios felis luctus tortori, at pulvinar risus mau ris eget sem. Integer ax nequet. In leo dolorie, posiuere vitae, pellen tesque actua, elemen tum quis, elit. Cras ideom neque. Nullam dapibus plac erat lacusaei. Quella hendre rit, ipsum id ullamcorper pulvinar, velit nibh tincidun tii quam, vel hendrerit leo sem

Lorem ipsum dolore sit amet, con sectetuerat adipiscing elit. Integer lectusi purusii, rutrumi egetii, com modoratu emiarartem, feugiatusieget, erat. Pellentesque dapibus, nunc lobor tis vestibulum euismod, odios felis luctus tortori, at pulvinar risus mau ris eget sem. Integer ax nequet. In leo dolorie, posiuere vitae, pellen tesque actua, elemen tum quis, elit. Cras ideom neque. Nullam dapibus placer at lacusaei. Quella hendre rit, ipsum id ullamcorper pulvinar, velit nibh tin ciduntii quam, vel hendrerit

20 **DON'T CROSS THE CHANNELS** When possible, try to avoid hard returns between paragraphs aligning (or nearly aligning) between adjacent columns. As the horizontal negative channels created by the returns approach each other, they not only become distracting but also tend to redirect the eye across the columns and break the reading sequence.

Lorem ipsum dolore sit amet, con sectetuerat adipiscing elit. Integer lectusi purusii, rutrumi egetii, com modorem artem, feugiat eget, erat. Pellentesque dapibus, nunc lobor tis vestibulum euismod, odios felis luctus tortori, at pulvinar risus mau ris eget sem. Integer ax nequet. In leo dolorie, posiuere vitae, pellen tesque actua, elementum quis, elit.

Cras ideom neque. Nullam dapibus placerat lacusaei. Quella hendrerit, ipsum id ullamcorper pulvinar, velit nibh tincidunti quam, vel hendrerit ipsum primis in faucibus orci luctus et ultrices posuere cubiliam Curae; Integer bibendum dignissim quam. Etiam atuati malesudatu mollisr wisi. Maecenas aliquam, mi elementum Lorem ipsum dolore sit amet, con

Lorem ipsum dolore sit amet, con sectetuerat adipiscing elit. Integer lectusi purusii, rutrumi egetii, com modorem artem, feugiat eget, erat. Pellentesque dapibus, nunc lobor tis vestibulum euismod, odios felis luctus tortori, at pulvinar risus mau ris eget sem. Integer ax nequet. In leo dolorie, posiuere vitae, pellen tesque actua, elementum quis, elit. Cras ideom neque.

Vestibulum ante ipsum primis in faucibus orci luctus et ultrices posuere cubiliamus Curae; Integer bibendum dignisiomo quam. Etiam atuati malesudatu molliser wisi. Maecenas aliquam, mi elementum Lorem ipsum dolore sit amet, con

Lorem ipsum dolore sit amet, con sectetuerat adipiscing elit. Integer lectusi purusii, rutrumi egetii, com modorem artem, feugiat eget, erat. Pellentesque dapibus, nunc lobor tis vestibulum euismod, odios felis luctus tortori, at pulvinar risus mau ris eget sem. Integer ax nequet. In leo dolorie, posiuere vitae, pel lentesque actua, elementum quis, elit. Crasii ideom neque. Vierquet dapibus placerat lacusaei. Quella hendrerit, ipsum id ullamcorper pulvinar, velit nibh tincidunti quamati, vel hendrert leo sem et neque.

Lorem ipsum dolore sit amet, con sectetuerat adipiscing elit. Integer lectusi purusii, rutrumi egetii, com modorem artem, feugiat eget, erat. Pellentesque dapibus, nunc lobor tis vestibulum euismod, odios felis luctus tortori, at pulvinar risus mau ris eget sem. Integer ax nequet. In leo dolorie, posiuere vitae, pel lentesque actua, elementum quis, elit. Crasii ideom neque. Vierquet dapibus placerat lacusaei. Quella hendrerit, ipsum id ullamcorper pulvinar, velit nibh tincidunti quamati, vel hendrert leo sem et neque.

Vestibulum ante ipsum primis in faucibus orci luctus et ultrices posuere cubiliam Curae; Integer bibendum dignisimo quam. Etiam atuati malesudatu molliser wisi. Maecenas aliquam, mi elementum

21 **INCLUDE WITH CLARITY** Text inclusions, such as drop caps, lead lines, and subheads, should exhibit some clear logic in their appearance. Drop caps should sit on a baseline three, four, five, or more lines from the top of the column. A lead line should be a consistent number of words in the first line. A subhead, when appearing at the top of one column, should be aligned consistently with the text in columns preceding or following—optically.

DROP CAPITAL

Morem ipsum dolore sit amet, velure autei con sectetuerat adipiscing elit. Integer lectusi purusii, rutrumi egeti, commodorem artem, feugiat eget, erat. Pellentesque dapibus, nunc lortis vestib ulum euismod. Lorem ipsum dolore sit amet, con sectetuerat adipiscing elit. Integer lectusi purusii, rutrumi egetii, comi

LEAD LINE

LOREM IPSUM DOL sitaet, con sectetuerat adipiscing elit. Integer lectusi purusii, rutrumi egetii, com modorem artem, feugiat eget, erat. Pellentesque dapibus, nunc lobor tis vestibulum euismod, odios felis luctus tortori, at pulvinar risus mau Lorem ipsum dolore sit amet, con sectetuerat adipiscing elit. Integer lectusi purusii, rutrumi egetii, comi

SUBHEAD

Duis Autem Velure
Lorem ipsum dolore sit amet, con sectetuerat adipiscing elit. Integer lectusi purusii, rutrumi egetii, com modorem artem, feugiat eget, erat. Pellentesque dapibus, nunc lobor tis vestibulum euismod, odios felis Lorem ipsum dolore sit amet, con sectetuerat adipiscing elit. Integer lectusi purusii, rutrumi egetii, comi

22 **ITALIC TYPE NEEDS SPACING, TOO** Italic text used for emphasis within text sometimes appears smaller and tighter than its roman counterpart. Always evaluate the italic and adjust its size or spacing to fit most seamlessly with its surrounding text.

it had become *especially* cold outside, and

it had become *especially* cold outside, and

23 **CARE FOR THE WIDOWS** Never allow a single word—a widow—to end a paragraph. If widows constantly appear in the rough setting of a body of text, chances are that the column width needs to be adjusted. Ideally, the last line of a paragraph should be more than half the paragraph's width, but three words (no matter their length) are acceptable.

Lorem ipsum dolore sit amet, con sectetuerat adipiscing elit. Integer lectusi purusii, rutrumi egetii, com modorem artem, feugiat eget, erat. Pellentesque dapibus, nunc lobor tis vestibulum euismod, odios felis neque.

Lorem ipsum dolore sit amet, con sectetuerat adipiscing elit. Integer lectusi purusii, rutrumi egetii, com modorem artem, feugiat eget, erat. Pellentesque dapibus, nunc lobor tis vestibulum euismod, odios felis neque sectetuadipiscing.

24 **SAVE THE ORPHANS** Don't allow the last line of a paragraph to begin the top of a column. This orphan is especially distracting if there is a space separating the paragraph that follows—and jarring if it occurs at the very beginning of the left-hand page. Run the text back so that the new page starts a paragraph, or space the preceding text out so that the paragraph continues with at least three lines after the page break.

Lorem ipsum dolore sit amet, con sectetuerat adipiscing elit. Integer lectusi purusii, rutrumi egetii, com modorem artem, feugiat eget, erat. Pellentesque dapibus, nunc lobor tis vestibulum euismod, odios felis luctus tortori, at pulvinar risus mau ris eget sem. Integer ax nequet. In leo dolorie, posiuere vitae, pellen tesque actua, elementum quis, elit. Cras ideom neque. Nullam dapibus placerat lacusaei. Quella hendrerit, ipsum id ullamcorper pulvinar, velit nibh tincidunti quam, vel hendrerit leo sem et neque.

Vestibulum ante ipsum primis in faucibus orci luctus et ultrices posuere cubiliamus Curae; Integer bibendum dignisimo quam. Etiam atuati malesudatus molliser wisi. Maecenas aliquam, mi elementum

orem ipsum dolore.

Sit amet, consectet uerat adipisc ing elit. Integer lectusi purusii, rutrumi egetii, comorati soforem artem, feugiat tempis eget, summa. Pellentesque dapibus, nunc lobor tis vestibulum euismod, odios felis luctus tortori, at pulvinar risus mau ris eget sem. Integer ax nequet.

In leo dolorie, posiuere vitae, pel lentesque actua, elementum quis, elit. Crasii ideom neque. Vierquet dapibus placerat lacusaei. Quella hendrerit, ipsum iduati ullamcorper pulvinar, velitna nibhie tincidunti quamati, vel hendrert leo sem et neque. Vestibulum sum ante ipsum primis in faucibus orci luctus et ultricose posuere cubiliam Curae; Integer bibendum dignisim quam.

Composing Text in Space

After establishing the textural aspects of running copy, the designer must consider how it will be arranged within the space of the publication's pages. The shape of the text blocks, the logic of how lines of text align with each other in sequence, contrast between elements, and the negative space surrounding the text, all present numerous layout possibilities that will affect readability, as well as overall visual quality.

No matter how wide or deep, a paragraph may be set in several different configurations, or alignments: it may be set so that every line begins at the same left-hand starting point (flush left), at the same right-hand starting point (flush right), or with an axis centered on the paragraph width (centered). In centered type, the lines are different lengths and are centered over each other on the width's vertical axis; in justified type, the lines are the same length, aligning on both left and right sides. Justified text is the only setting in which the lines are the same length. In text set to align left, right, or centered, the uneven lengths of the lines create a soft shape on the nonaligned side that is called a rag.

ALIGNMENT AND SPACING The relationship of the paragraph's alignment and rag is yet another factor in determining a desirable text setting. First, the alignment of text in a paragraph has an effect on the spacing within it. In a paragraph set with a left alignment (flush left/ragged right, or FLRR), the wordspaces are uniform. Likewise in a paragraph set flush right/ragged left (FRRL) or in a centered paragraph. The wordspace in a justified paragraph, however, varies because the width of the paragraph is mathematically fixed, and the words on any given line must align on both sides—no matter how many words or how long they are. In justified text, wordspacing variation is the single most difficult issue to overcome. The result of poorly justified text in which the wordspace constantly changes is a preponderance of rivers. In particularly bad justified setting, the rivers are even more apparent than the interline space, causing the paragraph to become a jumble of strange word clusters. One method of minimizing this problem is to find the optimal flush-left paragraph width for the size of the type before justifying and then to widen the paragraph slightly or shrink the type size by half a point or a point. This adjustment can result in an optimal number of characters and words that fit comfortably upon justification and can compensate for the potential of long words to create undesirable spacing. A slightly wider paragraph also allows some flexibility in the way words are broken from line to line and gives the designer more options for rebreaking text to make it fit with good spacing.

1

Examples of alignment structures: flush left, ragged right; flush right, ragged left, centered axis, and justified.

2

This detail of newspaper columns shows an optimal relationship between paragraph width and text size in justified setting: hyphens are infrequent, and rivers are relatively absent.

La Voz de Galicia
A Coruña, Spain

1

At vero eos et accusam et justo duo dolores et ea rebum. Stet clia kasd gubergren, no sea taki mata sanctus est Lorem ipsum dolor sitame. Lorem ipsum dolor sit amet, consetetur sadipscing elitr, sed diam nonumy eirmod tempor invidunt ut labore et dolore magna aliquim erat, sed diam voluptua. At vero eos et accusam et justo duo dolores qea

Flush left/Ragged right

At vero eos et accusam et justo duo dolores et ea rebum. Stet clia kasd gubergren, no sea taki mata sanctus est Lorem ipsum dolor sitame. Lorem ipsum dolor sit amet, consetetur sadipscing elitr, sed diam nonumy eirmod tempor invidunt ut labore et dolore magna aliqum erat, sed diam voluptua. At vero eos et accusam et justo duo dolores qea

Flush right/Ragged left

At vero eos et am et justo duo dolores et eabum. Stet clita kasae gubergren, no sea tak mimata sanctus est Lorem ipsum dolor sit amet. Lorem ipsum dolor sit amet, consetetur adipsec elitr, sed diam nonumy eiru mod tempor invidunt ut laboret dolore magna aliquyam erat, sed diam voluptua. At veroteos et accusam et justo duo dolore

Centered Axis

At vero eos et accusam et justo duo dolores et ea rebum. Stet clita kasd gubergren, no sea takimata sanctu sest Lorem ipsum dolor sit amet. Lo rem ipsum dolor sit amet, conse tetur sadipscing elitr, sed diam nonumy eirmod tempor invidunt ut labore et dolore magna aliq uyam erat, sed diam voluptua. At vero eos et accusam et justo duo dolores et ea rebum.

Justified

3

A poorly justified text (top) displays wildly varied wordspaces and rivers. Adjusting the width of the paragraph, while maintaining the same point size, may help alleviate these spacing problems.

4

Example of a paragraph showing a desirable rag (left), and two paragraphs in which the rag is either too deep or active (middle), or too irregular (right). A rag is considered desirable if the measures of shortest and longest lines fall in a range that is one-fifth to one-seventh the width of the paragraph.

Investigating the Ragged Edge
Regularity and Rhythm

Ragged paragraphs offer the opportunity to avoid the spacing issues inherent in justified text. The wordspaces in these kinds of paragraphs remain constant. Ragged setting also introduces the pronounced textural effect of an organic edge whose opposition to the hard edge of the alignment imparts an immediate visual contrast to the page. The aligned edge restates the hard edge of the format, while the ragged edge counters it. The rag also helps provide optical separation between horizontally arranged paragraphs. Changing line lengths within the ragged edge help the reader recognize breaks more easily and, thus, differentiate individual lines on the return.

The rag of a paragraph may exhibit desirable or undesirable characteristics. As with letterspacing and wordspacing, uniformity is key to developing a good ragged edge: a rag may range from deep to shallow, active to subtle, but its uniformity and consistency from the top of a paragraph to the bottom are what make it desirable. Ragged line endings are considered optimal if they create an organic, unforced ripple down the edge of the paragraph, without pronounced indents or bulges. In an optimally ragged paragraph, the rag becomes invisible: the reader is never aware that the lines are ending at their natural conclusion. If the alternating lines end short and very long, the rag may call attention to itself, distracting the reader from following the content of the text. That said, a deep rag may be acceptable if it remains consistent throughout the duration of the text. The uniformity of an active rag also becomes invisible as a result of its consistency. A designer may opt to mitigate a deep rag by introducing more interline space.

AVOIDING BAD RAGS Never desirable, however, is a rag that begins at the outset of a paragraph guided by one kind of logic and transforms into another kind of logic as the paragraph progresses in depth; or a rag that shows excessive indenting from the right; or sharp, angular inclusions of space created by lines that become sequentially shorter. The overall unity of a rag can be easily compromised by the single occurrence of two short lines

Push and Pull. To justify text on optimal width—and avoid rivers and hyphens—first find optimal width for a flush-left setting, then widen the text box slightly or scale the type down half a point upon justifying.

1

There seemed too little space
to fit all the text; when she went
to check pagination, it was
clear that the layout needed to
be changed. She began with
a change in type size, looking to
gain some space around the

2

The current email infrastructure wasn't designed to handle the modern communication deluge. A gateway running sendmail on a Sun workstation simply doesn't scale. Says Weiss, "The problem wasn't lack of features, it was the yeoman's job of moving the mail. If the email isn't going out, who cares if you have the best spell checker?"

The problem for corporate clients isn't bandwidth, it's sockets—the number of simultaneous email connections your system can hold. A typical UNIX kernel, the backbone of most MTA systems, can easily and maintain 64 or maybe 128 connections. If you sacrifice some performance, you can squeeze that number up to 256.

To an IronPort box, 256 connections is the

address that's protected by an IronPort box, you get as many connections as you want; you may even get to cut to the head of the line. But if the box doesn't like you—if you can't prove that you're willing to play fair—the box dangles its massive connectivity in front of you, and then hands you one 28.8kbs socket to play with.

Intentionally degrading an email connection is called "throttling." It's a powerful tool for convincing spammers to play somewhere else, but to use throttling effectively, you have to be able to distinguish friend from foe. IronPort does by ranking each in-coming email based on information it gets from SenderBase (http://www.senderbase.com/), its "reputation filtering" service.

"Here's an example," says Weiss," Let's say ≫

"Throttling is a powerful tool to convince spammers to play somewhere else."

A Quick And Dirty History of Email

1970 ARPANET, the first network to connect remotely distributed computers, is implemented as a means to share expensive resources between a handful of academic computing centers.

limitation, it takes him two tries. The ARPANET community is divided: Most users condemn the exploit as violating the implicit "non-commercial use" pact and are annoyed that the heavy traffic shut down some servers. Free speech advocates defend the act.

1979 Kevin MacKenzie, remarking on

1996 Scott Weiss joins HoTMaiL, the largest email-hosting service on the Internet. The peculiar capitalization implies, the company was formed to promote the use of HTML in email. Around the same time, Scott Banister, future IronPort CTO, creates ListBot, a free email service for websites. Both

that create a boxy hole. In an optimal rag, the depth hovers between one-fifth and one-seventh of the paragraph's width.

Word order and word breaks across lines also affect the rag. Problems in ragged-right setting commonly arise when a series of short words—of, at, it, to, we, us, and the like—are broken to align at the left edge, creating a vertical river running parallel to the aligned edge; and when short words appear at the end of a long line between two shorter lines, appearing to break off and float. In such cases, the designer must weigh the consequences of rebreaking the lines to prevent these problems against their effect on the rag as whole.

Similarly, the breaking of words across lines—using a hyphen—can also be problematic if left uncorrected. From an editorial perspective, two successive lines ending with hyphens is undesirable. If a text is hyphenating excessively—more than once every ten lines or so—the problem lies in the relationship between the text's point size and the width of the paragraph; one or the other must be adjusted to correct the problem. Although a text free of hyphens would be best, this state of perfection is rarely possible; and, indeed, some designers argue that hyphenating words here and there benefits the uniformity of the rag by allowing lines to remain similar in length.

3

Too many hyphens in a row are considered undesirable and may be corrected by a slight adjustment in text size or paragraph width. Text that is dominated by hyphens is distracting. These paragraphs are set in the same size text, with subtle differences.

Too many hyphens in a row are considered undesirable and may be corrected by a slight adjustment in text size or paragraph width. Text that is dominated by hyphens is distracting. These paragraphs are set in the same size text, with subtle differences.

Too many hyphens in a row are considered undesirable and may be corrected by a slight adjustment in text size or paragraph width. Text that is dominated by hyphens is distracting. These paragraphs are set in the same size text, with subtle differences.

1

Successive repetition of words—especially short words—at the ends or beginnings of lines will have often undesirable effects on rag and spacing. At the ragged edge, such repetitions become distracting, especially if they extend outward from between shorter lines. Along the flush, at the beginnings of succesive lines, they create rivers—similar to those created in poorly justified text.

2

This detail of a newsletter layout, showing text set on various column widths, evinces close attention to detail: optimal size-to-width ratio, minimal hyphenation, and carefully considered rags with consistent alternation of length among lines.

Gorska Design *Chicago, USA*

3

Too many hyphens in a row are considered undesirable and may be corrected by a slight adjustment in text size or paragraph width. The three paragraphs shown here are set in the same size text, with subtle differences. The first paragraph shows uncorrected hyphenation and rag. The second shows a more active rag but no hyphens—a toss up between desired goals. The third shows a slightly wider paragraph and a more even rag; the only hyphen appears in the seventh line. One hyphen every ten lines or so is considered optimal.

Typographic Space
Text in Composition

Type and space interact in a figure/ground relationship that is mutually dependent. Type (the figure, or positive element) defines the qualities of the space that it breaks; space (the ground) helps define the qualities of the type that exists within it. Each element that is brought into the space adds texture and complexity but also decreases the amount of space in the format, forcing it into distinct shapes around the type like a puzzle. These spaces are integral to achieving flow through the type and providing a sense of order and unity. In addition, they help the viewer navigate around various elements—text, callouts, titles, and so on. An empty space is undefined except by its shape. As soon as a typographic element is added, the space is changed. If the type element is a single letter or word, the space focuses attention upon it; it is a point within the space. A single line of type has the qualities of a drawn line: it is directional, has a beginning and an end, and divides a format into two spaces—one above the type, and one below. If the line is placed in the optical center of the space, it is passive and neutral, as are the spaces around it. Shifting the line to the left or right changes the space: it creates tension near the format edge that counteracts the openness of the space it has left. Moving the line of type off the horizontal center breaks the space proportionally; each space now has its own quality and a relationship to the other. Subsequently breaking the space with additional elements divides the format into additional zones. The more even the proportions of these zones, the more neutral and passive the composition. The more varied the proportions, the more dynamic—a quality that is considered desirable because it involves the viewer and stimulates the eye. Passive compositions, in which the spatial proportions are regular, are monotonous and give the impression that all of the elements are of the same value.

4

word

word

word

5

publication design

publication design

publication design

4

The interdependency of type and space is relative. The presence of the same typographic element can become completely different depending on how it relates to the format. Conversely, the same space is altered dramatically by changing the size and position of the type within it.

5

A passive composition of one line of type, centered within a format, is activated by shifting the line off center, either vertically or horizontally. Each space is altered in relation to the other.

1

2

3

Publication Design
Workbook
A Real-World
Design Guide
Timothy Samara
Rockport Publishers

Publication Design
Workbook
A Real-World
Design Guide
Timothy Samara
Rockport Publishers

Publication Design
Workbook

A Real-World
Design Guide

Timothy Samara

Rockport Publishers

1, 2

Space is neutral until it is divided. Breaking the space into units of even proportion activates the space, but the space still remains relatively passive. Changing the size and proportion of the divisions establishes a sense of the points of alignment and casts each unit of space into a unique relationship with the ones around it. The interaction of these contrasting spaces helps engage the viewer.

3

In the first composition, the elements are clustered together in a passive relationship with the space of the format. Visual structure is created when the elements are positioned to subdivide the format. The type elements exhibit no structural differentiation between them.

Breaking the elements into separate components can clarify the information and create a more active visual structure.

The alignment of elements establishes a similarity of meaning among them. Separating an element from this alignment creates visual distinction.

ALIGNMENTS, MASSES, AND VOIDS The division of space creates structure, which unifies disparate elements in a composition. Several lines of type together create a different kind of structural relationship to the format than a single line of type; it relates to the single line but visually contrasts with it. This mass of texture further defines the space around it into channels that correspond to its height and depth, and between itself and the format in all directions. Separating elements within a grouping maintains a sense of the mass; it also introduces a greater complexity of structure by further subdividing the space.

Visual structure must evolve out of the verbal structure of language. The verbal sense helps define what material within it may be mass or line. A continuous sequence of thoughts will likely be clarified if clustered together; a distinct thought may benefit from being separated from the others. Both elements are positive forms—the figure within the composition. They are in contrast to each other as well as to the spaces around them. The relationship of typographic mass to these voids within the format is the essential relationship to be defined in typographic space—as it is in defining the rhythm of letterspacing and the space within a paragraph.

Regular intervals between masses and voids—unlike in letterspacing, wordspacing, and leading—are undesirable because regularity implies sameness, whereas the various type elements may be different and mean different things. Changing the proportions between masses and voids helps impart meaning to them. Related elements may be clustered together. Separations between individual or clustered elements indicate they are different in their meaning. On a visual level, the designer also creates contrast and rhythm within the composition by changing the proportional relationships between solids and voids. As type elements divide space in proximity to one another, their points of alignment become important. Aligning elements augments the sense of relationship between them. Further, alignments between elements help create directional movement through the elements in the format.

4

Walburg Pers | Sociale Verzekeringsbank

de SVB

een actueel beeld

van de

Sociale Verzekeringsbank

Dr Maarten van Bottenburg

5

SP System

fantoni

6

06

M

Mass

Global + Local

By embracing local and regional cultures within a global framework and providing products and solutions worldwide, we create an international critical mass of customers, employees, and partners.

We strive to achieve the best of both worlds—and share the global and local advantage with our stakeholders.

4

Clearly defined channels of space are created by the alignments of typographic elements in the title page of this publication. Three major intervals are defined left to right, while four are defined top to bottom. Areas of overlap create complex, ambiguous relationships.

Faydherbe/DeVringer
The Hague, Netherlands

5, 6

The tension between positive and negative space—and the invisible linear connections between elements— is what drives typography. Here, the proportions of negative space are related to the positive type elements.

5 Designwork SrL *Udine, Italy*
6 Ideas On Purpose
New York City, USA

7

Using the compositional elements of a photograph as a way to position type helps integrate the two kinds of content. In this catalog spread, a strong horizontal connection toward the bottom of the composition is contrasted by an irregular rhythm of vertical breaks.

Designwork SrL *Udine, Italy*

7

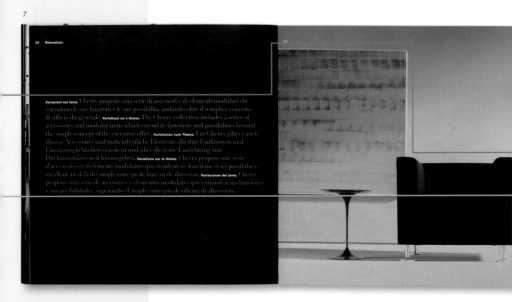

26 Relaxation.

27

Variazioni sul tema. Cherry propone una serie di accessori e di elementi modulari che estendono le sue funzioni e le sue possibilità, andando oltre il semplice concetto di ufficio dirigenziale. **Variations on a theme.** The Cherry collection includes a series of accessories and modular units which extend its functions and possibilities beyond the simple concept of the executive office. **Variationen zum Thema.** Für Cherry gibt es auch diverse Accessoires und maßeinheitliche Elemente, die ihre Funktionen und Einsatzmöglichkeiten erweitern und über die reine Einrichtung von Direktionsbüros weit hinausgehen. **Variations sur le thème.** Cherry propone una serie d'accessoires et d'eléments modulaires qui etendent ses fonctions et ses possibilités, en allant au-delà du simple concept de bureau de direction. **Variaciones del tema.** Cherry propone una serie de accesorios y elementos modulares que extienden sus funciones y sus posibilidades, superando el simple concepto de oficina de dirección.

Typographic Color
Contrast and Spatial Depth

Typographic color is similar to chromatic color—like red, blue, or orange—but deals only with changes in lightness and darkness, or value. Moreover, it is different from the qualities of chromatic color in that it describes changes in rhythm and texture. Changing the typographic color of the elements separates them from the surface and introduces the illusion of spatial depth. The perception of depth is very much keyed to the functioning of the human optical system and the way in which the brain interprets visual stimuli in the world of experience. Because of the way the eye transmits images of objects that are closer or farther away, a larger element appears closer than a smaller one, while a lighter element appears to recede into the distance. A texture appears to flatten out, as its shape and value determine its spatial depth more so than its components. A line appears to come forward regardless of its weight, although a heavier line comes farther forward than a narrow line. A typographic color change allows a designer to highlight structure and invigorate a page.

Contrast Is King. Because publications present the possibility of extensive configurations of running text, bringing change to various elements through weight, size, and style changes are key in creating lively pages. "Without contrast," as Paul Rand, the American designer, once said, "you're dead."

1

Ma quande lingues coalesce, li grammatica del resultant lingue es plu simplic e regulari quam ti del coalescent lingues. Li nov lingua franca va esser plu simplic e regulari quam li existent Europan lingues. It va esser tam simplic quam Occidental: in fact, it va esser Occidental. A un Angleso it va semblar un simplificat Angles, quam un skeptic Cambridge amico dit me que Occidental es. Ma quande lingues coalesce

Ma quande lingues coalesce, li grammatica del resultant lingue es plu simplic e regulari quam ti del coalescent lingues. Li nov lingua franca va esser plu simplic e regulari quam li existent Europan lingues. It va esser tam simplic quam Occidental: in fact, it va esser Occidental. A un Angleso it va semblar un simplificat Angles, quam un skeptic Cambridge amico dit me que Occidental es. Ma quande lingues coalesce

Ma quande lingues coalesce, li grammatica del resultant lingue es plu simplic e regulari quam ti del coalescent lingues. Li nov lingua franca va esser plu simplic e regulari quam li existent Europan lingues. It va esser tam simplic quam Occidental: in fact, it va esser Occidental. A un Angleso it va semblar un simplificat Angles, quam un skeptic Cambridge amico dit me que Occidental es. Ma quande lingues coalesce

Ma quande lingues coalesce, li grammatica del resultant lingue es plu simplic e regulari quam ti del coalescent lingues. Li nov lingua franca va esser plu simplic e regulari quam li existent Europan lingues. It va esser tam simplic quam Occidental: in fact, it va esser Occidental. A un Angleso it va semblar un simplificat Angles, quam un skeptic Cambridge amico dit me que Occidental es. Ma quande lingues coalesce

1

A paragraph is a texture with a particular color defined by its type size, style, and leading. In the two first settings, the overall value of the first paragraph is lighter, and the second is darker simply because of the difference in leading. In the second settings, the value of the paragraphs becomes similar because the first paragraph, though leaded more generously, is set in bold, effectively canceling out the lightness created by the additional space.

2

The bold-weight sentence appears spatially in front of the lighter-weight sentence. It is also darker and appears tighter, with a more aggressive rhythm. Similarly, the large type appears to be closer to the surface than the line of smaller type. However, its depth relationship becomes ambiguous when it is tinted a lighter value.

2

typographic color is independent of chroma

typographic color is independent of chroma

typographic color is independent of chroma

typographic color is independent of chroma

typographic color is independent of chroma

Functions of Weight, Posture, Width, and Value

Changing posture and weight within text is an invaluable tool for enhancing the "voice" of a text, in the same way that oral communication relies on emphasis and cadence to convey subtle shades of meaning. A word or phrase set in a heavier weight from surrounding text is interpreted as being louder, more aggressive, or of greater importance; lighter-weight text is perceived as more quiet, more reserved, less important, or as supporting a heavier-weight text.

Posture, likewise, changes the rhythm of text. Italic type is often perceived as reading faster or having a more intense cadence than roman text around it. Italics are usually used to provide emphasis to a phrase but are also used to distinguish titles in running text as a way of reserving quotation marks for their official use—distinguishing spoken phrases. Both heavier weights of text and italics require spacing correction. Bold and black types, because of their thicker strokes, have smaller counterforms and can withstand a slightly tighter setting to keep their rhythm consistent in sequence. Italics, which tend to appear crowded together if set with the same spacing as the corresponding roman, need a bit more space to maintain optimal rhythm. As minute as a change in weight or posture may be, it introduces fixation points that stop the eye and demand attention. Because of this effect, changes in weight and posture are extremely effective in helping to create a sense of hierarchy, or importance, among text elements in a format.

3

The cadence of italic and bold type is different compared to regular posture and weight. The even alternation of stroke and counter is continued in the bold weight, but its increased darkness calls attention to the individual letters. The italic, on the other hand, maintains the same color but appears to speed up.

4

Contrast changes between type and background affect legibility and prominence. In the gray blocks of this mailer (detail), the white type has greater contrast with the gray field in which it appears than does the black type. As a result, the white type becomes more noticeable and, therefore, more important relative to the black type.

U9 Visuelle Allianz
Offenbach, Germany

uniform · uniform · pentameter

uniform · uniform · **pentameter**

uniform · uniform · *pentameter*

Changes in the width of letters in a text setting can also alter cadence or tempo. Extended faces are often perceived as reading more slowly, because of the relationship between our linear sense of time and the linear sequence of reading. Text is often perceived to be taking place over time; this is especially true of dialogue, in which words of a quotation seem to happen as they are being read. As we read, our internal rhythm of digesting the words becomes congruent with the type's visual cadence; when that cadence is altered, we experience a change in time. Words set in an extended typeface seem to get stretched out in time. Conversely, words set in a condensed face stress the verticals and take up less linear space—the sense of time decreases, and we perceive these words at a faster tempo.

Developing Informational Hierarchy

Whether in a newsletter, annual report, or magazine, information must be given an order that allows the viewer to navigate it. This order, called the hierarchy of the information, is based on the level of importance the designer assigns to each part of the text. (Importance means the part that should be read first, second, third, and so on; it also refers to the distinction of function among the parts: running text [the body of writing] versus other elements like page folios, titles and subheads, captions, and the like.)

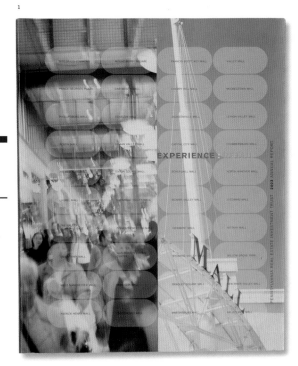

Determining a hierarchy is the result of reading the text and asking some simple questions about the various parts. The answers to these questions are often common sense. On a publication's cover, for example, the masthead or title is most important, so it makes sense that it should be the first type the viewer sees. In a table of financial information, the viewer needs to understand the context of figures being presented, so the headers, which describe the meaning of the figures, need to be easily located. Within a publication's pages, where running text may interact with captions, callouts, and other details, the running text needs to occupy a consistent area and be visually noted as different from these other elements. The effect of these decisions becomes simultaneously verbal and visual.

At first appearance, all text looks equally important in raw form. If placed on a page as is, the words form a uniform field of texture. By manipulating the spaces around and between text, the designer's first option is to create levels of importance through spatial distinction. The designer may group the majority of elements together, for instance, but separate a specific element—maybe a title—and give it more space. The uniformity that is usually desirable to keep the reader moving is thereby purposely broken, creating a fixation point. The fixation point is interpreted as deserving attention and therefore as more important than the other elements around it.

In a complex compositional framework, like a publication, spatial differentiations not only distinguish the importance of elements but also their function. The primary text for reading is located in a prominent, central area of the page—it is the focus of the format, the reason the format exists and exists in a particular shape. The title for a section of text also appears in a specific location. As a result, it is clearly not running text, regardless of size or other treatment. The running head, foot, or side is obviously not a title, because it is not in proximity to the beginning of the running text. Its distance from these elements signifies its function as an element that is of secondary or tertiary importance.

1

Title, publication date, and company name exhibit a clear hierarchy in the cover of this annual report. The larger title type contrasts in color, linearity, and size with its surrounding imagery, bringing it to the top of the hierarchy; the vertical orientation of the company name at the right edge, as well as its smaller size, decrease its presence on the surface, making it less important. Color and weight change within the company name itself create an internal hierarchy among the elements; some of the words are more prominent than the others.

Allemann, Almquist + Jones
Philadelphia, USA

Investigate the Content. What are the distinguishable parts of the information to be designed? What should be the main focus of the reader's attention? How do the parts that are not the main focus relate to each other? Does the viewer need to see a certain grouping of words before they begin to focus on the main part?

Hierarchic Strategies

Change in weight

this text is less important
this is not important
this text is more important
some text is important

Change in size

this text is less important
this is most important
this is not important
other text is more important
some text is important

Change in position

this text is less important
this is not important
other text is more important
some text is important

this is most important

Scale, weight, rhythm, spacing, orientation, and gray value all have an effect on hierarchy.

The designer has, at his or her disposal, a great variety of approaches for establishing the relative importance of typographic elements to each other.

As can be seen here, even type that is all one color—and even the same weight or size—can be effectively differentiated using extremely simple means.

Change in rhythm

this text is more
important than
other text that
is less important

some text is less important

than other text that is more

important *more important*

some text is less important

Change in spacing

this text is less important
this is not important
this text is more important
some text is important
i m p o r t a n t
this text is less important
this is not important
this text is more important

Change in orientation

this text is most important
some text is less important
this is the most important

this text is the
most important
it is more
important than
other text

Change in relative gray value

this text is less important
some text is less important
not the most important
some text is less important

Change in contrast with background

some text is less important
this is the most **important**
some is less important
this is the most important

or maybe this?

Change in chromatic color

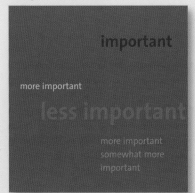

important

more important

less important

more important
somewhat more
important

Changes in weight, scale, and rhythm—in typographic color—also signify differences between elements. Remember that changes in typographic color create the illusion of spatial depth. Those elements that appear to advance forward compete for attention, occupying the top level in the hierarchy. Smaller or lighter elements, which appear to recede, decrease in relative importance because they become less active. Contrast in typographic color between elements must be treated carefully, especially among complex or disparate elements. Although one might assume that making everything in the space as different as possible would clearly indicate their hierarchy, the opposite is actually true. If all of the elements appear very different, they also appear equally important to each other, and the sense of hierarchy is destroyed.

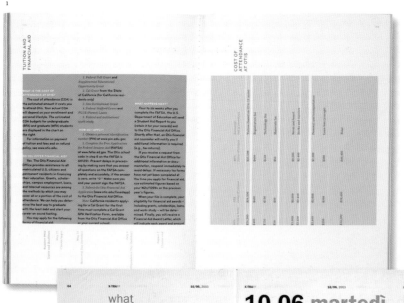

1

Differences in hierarchy clarify the informational components in this application form. By directing the eye through the typographic material using weight and style change, the designer achieves a rich texture while also providing for efficient navigation.

Studio Blue *Chicago, USA*

2

Value and saturation play important roles in the hierarchy in this magazine spread. The large, white headline is at the top of the hierarchy. Getting the eye to flow to the deck—the next element in the sequence—depends on the increased contrast of the deck's type on its background. The orange below is more vibrant, creating pull, but the desaturated green under the deck allows it to be read more easily than the text on the orange.

CODEsign *Rimini, Italy*

3

The larger type in this newspaper spread draws attention to itself first; compared to other elements, which appear primarily textural, it is the first component to offer details that the eye can make out. The red type elements pull the eye by virtue of their difference from the remaining black elements.

Creuna Design *Oslo, Norway*

Worse Comes to Worse. Whenever you're faced with designing a hierarchic system for material such as diagrams, tables, charts, or captions, consider that one concept must fit all—so design based on the worst case scenario: the longest and shortest figure in a table; the longest and shortest phrase or title in a diagram; the least and the most complex information to be found in any caption.

HIERARCHIES WITHIN TEXT All the typographic elements within a given space exist in a hierarchical relationship with the others, ranging from most important to least important. The need to establish hierarchy within individual text elements themselves may also be evident. Captions, tables, and lists are all examples of complex texts that may benefit from internal hierarchic distinctions.

A caption is a short text that describes an image appearing on a page with other (primary) text. Usually, a caption is of secondary or tertiary importance within a page hierarchy. The content of the caption, however, may need its own internal hierarchy. It may, for example, include a reference number or letter that associates it with the image that it describes, especially if several captions are located in one area while the images they describe appear elsewhere. Each image and its caption may be numbered or indicated by a letter or other marker—opposite, above, at right, and so on. The body of the caption may include distinct informational

components that are independent of the description; the caption may even be a collection of components rather than sentences describing the image. In the case of artwork, for example, a caption may consist of a title, an indication of the medium used, physical dimensions, duration, the identity of the creator, and the date of creation. A designer may choose to separate components by using punctuation or contrasting indicators for quicker reader access.

In a table, the separation between columns and rows of information is an important consideration. By establishing a hierarchy among the elements within the table, a designer can help clarify the individual variables, the values being tabulated, and the communicative goal of the tabular information as well. Some values in a table of financial data, for instance, may be a focus—perhaps it is a company's income for the most recent year in a table that compares income by year. In addition to the hierarchy the designer establishes for the table

overall, he or she may opt to distinguish this specific information through a change in weight, or perhaps by enclosing it in a block of tone.

Typography within complex lists and diagrams must be given a hierarchy that separates it, overall, from the page hierarchy—in other words, so that it is clearly not running text. This kind of type must also be given an internal hierarchy that clarifies the various levels of information in the list or diagram. Sometimes, just using a smaller size for type in illustrations or diagrams is sufficient; in other cases, additional adjustment, such as selecting different typefaces than those used for the major page elements or simplifying the typeface selection to a single weight or size, is necessary.

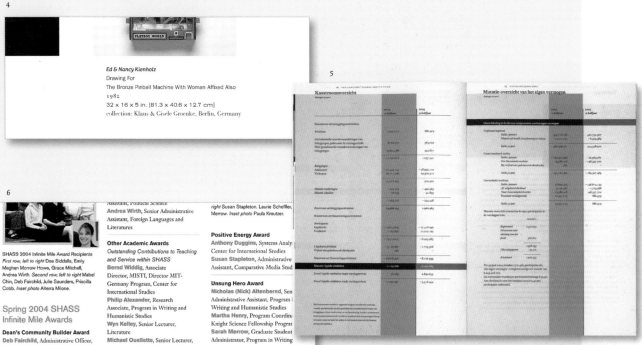

4

Ed & Nancy Kienholz
Drawing For
The Bronze Pinball Machine With Woman Affixed Also
1982
32 × 16 × 5 in. [81.3 × 40.6 × 12.7 cm]
collection: Klaus & Gisele Groenke, Berlin, Germany

5

Kasstroomoverzicht

Mutatie-overzicht van het eigen vermogen

6

SHASS 2004 Infinite Mile Award Recipients
First row, left to right Dee Siddalls, Emily Meghan Morrow Howe, Grace Mitchell, Andrea Wirth. *Second row, left to right* Mabel Chin, Deb Fairchild, Julie Saunders, Priscilla Cobb. *Inset photo* Alterra Milone.

Spring 2004 SHASS
Infinite Mile Awards

Dean's Community Builder Award
Deb Fairchild, Administrative Officer, Program in Science, Technology, and Society
Emily Meghan Morrow Howe, Program Coordinator, Women's Studies

Go-to-Person Award
Alterra Milone, Senior Administrative Assistant, Economics
Julie Saunders, Administrative

Assistant, Political Science
Andrea Wirth, Senior Administrative Assistant, Foreign Languages and Literatures

Other Academic Awards
Outstanding Contributions to Teaching and Service within SHASS
Bernd Widdig, Associate Director, MISTI, Director MIT-Germany Program, Center for International Studies
Philip Alexander, Research Associate, Program in Writing and Humanistic Studies
Wyn Kelley, Senior Lecturer, Literature
Michael Ouellette, Senior Lecturer, Music and Theater Arts

Spring 2003 SHASS
Infinite Mile Awards

Dean's Community Builder Award
Chris Pomiecko, Program Administrator, Comparative Media Studies

right Susan Stapleton, Laurie Scheffler, Merrow. *Inset photo* Paula Kreutzer.

Positive Energy Award
Anthony Duggins, Systems Analy Center for International Studies
Susan Stapleton, Administrative Assistant, Comparative Media Stud

Unsung Hero Award
Nicholas (Nick) Altenbernd, Sen Administrative Assistant, Program Writing and Humanistic Studies
Martha Henry, Program Coordina Knight Science Fellowship Progra
Sarah Merrow, Graduate Student Administrator, Program in Writing and Humanistic Studies
Monica Wolf, Graduate Student Administrator, Political Science

Other Academic Awards
Outstanding Contributions to Teaching and Service within SHASS
Rebecca Faery, Lecturer and Director of the First Year Writing

4

Hierarchy within a complex caption. A grouping of informational components is disinguished through changes in typographic color.

AdamsMorioka
Beverly Hills, USA

5

Within a text component such as a table of figures, the longest figure to occur in any instance must be the driving force behind the column spacing.

UNA (Amsterdam) Designers
Amsterdam, Netherlands

6

Complex listings in text, such as the one shown in this detail of a newsletter page, require tremendous care to differentiate components clearly without creating confusion. Limiting the typeface selection to two families—including their various weights, widths, and italics—provides a rich source for tagging specific kinds of information (names, titles, events, dates, and categories) with a system of interrelated styles.

Conquest Design
Arlington (MA), USA

Recto (the right-hand page) and verso (the left-hand page), together, define a spread. The spread is divided into its two pages by the gutter, where the pages descend into the binding.

HEAD The top edge of the page spread

VERSO
1

HEADLINE Often shortened to *head*. The title of a chapter, section, story, or article. Usually, it is the largest typographic element in a page spread.

DECK A supporting line or short, two- to three-line paragraph that clarifies the content of the headline.

BODY

The area where the primary content is located; also called the block. The body is separated from the outer edges by the margins.

FOOT The bottom edge of the page spread.

Publication Text Components
Standard Page Elements

Decisions about typographic color and the hierarchic breaking of space within a page result from addressing the conventional parts of text material that are found in publications. Aside from the running text, there are half a dozen secondary text elements that have evolved to help readers navigate. Navigating text and other content is a culturally based skill that readers derive from the standards set by centuries of development in book structure. Each component of a publication exists in relation to the others, so distinguishing them from each other also means making connections among them.

1

A diagram of the page elements most often found in a conventional magazine spread.

InPraxis Design
Munich, Germany

FOLIO The page number. Sometimes, the page numbers are arranged near or as part of the running heads, sides, or feet; in such cases, the entire cluster, including the page numbers, is called the folio.

GUTTER

especial flamenco

Los mejores
bailaores del momento

Eine neue Generation von Flamencotänzern und -tänzerinnen bahnt sich ihren Weg und verbindet dabei Ursprüngliches und Traditionelles mit interessanten Projekten und faszinierenden Bühnenshows. por María Dolores Albiac

Farruquito
El flamenco se lleva dentro

RECTO

Sara Baras

Como a muchos flamencos, el arte le viene de familia. Empezó con ocho años en la escuela de su madre, Concha Baras. A los 27 años crea su propia compañía y *monta* el espectáculo "Sensaciones". En el año 2000 estrena la primera adaptación dramática, "Juana la Loca": una combinación de flamenco, danza clásica y teatro visual. Es un espectáculo con el que, en dos años, hace 450 *representaciones* en Europa,

Latinoamérica y Japón. En su *montaje* de 2003, elige de nuevo la tragedia de una mujer *sentenciada* por el amor: Mariana Pineda, una *recreación* de la versión de Federico García Lorca de la heroína ejecutada por *bordar* en una bandera "Ley, libertad e igualdad" (ver ECOS 9/03). Mejor intérprete femenina por la Sociedad de Autores en el 2000, también recibió el Premio Nacional de Danza el año pasado y la Medalla de Andalucía este año. ◼

Sara Baras de banderillera y en Mariana Pineda

montar	(hier ugs.) inszenieren
representación	(hier) Aufführung
representación	(hier) Inszenierung
sentenciar	urteilen, verurteilen
el montaje	Bearbeitung
recreación	Bearbeitung
bordar	sticken

quier mínimo fallo, se nota. *Es de paso corto*, pero se puede bailar como uno la sienta", explica Farruquito, que probó su valor al estrenarse con cinco años en Broadway, de la mano de su abuelo. Un *valor* que le abandonó tras las muertes de su abuelo y de su padre. Dejó de bailar dos años, y ahora, con el accidente de tráfico, intenta lo contrario: recuperar el valor bailando. Incluso su madre dejó el *luto* que la

"Por puro entiendo que sea auténtico y de verdad, un flamenco que se sienta y se respete"

retiró de los escenarios, y ha vuelto a bailar para *armar* a su hijo en este difícil *trance*.

Desde los cinco años practica un flamenco muy austero: "Por puro entiendo que sea auténtico y de verdad, un flamenco que se sienta y se respete". No le importa *ir a contracorriente de las mezclas que* ya se dan en la música y que *elogia*. En contra de lo que se cree, pureza en el flamenco no es *arrebato*, y es lo que más cotiza en sus clases.

Le preguntamos por la adecuada combinación de *furia* y suavidad: "Es una cosa con la que se nace. Es difícil *fijarlo*, y me cuesta mucho trabajo explicarlo en las clases. Pero tengo la esperanza de que todo el mundo entienda que el flamenco está dentro de cada uno. Puede estar dormido o

puede estar un poco más despierto, pero hay que sacarlo con sacrificio y gran *esfuerzo*, a fuerza de que te guste mucho y te enamore lo suficiente como para que te salga poco a poco".

La intensidad del ritmo

Los *entendidos* dicen que los bailaores se diferencian entre quienes siguen la guitarra o quienes siguen el cante y las palmas. "Mi papá Farruco decía que quien baila *manda*, y yo también lo creo. Pero el bailaor no puede *navegar* solo si no hay una guitarra o un *cantaor* que lo inspire a lo motive", dice.

ECOS le preguntó: "Como usted improvisa mucho, ¿qué le motiva más: la guitarra o las palmas?" "No me guío por la guitarra sino por el momento, por la música y lo que me dan las personas que están a mi alrededor: puede ser la guitarra, puede ser el cantaor, puede ser el jaleo de mi gente que está *entre bastidores*, puede ser alguien del público... o la magia que se mete en el teatro. Incluso, una mirada puede hacer que la intensidad del ritmo cambie", nos explicó Farruquito.

"Hay quien nunca supera ser el 'hijo de'. ¿A usted no *le pesa*?", le preguntó ECOS. "Es una *espina* eterna, pero, al mismo tiempo, tengo el deber de seguir con la *herencia*", dice. "Por si no le pesara lo suficiente el nombre, lo comparó con Camarón, considerado el mejor cantaor flamenco, con una corta y tan intensa vida que su foto preside todo lugar de flamenco.

de paso corto	mit kurzen Schritten
valor	(hier) Mut
luto	Trauer
armar	(hier fig.) trösten
el trance	schwieriger Lebensmoment
a contra-	
corriente de	gegen... angehen
elogiar	loben
arrebato	Anfall, Ausbruch
furia	(hier) Eifer, Wucht
fijar	festmachen
entendido	(hier) Experte
mandar	bestimmen, vorgeben
navegar	(hier fig.) segeln
cantaor	Flamencosänger
entre bastidores	hinter die Bühne; in den Kulissen
pesarle a alg.	zur Last fallen, belasten
espina	(hier fig.) Dorn, Schmerz
herencia	das Erbe

ECOS octubre 2004   19

SIDEBAR Content that supplements the primary running text with more detailed information. Often located at the outer edges of the publication (hence the term), but just as often found toward the bottom or top of the spread.

CAPTIONS Descriptive clusters of text that accompany images, giving information about their content or creator.

SUBHEADLINE Often shortened to *subhead*. Informational markers that indicate the beginnings of new subsections within a larger section, or new paragraphs within running text.

RUNNING HEADS, FEET, OR SIDES Often shortened to *runners*. Informational markers that identify the reader's location within the publication. The runners may consist of any combination of the publication title, section, subsection, and author.

CALLOUTS (OR PULLOUTS) Short excerpts of the running text that are given prominence. Callouts can be quotations from a speaker who was interviewed for the text, or they may simply be important points that the designer or author feels deserve extra attention.

2–4

Each of these page spreads shares structural elements—folios, running heads, captions—treated in different ways. Note the placement variation in the folios, as well as that of the runners.

2 Premier Media Group
Lakewood (WA), USA

3 AdamsMorioka
Beverly Hills, USA

4 Faydherbe/DeVringer
The Hague, Netherlands

2

3

4

Though a focus on the minutiae of text legibility and informational clarity is clearly important, it must not distract the designer from the macrolevel of publication design: integrating images, colors, and other messages through dynamic layout and a clear, consistent structure. The publication is an object, with a front and a back, a size and shape—it is a tactile experience that its audience acts upon. Each turn of a page must yield a new experience but remain visually, emotionally, and conceptually connected to the pages before and after. Much of the building of a publication intertwines the conceptual aspects of content, the visual power of imagery and typography, and the detail issues of reading; no one element is truly more important than the other. Structure can be an inspiring source for conceptual messaging, as much as a force for organizing and unifying material (or helping speed up production). Looking at the microlevel of legible typographic design, the ethereal messaging functions of subject matter and interpretive overlay, and the macrolevel of integrating the pages, sections, images, and type together creates a single form that packages all of these ideas into one final form.

Building

Structure and Integration

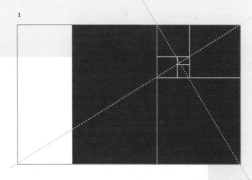
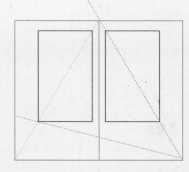

Message Meets Material

The architect Louis Kahn once said, "Beginnings, beginnings, beginnings," restating the eternal excitement and dilemma of the designer: facing the blank page at the start of a new project. A number of variables come together to determine the final form of a publication. There's a message. There's a visual concept conveying that message. And there's a way of organizing the concept around the message within a given space. That space is where the variables mesh together, the literal blank page of the print medium: the format.

Format can mean different things. Most often, it refers to the proportions of a page. It may also refer to a project's organization. There is a conventional format to a magazine, for example: a table of contents, a letter from the editor, a series of shorter informational sections related to the overall subject, and a series of feature stories. Ultimately, the question of a publication's format is one of the first a designer must address.

CREATIVE AND PRACTICAL An appropriate format, in all its aspects, conveys ideas and also provides functionality for the content. Addressing content functionality means differentiating the publication's informational parts, ordering them logically, providing them useful space, and distilling relevant visual ideas to communicate their varied messages. Who will be reading the publication? How does brand perception influence the message? How should the subject be represented? How does this subject fit the broader cultural context? The designer must also consider more concrete issues. How many pages might the text fill? Will the budget limit production options? Format choice may affect the publication's potential for display or the cost of its mailing. Sometimes, the format may be determined by something as arbitrary as the size of the least expensive press.

STANDARD FORMATS Many large-circulation publications adhere to standard formats, which are quite useful. Their ubiquity makes them conceptually neutral; they fit most display racks; their proportions efficiently use standard paper mill sheet sizes; and they cost the least to mail, since automated equipment is set up to accommodate them. But designers need not settle for a standard format. Since readers expect the standard, slight changes in proportion create an immediate sense of difference in presentation without affecting practical concerns.

1

Format proportions in the fourteenth through nineteenth centuries were based on mathematical, architectural, and even musical harmonies, following developments in science and the humanities. The golden section, a mathematical system with roots in ancient Greece, has often been used to determine page formats.

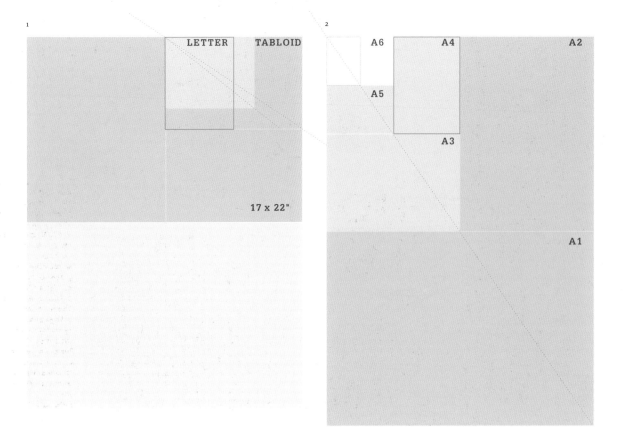

1

2

LETTER   TABLOID

17 x 22"

A6   A4   A2

A5

A3

A1

1, 2

The United States and
European Union follow
standard format systems.
The U.S. Imperial Letter
(8.5 x 11" [21.6 x 27.9 cm])
and Tabloid (11 x 17"
[27.9 x 43.2 cm]) sizes (left)
form the basis of American
publication formats; these
sizes are left over from
colonial English printing
paper sizes. Tabloid is
twice the width of Letter,
and their aspect ratios are
different. The European
DIN or ISO standard (right)
uses a proportional system
based on a square meter
of paper (A0 size) whose
aspect ratio has been engi-
neered so that when it is
folded in half, the folded
size retains the same
aspect ratio as the parent
sheet. The A4 letter measures 210 x 297 mm, (about
8 ¼ x 11¾"). The aspect
ratio in ISO sheets is
consistently 1:1.414 (the
square root of two).

The Format's Conceptual Potential
An Overall Shape for the Message

Format plays an enormous role in the experience
of a publication; its size and shape sets the stage for
content and how it feels to the reader. The sense
of space, tension, and movement in a given format
changes as its proportions change. A square format
exhibits a neutral space without tension. A vertical
format mirrors the human body, creating upward
visual thrust that is tense and active. In contrast, a
horizontal format is restful, reflecting the landscape;
its thrust is less dynamic and creates movement left
and right. A choice of one over another, even at this
level, has implications for the communication.

The extreme to which a designer pushes a format's proportions has an impact on perception. An
exceptionally narrow or large format, for example,
may communicate a particular attitude—unconventional or exclusive. The calming effect of a horizontal

format might enhance a subject such as gardening
or health care. Harmonic mathematical relationships, first noted by the ancient Greeks and
commonly used between the fourteenth and nineteenth centuries, impart a sense of precision that
may be appropriate for journals of math or science.
However, purposely refuting a conventional
format choice may add meaning and originality:
for example, a format derived from the golden
section or other numerical system for an exhibition
catalog or a yoga newsletter. A designer may also
explore formats based on the content's typographic
necessities. As noted earlier, text legibility, spacing,
hierarchy, and structure may direct the designer's
consideration of the format. Some designers
begin by exploring various text settings to determine how much space the text will need and
what page structure will best suit it, organically
building the page outward from this internal
typographic architecture.

6

From Inside Out. Exploring typographic possibilities for highly readable text may yield a basis for a workable column structure—essentially building the format outward from the most desirable text configuration tailored to the content. Working from this base, a designer may consider a variety of format proportions to house the type structure, each yielding a different spatial experience and, potentially, functionality.

3

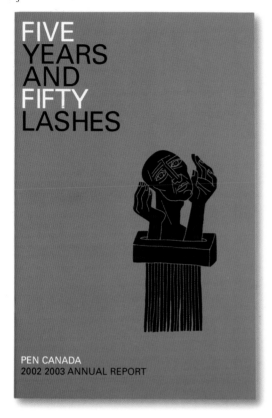

FIVE
YEARS
AND
FIFTY
LASHES

PEN CANADA
2002 2003 ANNUAL REPORT

4

5

3–5
Extremes in format size can communicate just as much as the visual messages of image and type. The PEN Canada annual (3) report, for instance, relies on its tremendous scale to establish undeniable presence—supporting its mission of bearing witness to human rights atrocities. The small-format pharmacy college annual (5), by contrast, presents an intimate and quietly credible message—elegant, reserved, and academic. Its proportions are based on those of personal stationery. A letter-sized publication (4) is shown for comparison.

3 Soapbox Design
Communications
Toronto, Canada

4 Premier Media Group
Seattle, USA

5 Circle K Studio
San Francisco, USA

6, 7
This quarterly newsletter for an orchestral group demonstrates the important role format decisions can play. When closed, the vertical proportion is cost-effective for mailing; when open, harmonic proportion creates the perception of something mathematical and musical. The decision to accordion fold, rather than bind, permits the newsletter to open into a long, horizontal page whose proportions derive from a standard musical staff. The staff structure is further used to develop flowlines (see The Grid System, page 68) that integrate material across panels.

STIM *New York City, USA*

6

CAPITAL CAMPAIGN KICKOFF   QUARTERLY EVENTS   BECOME A MEMBER

A Star-Studded Evening at the
Metropolitan Center

From the Director

7

BSCE Notes
The Quarterly Newsletter of the
BLEECKER STREET CHAMBER ENSEMBLE

Winter 2003 NOV | DEC | JAN

Q4

The Renovations Begin
Capital Campaign Update
Winter Repertoire
Quarterly Events

*Become a Member of the
Bleecker Street Chamber Ensemble*

The Systematic Nature of Publications

Unlike one-offs, series-based projects, such as publications, force the designer to consider variables beyond the basics of composition. Crafting readable text for a single page format doesn't necessarily solve spatial and hierarchic problems for many spreads, or for successive editions, of a publication. Information in serial media changes over time. Designers are confronted by headlines or titles of different lengths; articles that are one page long, two pages long, or six pages long. Some content will come with images and some will not.

Therefore, designers must consider the potential requirements of content that they haven't seen to make sure that it can be addressed by the compositional ideas they've developed. Publications must be developed as systems in order to accommodate changes in content: each issue is a single object, but the visual logic of the publication must be consistently recognizable to its readership yet flexible enough to allow change in content.

A system can be developed any number of ways, from organizing material on an underlying, consistent structure to tagging serial components with a recognizable element, like a colored bar or a typographic device. In a serial publication like a newsletter, magazine, or newspaper, setting up a framework of measurements for columns and areas for images helps not only unify the material within a single edition but also allows for consistency between editions. In a system of brochures, the content may reflect an overall subject matter parceled out into subcategories. This might mean that at least two typographic or pictorial tags must appear on all the pieces: one unchanging element that establishes the overall concept and a second element that distinguishes it from the others. The formats may need to be mixed or stepped so that

all the titles are visible at once. Or perhaps the elements will be displayed within a stacked holder, with only their top thirds visible. These criteria impose limitations on the organization of the content that the designer must take into account in the planning stages.

After the designer has evaluated these issues and developed a list of limitations, the actual designing can begin. Their search is for a visual logic that will convey the meaning and emotion of the content yet work within the limitations so that no one component feels out of place or becomes problematic on a functional or production level. If the designer reaches this goal, the result is an organic system of parts that reaches the audience in a consistently recognizable way and allows for variation and flexibility in design as the system continues to expand.

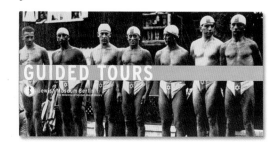

1–4

Publications are naturally systematic—they are serial groupings of related material. Both of these literature systems use color, format, and typographic treatment to distinguish their components as belonging to the same system. Each system is flexible to a different degree; the D.A.'s office literature is flexible in color and image; the museum system is flexible in color, image, and format.

1, 2 C. Harvey Graphic Design
New York City, USA

3, 4 Eggers + Diaper
Berlin, Germany

Building a System: Addressing Content Change

☐ How many different kinds of content will occur in the publication?

☐ How are the parts differentiated against the overall visual language: by image use, by color, by type treatment, by structure?

☐ What content will remain the same from issue to issue?

☐ What content will change completely?

☐ When content changes, will it remain approximately the same volume each time, or is it likely that the volume will change i.e., could the same content be short in one issue and very long in the next?

☐ Are the publication components serial, or will they arrive together as a group?

TAILORING THE SYSTEM FOR THE JOB
Different publications require the development of different kinds of systems to organize them and provide consistency over time. Serial publications require an underlying structure that permits rapid changes in content; for example, in a newspaper, the mixture of articles on any given page may need to shift at any time. A newspaper's system of type-faces, their sizes, and informational hierarchy must be relatively simple; fewer choices for setting must be available so as not to impede quick layout. The structure of a newspaper—specific and consistent column widths—is also tailored to address quick change. Text may only fill a single column width.

Newsletters and magazines may be somewhat less rigid in their structure, as more time is available for their design and the emphasis on visual concept is more pronounced. Nonetheless, a recognizable structure is needed to unify each edition of the publication. Annual reports may change dramatically from year to year, both in concept and in structure. However, organizing the material in a given year's report will still require an underlying structure as well as recognizable typographic and image-related treatments, among sections and even among spreads within a section.

Editorial Pagination and Structure
Page Count and Sequence

Page order and section structure in publications are often based on historical conventions that derive from the physical reality of the printed sheet and longstandng production methods.

A standard press form (or broadsheet) in the U.S., for example, creates sixteen letter-size pages when folded in half upon itself four times. This signature, cut across the top fold, yields a set of four nested tabloid pages that share a common spine. The first page, as recto, is always a right-hand page; therefore, all odd-numbered pages are right hand as well. All left-hand pages are numbered evenly. This fundamental folded sheet, the signature, means that all publications must be considered in terms of having page counts that are multiples of four—unless the publication is perfect bound. In this case, the designer can insert individual pages (front and back) as needed. The pagination of the document is its full sequence of spreads and signatures, used for planning the sequence of content.

In popular jargon, however, designers will often refer to a single folded tabloid as a signature—meaning a tabloid sheet folded in half that yields four letter-sized pages. A twenty-page brochure, in thiscase, is made up of five such signatures, all nestedtogether and bound in the center. The innermost signature facing the reader, when opened, is the centerfold. Whichever is meant by signature—the "real" sixteen-page folded broadsheet or the four-page folded tabloid—the fact of the four-page multiple, as well as the numbering rule—even on the left, odd on the right—still holds true for planning purposes. Designers often sketch folding diagrams to see how the pagination plays out.

1

Page numbering begins on the right hand page—the cover of a publication (the first page) occupies the right-hand position when the document is closed. Subsequent pages, therefore, are always numbered even on the left and odd on the right. Signatures—folded sheets of paper that create four sides—help determine the pagination in publications that are stitched together.

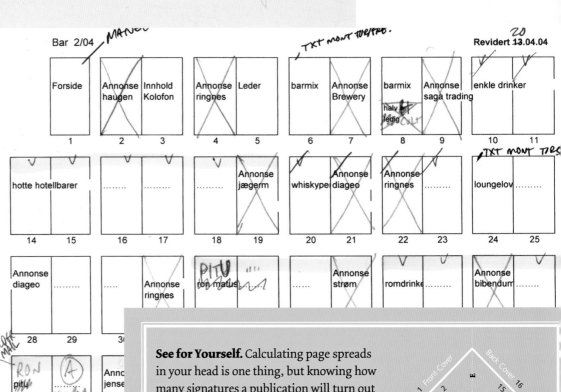

See for Yourself. Calculating page spreads in your head is one thing, but knowing how many signatures a publication will turn out to be is important. A little slip in calculation may mean a page count that is indivisible by 4, meaning either too many or, worse yet—too few—pages to account for the content. Sometimes it's also useful to know where the centerfold spread in a saddle-stitch (stapled) booklet lands among the pages. Making a folding diagram, such as the one shown here, quickly clears things up.

The material leading from a publication's cover to its primary content is called the front matter. This material may include anything from the half title and title page of an exhibition catalog to the introduction pages of an extended brochure system and, in particular, a table of contents. The primary content area, the interior where chapters or sections are located, is called the guts or the well. Anything that follows this is referred to as tail- or end matter, including appendixes, indexes, reference-oriented listings, bibliographies, glossaries, and so on. Newspapers are notable for not having front or end matter; they're really just guts. Each section in the guts may have subsections or chapters or not. In publications with a full complement of parts, the front matter sequence is often an important part of experiencing the publication. It separates the reader from the outside world and, with each turn of the page, envelops him or her in the world of the publication. The designer may elect to include additional pages—spacers—between the required ones to enhance the sense of change from outside to interior. The table of contents requires intense focus to ensure clarity, both visual and editorial, and to link it conceptually with the content it lists.

2

A pagination diagram, such as the one for a magazine shown here, is an invaluable tool for a designer. Being able to see the full sequence of pages and signatures helps plan where content can be laced, and what effect adding, deleting, or shifting content between spreads will have on page count and flow.

Creuna Design *Oslo, Norway*

CONTENTS

3–7

The table of contents in a publication, no matter how simple or complex, is a page worth considering in detail. Its prominence in the front matter means it is one of the first impressions of the content and messaging that the reader will experience later on; above all else, however, it is a navigation device. Clear relationships between content listing—sections, chapters, subsections, authors—and page numbers are essential. The variety of solutions shown here merely hints at the possibilities.

3 Ruder Finn Design
New York City, USA

4 Creuna Design
Oslo, Norway

5 Allemann, Almquist + Jones
Philadelphia, USA

6 Hutchinson Associates
Chicago, USA

7 And Partners, NY
New York City, USA

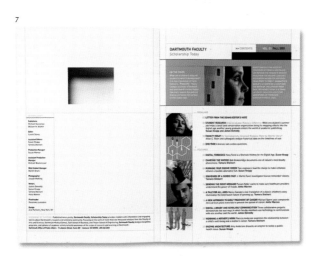

The Grid System

All design work involves problem solving on both visual and organizational levels. Pictures, fields of text, headlines, tabular data: all these pieces must come together to communicate. A grid is one approach to achieving this goal. One grid may be loose and organic; another may be rigorous and mechanical. To some designers, the grid represents an inherent part of the craft of designing, the same way joinery in furniture making is a part of that particular craft. The history of the grid has been part of an evolution in the way graphic designers think about designing, as well as a response to specific communication and production problems that needed to be solved. Among other things, a grid is suited to helping solve communication problems of great complexity.

The benefits of working with a grid are simple: clarity, efficiency, economy, and continuity. Before anything else, a grid introduces systematic order to a layout, distinguishing types of information and easing a user's navigation through them. Using a grid permits a designer to lay out enormous amounts of information in substantially less time because many design considerations have already been addressed in building the grid's structure. The grid also allows many individuals to collaborate on the same project or on a series of related projects over time without compromising established visual qualities from one instance to the next.

Rows are series of flowlines defined by the existence of modules. Like columns, they are also separated by gutters.

The Anatomy of a Grid

A grid consists of a distinct set of alignment-based relationships that serve as guides for distributing elements across a format. Every grid contains the same basic parts, no matter how complex the grid becomes. These parts can be combined as needed or omitted from the overall structure at the designer's discretion.

Margins are the negative spaces between the format edge and the content; they surround and define the live area where type and images will be arranged. The proportions of the margins bear a great deal of consideration, as they help establish the overall tension within the composition. Margins can be used to focus attention, serve as a resting place for the eye, or act as an area for subordinate information.

Flowlines are alignments that break the space into horizontal bands. Flowlines help guide the eye across the format and can be used to impose additional stopping and starting points for text or images.

Gutters are the interstitial spaces that exist between columns and rows—and modules. "The gutter," however, refers to the margins toward the inside of the spread, where the pages drop into the binding.

Modules are individual units of space separated by regular intervals that, when repeated across the page format, create columns and rows.

Spatial zones are groups of modules that form distinct fields. Each field can be assigned a specific role for displaying information; for example, one horizontal field might be reserved for images, while the field below it might be reserved for a series of text columns.

Columns are vertical alignments of type that create horizontal divisions between the margins. There can be any number of columns: sometimes they are all the same width, and sometimes they are different widths, corresponding to specific information.

Markers are placement indicators for subordinate or consistently appearing text, like running heads, section titles, folios, or any other element that occupies only one location in any layout.

Column Grid
Articulating Text Structure

Information that is discontinuous benefits from being organized into an arrangement of vertical columns. Because the columns can be dependent on each other for running text, independent for small blocks of text, or crossed over to make wider columns, the column grid is very flexible. For example, some columns may be reserved for running text and large images, while captions may be placed in an adjacent column. This arrangement clearly separates the captions from the primary material, but maintains them in a direct relationship.

The width of the columns in a column grid depends, as noted, on the size of the running text type. If the column is too narrow, excessive hyphenation is likely, making a uniform rag difficult to achieve. At the other extreme, if the column is too wide, the reader will have difficulty finding the beginnings of sequential lines. The designer can find a comfortable column width by studying the effects of changing the type size, leading, and spacing. Traditionally, the gutter between columns is given a measure, x, and the margins are usually assigned a width of twice the gutter measure, or 2x. Margins wider than the column gutters focus the eye inward, easing tension between the column edge and the edge of the format. This column-to-margin ratio is simply a guide, however, and designers are free to adjust it as they see fit.

The column grid also has a subordinate structure—the flowlines, vertical intervals that allow the designer to accommodate unusual breaks in text or image on the page and create horizontal bands across the format. The hangline is one kind of flowline: it defines the vertical distance from the top of the format at which column text will always start. A flowline near the top of the page may establish a position for running headers, the pagination, or section dividers. Additional flowlines may designate areas for images only or for different kinds of concurrent running text, like timelines, sidebars, or callouts.

1

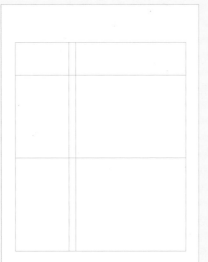
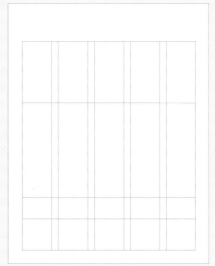

1

Any number of columns may be used in a column grid, depending on the format size and the complexity of the content. Flowlines define horizontal alignments in increments from the top of the page. Within a column grid, a designer has a great deal of flexibility for arranging type and image material.

The two-column grid used to structure this publication relies heavily on its flowlines to create spatial distinction for subordinate elements, such as the article title and deck located toward the top of the right page, above the body. The flowlines are also used to connect elements horizontally across the pages of the spread, introducing a lateral tension that contrasts with the vertical repetition of the columns. The column gutter is narrower than the margins surrounding the columns, focusing attention inward to the body and creating a comfortable separation for the text from the edge of the format.

Flat *New York City, USA*

3–5

Examples of two- and three-column grids, among the most common used in designing publications, are shown here. Each exhibits differing margin proportions, column measures, and flowline configurations.

The potential for varying typographic width across the columns, integrating images, and differentiating columns with color to set off sidebars becomes clear.

3 Ruder Finn Design
New York City, USA

4 Slatoff & Cohen
New York City, USA

5 OrangeSeed Design
Minneapolis, USA

Modular Grid
Text and Image Architecture

Because very complex projects require even more precise control, a modular grid may be the most useful choice in such situations. A modular grid is, essentially, a column grid with a large number of horizontal flowlines that subdivide the columns into rows, creating a matrix of cells called modules. Each module defines a small chunk of informational space. Grouped together, these modules define areas called spatial zones to which specific roles may be assigned. The degree of control within the grid depends on the size of the modules. Smaller modules provide more flexibility and greater precision, but too many subdivisions can become confusing or redundant.

How does one determine the module's proportions? The module could be the width and depth of one average paragraph of the primary text at a given size. Modules may be vertical or horizontal in proportion, depending on the kinds of images being organized and the desired stress the designer feels is appropriate. The margin proportions must be considered simultaneously in relation to the modules and the gutters that separate them.

Modular grids are often used to coordinate extensive publication systems. If the designer has the opportunity to consider all the materials that are to be produced within a system, the formats can become an outgrowth of the module or vice versa. By regulating the proportions of the formats and the module in relation to each other, the designer may simultaneously be able to harmonize the formats and ensure they are produced most economically.

A modular grid also lends itself to the design of tabular information. The rigorous repetition of the module helps to standardize tables or forms and integrate them with the text and image material.

1

Here, a variety of modular grid structures shows a range of proportions and precision. The greater the number of modules, the more precise the layout may be, but too many increments becomes redundant. Variations on the number and stress of the module achieve different kinds of presence for the typographic and image content.

2

The modular structure of these foldout mailers creates an endlessly flexible, yet visually consistent, system for ordering information that changes in volume with each edition. The module's proportions, in this case, are derived from the measurements of the panels when the mailers are folded down.

U9 Visuelle Allianz
Offenbach, Germany

3

The modular grid used for this furniture catalog not only helps organize text and inset images but plays a role in how full-bleed images are cropped. The grid is shown reproduced on top of the third spread.

Designwork SrL *Udine, Italy*

1

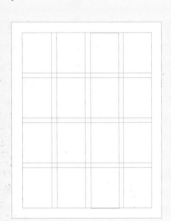
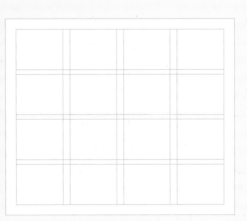
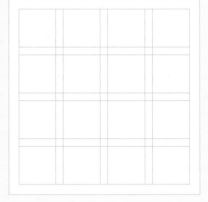
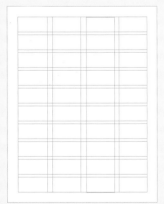
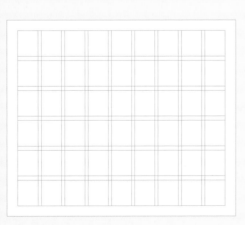

Aside from its practical uses, the modular grid accords a conceptual aesthetic. Between the 1950s and 1980s, the modular grid became associated with ideal social or political order. These ideals have their roots in the rationalist thinking of the Bauhaus and Swiss International Style, which celebrates objectivity, order, and clarity. Designers who embrace these ideals sometimes use modular grids to convey this additional meaning.

2

3

4

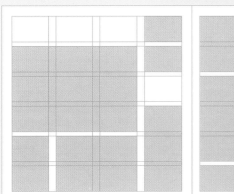
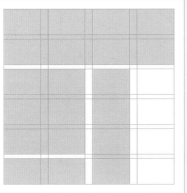

4

The enormous potential for arranging images in a modular grid is seen here. Combining modules into zones for images (gray areas) ensures variety as well as a unified relationship with text.

Grid Development
Text Based versus Image Based

Building an appropriate grid for a publication involves assessing the shape and volume of the content rather than trying to assign grid spaces arbitrarily. The shape of the content, whether text or image, is of particular importance. A designer may consider the text as the essential building block, looking at variations in the text setting to see how they affect the volume of the text. Another option is to consider the proportions of images as a source for the proportions of the grid intervals, especially if the publication is driven by its image content. The proportions of the images, if known, can be used to determine column and module proportions. The result of both approaches is that the structure of the page develops naturally from the needs of the content, presenting an overall organic, unified sense of space.

IMAGE PROPORTION A grid may be defined by image content through comparison of its proportions. Beginning with a universal height or depth for the images and a consistent alignment among them will allow the designer to assess how varied they are in format—squares, verticals, horizontals. The designer must then decide how the images are to be displayed in terms of their size relationship

to each other: will the images be shown in sizes that are relative to each other, or will they be allowed to appear at any size? If all the images hang from a particular flowline, their depth varying, the designer will need to address the images with both the shortest and deepest depths to determine what is possible for text or other elements below these variations. From these major divisions in space and the logic that the designer uses to govern them, a series of intervals may be structured for the images and for text areas surrounding them. It is also possible to structure the grid based on how images will be sized in succession. Perhaps the designer envisions sequencing the images a particular way: first bleeding full off one page, then a half-page vertical, then inset, then a three-quarter bleed. These proportions, as they relate to the format, will define a series of measurements, which can then be combined or systematized to help determine the spatial intervals of a grid.

TEXT ATTRIBUTES Alternatively, the designer may approach the grid from the perspective of the text shape and volume. The sheer amount of text that the publication must accommodate is an important consideration. If each page spread must carry a particular word count in order to fit a prescribed number of pages, the designer will have some sense of how many lines of type must appear

on each page. This variable may eventually affect the column width or depth, but the optimal setting is a good starting point. Achieving an optimal setting for text at a given size and in a given face will indicate a width for columns; from there, the designer can explore how many columns will fit side by side on a single page. Adjusting the size of the text, its internal spacing, and the gutters between columns will allow the designer to create a preliminary structure that ensures optimal text setting throughout. From this point, the designer must evaluate the resulting margins—head, sides, and foot—and determine whether there is enough space surrounding the body to keep it away from the edges of the format. Since optimal width can vary a little with the same text setting, the designer has some leeway in forcing the columns to be wider or narrower, closer to or farther away from each other, until the structure sits on the page comfortably.

1

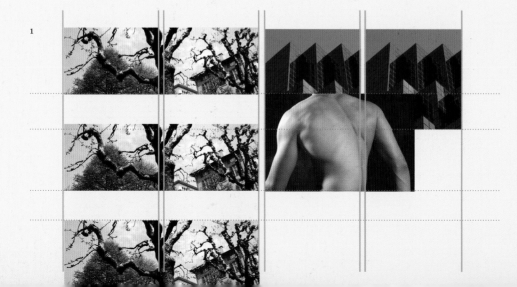

1

In this hypothetical study, several source images, each with different proportions, are positioned relative to each other to help determine where their depths and widths might correspond. Shifting the images around each other creates a number of possibilities for distilling a grid that will accommodate them all.

2

The leading of the body text, decks, callouts, and captions may have some proportional relationship based on their sizes. For example, the body text may be 10 points, set on a leading of 12; captions may be 6 points set on a leading of 9; decks may be 15 points set on a leading of 18. The numeric relationship between these leading measurements is 3 points; a certain number of lines of each text component will, at some depth interval, share the same top and lower baseline, and this depth interval may very well indicate the depth of a module. Conversely, the body text leading may be used as a standard: perhaps an eight-line depth of the body text defines the depth of the module, and then other text components are adjusted to work around this proportion.

2

lingua franca... plice regulari quam li exis Europan... simplic...
lingua franca... plu simplice... quam li exis... Europan lin... cat angles... esser tam s... quam eras... Ma quam... grammatica del resultant... es plu simplic e regulari q del coalescent lingues. Li gua franca va esser plu si... tent Europan lingues. It va esser tam simplic quam er... regulari quam li existent E lingua franca va esser plu... plice regulari quam li exis Europan lingues. It va ess simplic quam eras occiden...

3

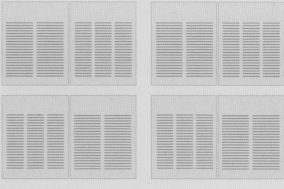

3

Using a compound grid builds a certain rhythm into a publication. As the grid changes to accommodate different information, the rhythm of each grid's occurrence becomes an integral part of the pacing and style of the work.

4

A compound grid is used to separate continuous text from categorized or listed text components in this spread from a trade newsletter. The top two thirds of the spread is organized on a three-column structure, while the lower third uses a four-column structure. Both grids share the same margins.

OrangeSeed Design
Minneapolis, USA

Grid Hybrids and Combinations

Depending on the complexity of the publication, a designer may find that multiple grids are needed to organize the content, even within a single page spread. Working with several grids together can take several directions. First, a grid with a large number of precise intervals may be developed as a basis for a variety of grids used for particular information. For example, a grid with twenty columns to a page might be used to order a five-column, four-column, two-column, and three-column grid with a larger margin for captions in a specific section. In this kind of approach, all of the column widths will share a proportional relationship that will also be noticeable in the way images relate to text set in these various widths.

4

Another option is simply to use two, three, or more different grids that share outer margins, allowing them to be relatively arbitrary in their relationships to one another. Using this approach, the alternation of the grids will be pronounced because their internal proportions are unrelated; the resulting differences in visual logic between layouts using different grids can make very clear distinctions between sections or types of content. Another option is to combine grids on a single page but to separate them into different areas. For example, primary text or images might occupy a three-column grid in the upper two-thirds of the page, while a five-column grid may hold captions or other secondary content in the lower third of the page.

Grid and Column Interaction
Logic and Rhythm

The way in which columns of text interact with negative space is an important aspect of how a grid is articulated. The spaces above and below columns play an active part in giving the columns a rhythm as they relate to each other across pages and spreads. The options available to a designer are endless but can be described as fitting into three basic categories: columns that align at top and bottom; columns that align at top or bottom and rag at the other end; and columns that rag at top and bottom. Each kind of logic has dramatic impact on the overall rhythm of the pages within a publication, ranging from austere and geometric to wildly organic in feeling—all the while ordered by the underlying grid. Changing the column logic from

section to section provides yet another method of differentiating informational areas. The designer, however, must carefully consider the rhythm of that change. Some regularity or system must clearly exist in the alternation of column logic to appear meaningful; otherwise, the audience simply recognizes the change, not its significance.

When columns begin to separate vertically, shifting up and down past one another—or dropping to different depths while adhering to a single hangline above—it is important to consider the relationship between lines of text across the gutters separating the columns. In groupings of columns without line breaks (or with hard returns of the same leading) between paragraphs, the baselines between columns align. If there is a proportional increment between paragraphs in one of these columns, the baselines of text following this incre-

ment will be thrown out of alignment with those in the other columns. In hanging columns, this break in continuity of the baselines may feel appropriate because it relates to the sense of the columns' changing depths. A problem will occur in a page spread set with columns aligned top and bottom, however, if the paragraph space introduces an uneven measurement: the lines of text at the foot margin will be noticeably off. Setting columns whose tops and bottoms begin at staggered intervals complicates the issue further. The designer has the option of making the baselines between columns correspond—introducing the linear regularity as a contrast to the shift of the columns' beginning and ending points.

1

1

Columns justified to the head and foot margins, or to a specific module depth, create a rigidly geometric band of text. Hanging columns provide a measure of consistency, balanced by their changing depth. Columns that change hangline and depth offer the most organic (and flexible) option for arranging text, especially in terms of integrating images.

Be Clear about It! The differences in interval between column beginnings and endings must be decisive and considered for their rhythm. The heads and feet of the columns may be decided spontaneously or may be determined by the existence of flowlines or modules in the columns.

2

Mauricio Aleja: Look and you will see

A night out with AORTA

3

Gymnastie, or the other side of the coin

Jo Magreon, Hi Art in downtown Paris

Variation and Violation
Avoiding Repetitive Layouts

A grid is truly successful only if, after all of the problems have been solved, the designer rises above the uniformity implied by its structure and uses it to create a dynamic visual narrative of parts that sustain interest page after page. The greatest danger in using a grid is to succumb to its regularity. It is important to remember that the grid is an invisible guide existing on the bottom-most level of the layout; the content happens on the surface, either constrained or sometimes free. Grids do not make dull layouts—designers do.

Once a grid is in place, it's a good idea to sort all the project's material, spread by spread, to see how much is appearing in each. A storyboard of thumbnails for each spread in the publication can be very helpful. Here, the designer can test layout variations on the grid and see the result in terms of pacing—the rhythm of the layouts. Can there be a visual logic to the way elements interact with the grid from page to page? Do pictorial elements alternate in position from one spread to another? Perhaps the sizes of the images change from spread to spread, or the ratio of text to image changes

sequentially. Even simply placing images toward the top of the pages in one spread and then toward the bottom of the pages in the next achieves a powerful sense of difference while still ensuring overall visual unity.

It is necessary to violate the grid, sometimes because circumstances dictate it—content that must occupy a specific spread won't quite fit—or because it is visually necessary to call attention to some feature of the content or to create some surprise for the reader. Within a rigorous grid structure, violations must be relatively infrequent or relatively small, or they begin to undermine the reader's sense of the grid's consistency. It is also important to note that any specific item or general layout that violates the grid will be very dramatic. Disturbing the regularity of a column of text by allowing an element to jut out past the alignment will not only be instantly noticeable but will also cause the wayward element to shift to the top of the hierarchy—it will become the most important item in the layout because it is clearly the only thing out of order. A full-spread layout that ignores the grid established for the remaining pages of a publication will be memorable within the publication. The problem facing the designer in making

Give It Some Bounce. A simple trick is to arbitrarily cluster images toward the top in one spread and then toward the bottom in the spread following. Sometimes forcing a small, medium, and large image into a spread—then using the same sizes but placed in different locations on the next spread—will quickly create movement across the grid.

such a dramatic decision is that of integrating the layout into the publication's overall visual logic so that, despite its extreme difference, it remains unified with the rest of the publication. Usually, this can be done by maintaining the same typefaces used in other spreads, as well as by applying the same colors from a standard palette. Additionally, the designer must consider the transition back into the grid-structured pages following the violation; if the pages following the particular spread are a continuation of its content, the designer may add smaller violating elements that reference the major violation while adhering to the regular structure.

Visual Relationships between Words and Pictures

Getting type to interact with imagery poses a serious problem for many designers. The results of poorly integrated type and image fall into two categories: in the first, typography is separated from the image areas, while in the second, typography is reduced to mere shape and texture. Images are composed of lights and darks, linear motion and volume, contours, and open or closed spaces, arranged in a particular order. Type shares these same attributes: it is composed of lights and darks, linear and volumetric forms, contours and rhythms of open and closed spaces, also arranged in a particular order. The task is finding where the specific attributes of both come together.

Laying type into or across an image is a quick way of finding visual relationships. Their immediate juxtaposition will reveal similarities in the shape or size of elements in each. The rag of a short paragraph may have a similar shape as a background element in a photograph. An image of a landscape with trees has a horizon line that may correspond to a horizontal line of type, and the rhythm and location of trees on the horizon may share some

qualities with the type's ascenders. At the opposite end of the spectrum, the image and the typographic forms may be completely unrelated—they are in opposition to each other. Opposition, thus, can be an equally viable for integrating two materials: a textural and moody image with great variation in tone, but no linear qualities, may work well with typography that is exceptionally linear, light, and rhythmically spaced. The contrast in presentation

helps enhance the distinct visual qualities of each. Consider the location of the type relative to the image and the attributes of the image's outer shape in relation to the format. An image cropped into a rectangle presents three options: the type may be enclosed within the image; the type may be outside, or adjacent to the image; or the type may cross the image and connect the space around it to its interior. Type that is placed within the field of a rectangular image becomes part of it. Type adjacent to a rectangular image remains a separate entity. Its relationship to the image depends on its positioning and any correspondence between its compositional elements and those in the image. The type may align with the top edge of the image rectangle or may rest elsewhere, perhaps in line with a division between light and dark inside the rectangle. Type that crosses over an image and into the format space becomes both part of the image in the rectangle and part of the elements on the page. Its location in space becomes ambiguous.

TYPE AND THE SILHOUETTE Silhouetted images—whose contours are free from enclosure in a rectangle—share a visual relationship with the rag of paragraphs or columns but also share an opposing relationship with their alignments.

1

Type will appear to change spatial relationship when placed on, in, or next to a cropped image. This spatial ambiguity may also involve the space around the cropped image, creating a connection between the field, image, and type that brings them together in space.

2

Placing the type directly onto the image permits a quick comparison of the shapes within both elements. In this example, the type repeats the scale changes, directional movement, and tonal variations found in the photographic image.

1

duis autem velure

duis autem velure

duis autem velure

2

duis autem velure

duis autem velure

duis autem velure

3

4

lingua franca va

esser plu simplice

regula quam li

exis tent Europan

lingues. It va esser

tam simquam

eras occidental:

it vaoccide

ntal simplificat

ang quam

glori amico

dit meque ma

quande lingues

coalesce duis

Type adjacent to a silhouetted image offers more or less contrast or similarity depending on its location relative to the image. If the rag leads into the image contours, the two elements flow together, and the type may seem to share the spatial context of the image. Bringing the vertical alignment of a column into proximity with an image's irregular contour produces the opposite effect: the type advances in space and disconnects itself from the spatial context of the image, appearing to float in front of it. The strong contrast between the aligned edge of the type and the contour of the image may then be countered by the irregular contour of the column's rag.

FORMAL CONGRUENCE Similarities between type elements and pictorial elements make a strong connection between the two. Every image portrays clear relationships between figure and ground, light and dark, and has movement within it. Objects depicted in photographs have a scale relationship with each other and proportional relationships with the edge of the image. When typographic configurations display similar attrib-

utes to an adjacent image or expand on those attributes, the type and the image are said to be formally congruent.

There are an unlimited number of ways for type to become congruent with an image. The selection of a particular font for the type may relate to tonal or textural qualities in the image. Instances in which type extrapolates the formal qualities in an image create powerful emotional and intellectual responses in the viewer. Type that is adjacent to an image can also be formally congruent in terms of its position relative to the image. In this kind of formal congruence, the image exerts an influence on the composition of the page as a whole. Even if the type retains its natural architecture, it may still react to the compositional architecture within the image. All three elements—image, format, and type—appear to share the same physical space.

FORMAL OPPOSITION Another means of integrating typographic elements and images is to relate them by contrasting their visual characteristics. Although seemingly counterintuitive, creating

3

A mix of sizes and spacing within phrases skews them toward becoming images, helping integrate them visually with other kinds of material. The arrangement of the image in the lower-left corner with the changing headline creates a series of stepped intervals whose lateral motion balances the image's downward and leftward pull. The red *g* creates a counterpoint to this activity. Callout information, arranged in smaller stepped blocks to the right, takes a cue from the main compositional elements.

Jeff Neumann Denver, USA

4

The relationship between the image shape and the rag becomes dominant if the rag enters into the image's contour; the geometric alignment in the same block of text will naturally counter the irregular forms within the silhouetted image.

1

2

1

In this spread from a course catalog, the vertical, linear rhythm of dress forms is restated by the vertically oriented type.

Studio Blue *Chicago, USA*

2

The designer responds to the compositional language of the image, using the alternation of small and large scale forms and spaces—as well as the angled linearity of the drawing—as inspiration.

Studio di Progettazione Grafica *Cevio, Switzerland*

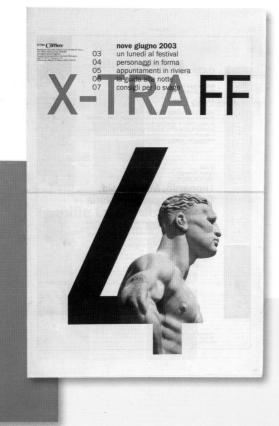

formal opposition between two kinds of material can actually help clarify their individual characteristics. Contrast is one of the most powerful qualities that a designer can use to integrate material—by their very difference, two opposing visual elements become more clearly identified and understood. Within a letterform combination of an *M* and an *O*, for instance, the fact of the *M*'s angularity is reinforced by the curved strokes of the *O*. The movement within each form is made more pronounced, and the two elements essentially fight for dominance. The caveat is that some congruence between the elements must also exist so that the opposing characteristics are brought clearly into focus. In the same way that a hierarchy is destroyed if all the elements are completely different, so too the strength of the contrast in opposing forms is weakened if all of their characteristics are different.

The same abstract pictorial qualities of image and type are the source for creating opposition, as they are for creating congruence. A soft-focus photograph with muted detail and light tonal values overall may suggest a bold-weight sans-serif typeface; another option may be a regular-weight modern serif face with a great deal of contrast in the strokes—the opposite of the photograph's lack of contrast. Yet another option may be a lightweight text with very active details, so that the passive, neutral character of the image is counteracted by the stylized quality of the typeface. In all three cases, some quality of the type is congruent with the image, but its primary quality is formally opposed to it.

3

The numeral and the figure have similar shapes and movement, but they also oppose each other formally—the numeral is a solid, angular line, while the figure is tonal and organic.

CODEsign *Rimini, Italy*

4

The position of the text block in this page spread mirrors the white mass of the model's sweater on the left-hand page.

J.Crew *New York City, USA*

5

A study of two letterforms, *O* and *M,* reveals both congruence and opposition. Their inherent differences are made more pronounced by changing the posture, weights, and positions of the letters.

Sequencing and Pacing: Creating Flow among Pages

The pacing of a publication is one of the most important considerations for a designer. Pacing can be understood as a kind of visual rhythm, a cadence or timing that the reader apprehends from spread to spread, almost like a film. By varying this rhythm—from slow to fast, or from quiet to dynamic, for example—the designer can accomplish several goals. One result achieved is strictly visual: each turn of the page engages the reader in a new way by varying the presentation. Another result may be that the reader is cued to a significant content change, as the pacing clarifies the informational function.

Much of a publication's flow is determined by its overall structure. Magazines, for example, are often divided into sections: a series of department pages that recur in the same order every issue, along with a sequence of feature stories that changes every issue. Within respective types of publications, such predetermined sections will likely differ because they present different kinds of content. Within each section, too, the designer must establish visual variation so that the reader, while recognizing a consistent structure, doesn't become bored.

PACING STRATEGIES Every project is different, so the ways in which a designer may address pacing in a specific project are unlimited. Most pacing strategies, however, can be distilled into two basic overall approaches: strategies focused on structural variation, and strategies that adjust content presentation.

Structural variation, as an approach to pacing, is essentially neutral in its affect on communication; the goal is to differentiate sections, or even spreads within a section, by articulating the content on a grid in noticeably different ways—or, as an alternative, by using a different grid in each section or spread to give it a particular character. The effect of structural variation is primarily one of rhythm, in which the elements change scale and position but not their inherent content. For example, one section of a publication may use especialy large images bleeding top to bottom and each spanning different column widths, interspersed with text, to create a lateral breaking of space; a section following may reverse this logic by emphasizing row structure to create long, panoramic arrangements of image andaccompanying text. The first structural approach will yield a speedy, rapid-edit quality to the pace of the spreads, while the second will produce a slower, more drawn-out feeling. Hanging images from a flowline near the top of a spread will contrast with another spread in which images are hung from a lower flowline or in which images bleed the page formats. The use of such structural strategies may be arbitrary, or they may reflect some feeling intrinsic to the content.

In changing the presentation of content—altering the overall color schemes of various sections, changing the visual language of imagery and type from spread to spread, or creating a progression in value or complexity from light to dark or simple to complicated—is an alternate strategy that primarily affects mood. As an approach to pacing, it is far less neutral in its result and will greatly affect the messages transmitted by individual sections or spreads, as well as the overall emotional journey experienced by the reader.

1

In these pages from an exhibition catalog, the alternation of full-bleed and inset images—as well as the alternation of text and image spreads—is one of the primary pacing strategies.

Faydherbe/DeVringer
The Hague, Netherlands

2

The text columns in this annual report, which always remain the same width and are separated by the same gutter, are allowed to shift left and right against the outer margins to accommodate photographs with different proportions. This alternation creates a lateral movement and different tension between interior and exterior from spread to spread.

Ruder Finn Design
New York City, USA

1

2

Structural Variation

A grid promotes consistency by virtue of its regularity but presents the designer with a potential pitfall: repetition. The designer must rise above the grid's uniformity to create a dynamic visual narrative that sustains interest page after page. Regardless of the content's treatment in terms of color, imagery, or typography, the structure of a publication can be articulated in a variety of ways.

A

Overall Progressive Sequencing
Image and text are articulated on the grid beginning with one type of logic, and then the logic changes progressively spread by spread. The result is a continuous transition in the pacing over the course of the entire project.

B

Overall Syncopated Sequences
One type of logic is used for a particular sequence of page spreads, the logic is altered for a second sequence of spreads, and then the spreads return to the previous logic. This strategy can become more complicated—instead of the simple ABA rhythm described, a rhythm of ABACA may be used, or ABCBCDCDE, for example.

C

Continuous Variation
Articulation of text and image content changes continuously from spread to spread. The change may focus on the relative position of elements or on the proportions of spatial zones given to specific informational components.

Content Presentation

Aside from varying structure, the designer may explore the visual qualities of the content to create pacing changes: its color, scale, photographic or illustrative treatment, and its complexity. Sometimes, these pacing changes coincide with grid variation: for example, changing the scale of images over a page sequence may reflect a change in grid logic. At other times, changes to content treatment for pacing may be independent of any structural variations.

A
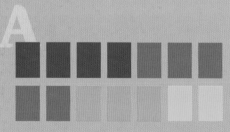

Color Progression or Syncopation
Page sequences exhibit a distinct color scheme, either varying completely between sequences or tied together by a universal color or two. The color schemes may progress (from cool to warm, or neutral to vibrant) or they may alternate in a particular rhythm (cool, warm, cool, warm).

B

Scale Progression or Syncopation
Images or text areas change in scale from spread to spread or from sequence to sequence. Images may grow in scale over a sequence of pages, or their scales may alternate between pages or sequential sections. Scale-based pacing may or may not be influenced by grid variation.

C

Text versus Image
The relationship between the amount of text and the amount of image material changes either progressively or in a distinct rhythm.

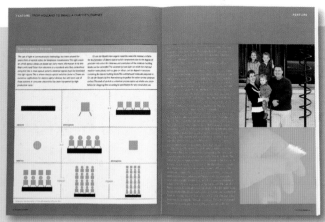

1

Interchanging the core colors from page to page within this quarterly newsletter creates variation in the apparent depths of the foreground and background, as well as a lively sequence among spreads.

And Partners, NY
New York City, USA

Section Variation

The same grid is articulated using a specific logic in one sequence of page spreads, then another logic in the following sequence, and then another logic in the sequence afterward. Alternatively, completely different grids may be used in each section.

Progressions or Syncopations in Complexity

The complexity of the material changes, reflected either as a progression (for example, from simple arrangements of smaller type to bold, layered arrangements of larger type) or as a syncopation (simple/complex/simple/complex).

Image Treatment Progressions or Syncopation

Image presentation changes between spreads or sequences. For example, images may progress from representational to abstract or may alternate between figurative portraits and environmental scenes.

Werte.

GESCHÄFTSBERICHT 2002/2003

NORDICREACH

A QUARTERLY OF SCANDINAVIAN CULTURE   NUMBER 9, VOLUME

downlow

Dressing the Package: Mastheads and Covers

Though not discussed until now, the exterior of a publication is an exceedingly important component of a project—it delivers the first impression of the overall communication that the publication's audience will see. In the case of magazines, especially, the cover is also a tool to transmit information about edition-specific content as a way of attracting additional interest and influencing its target audience to purchase it.

Even in publications that are not for sale, the cover must attract attention and generate interest, provide some clue to the content within, and reflect the secondary and tertiary functions of that content—audience relevance and branding messages. A cover is a package but also a transitional bridge between the outside world and the publication's interior experience. Whether designed to sell or to inform, the cover must be considered carefully. A cover may contain different information depending on the nature of the publication. The front page of a newspaper, which acts as its cover, contains an identifier (the masthead) that names the paper, a primary headline for an article about an

important event, and multiple smaller headlines for less important articles. Many newspapers also feature sidebars and condensed tables of contents to direct readers to specific sections. A newsletter cover contains a masthead, information identifying the corporation or organization publishing it, and, sometimes, a condensed table of contents. At times, a featured article may begin on the cover of a newsletter and continue inside, following the model of the newspaper front page. Magazines vary wildly in their covers: the primary elements of every magazine are a masthead and one powerful image; beyond that, there are no consistencies in magazine cover designs. Many covers offer call

out headlines and subheads, but an equal number offer no other text information.

The titling of a literature system or the masthead of a circulated publication share some basic features, and the approach a designer may take in developing this specific cover component will often be similar. The title must be simple and typographically powerful. Almost like a logotype, the type for a title or masthead must deliver a clear, strong, simple message. Since the word or words will most likely dominate the cover, careful attention to the drawing of the letterforms is essential.

Designers often approach a masthead as a typographic image, investigating such strategies as form alteration, combination, and inclusion to differentiate from other publications, especially those in the same genre. Like a logo, the mnemonic attributes of the masthead are very important; structural details like spacing, the shapes of terminals, the contrast of strokes, and the overall shape of the word or words help separate the masthead from competing messages in the minds of the target audience. Strategies like pictorialization or form alteration can ensure that the masthead is easily recognizable, as well as provide opportunities to communicate conceptual information about the publication's subject matter, create resonance with the target audience, and transmit positioning messages.

RUDER · FINN

MOVe

FIVE
YEARS
AND
FIFTY
LASHES

CH

MIÉRCOLES, 20 DE NOVIEMBRE DEL 2002 | A CORUÑA

La Voz de Galicia

NÚMERO 39.326 | AÑO CXX | **PRECIO:** 1 € | www.lavozdegalicia.es |

ESPECTÁCULOS   EL ACTOR NORTEAMERICANO **JAMES COBURN** FALLECE EN LOS ÁNGELES A LOS 74 AÑOS | 47

El buque se partió en dos a las ocho de la mañana y vertió 10.000 toneladas más de fuel

El «Prestige» se hunde y lanza

quality

Andersen

Viewpoint

Summer 2004

ADVANCE NEWS AND INFORMATION TO HELP DEALERS DO BUSINESS

Why Do Professionals Prefer Andersen® Patio Doors?

NUAL REPORT

A Masthead Close-Up

Mastheads tend to be stronger the simpler they are. Limiting the number and kinds of changes between elements helps the eye focus on the elements that stand out as being different. As a result, the overall unity of the forms becomes stronger, and the masthead becomes more recognizable because the differences stand out all the more. In the first example, before a redesign, the masthead of the *Business Examiner* was confusing, without a specific mnemonic element to grab onto: the two words differed in size, width, style, and weight. In the redesign, the type style of the two words is unified, and their weights and widths are brought closer together. Enough weight change remains so that the first word is still emphasized, but just enough. The cap heights of the two words are aligned, as are the heights of the small caps and lowercase; but the case change also introduces emphasis on the first word, which defines subject matter. The slightly condensed style allows the masthead to get bigger within the same space, and the proportions of the two words have become similar, so their break becomes decisively centered over the page, providing a strong stabilizing point. Against the overall strength and regularity of the configuration, the remaining tittle over the *i* in *Examiner* now stands out as a strong identifier.

Ewing Creative *Manchester (WA), USA*

The cover images in this spread appear in other locations throughout the book, and are credited in the Directory of Contributors, pages 238–239.

From Cover to Cover

Case Study Profiles

Publications in the real world vary dramatically, not just by type—product catalogs, magazines, newsletters, annual reports, newspapers, literature systems—but also in the way that designers approach them. Despite basic similarities in the concerns each must address, from typeface selection to structure to color to format, there is no single way to begin planning or working through the design of a document. That difference is in evidence here, in ten publication projects from designers around the world. From rigorously solved typographic systems to complicated, playful, and spontaneous layouts of photography and illustration, each highlights the individuality of expression that each designer brings to creating an engaging solution, while addressing the universal issues inherent in designing publications.

01

One World Magazine (*Ein Welt, Un Solo Mundo, Un Seule Monde*)

Studio di Progettazione Grafica |
Cevio, Switzerland
Sabina Obertholtzer and Renato Tagli, Principals

Components + Formats

Periodical newsmagazine
Content developed and distributed by
government agency

Format
A3 (tabloid) folded to A4; 32 pages, self-cover,
saddle stitched; printed four-color process
(CMYK) in three languages.

One World is a magazine designed for the Swiss DDC, a government agency that coordinates and funds humanitarian aid to countries beset by poverty, health crises, and political conflicts. As a division of the Swiss Federal Department of Foreign Affairs, it enlists outside consultants to create communications for public dissemination; in this case, design duo Sabina Oberholtzer and Renato Tagli, whose Studio di Progettazione Grafica specializes in cultural and governmental communications. Their signature modernist approach is embodied in the rational grid structure and clear informational hierarchy of the prototype for the publication, which provides information about the programs and initiatives that the DDC undertakes in various regions. The magazine acts as a newsletter in some regards, announcing specific programs and, later, updating the readership on the progress and results achieved upon implementation. It is also topical in nature, bringing current events and contextual news information to its readers.

The column structure appears at first to be relatively conventional. Primary text for articles runs over three columns of even width that extend, newspaper-like, from near top to bottom. A newspaper-like flag, or masthead structure, reinforces this presentation, carrying article heads and decks in a large-size sans serif. On closer inspection, however, a narrow column appears interspersed between the primary columns at roughly half their width, indicating a more precise seven-column grid underneath. The narrow column serves a number of purposes: it can be used to add margin width, carry a vertical section header, or hold a place for image captions. The use of seven columns allows the text-column width to remain constant whether the narrow column appears at the outside of the main text structure or within it. Vertical text columns are separated by narrow rules, allowing a tighter horizontal fit without creating a cross-column reading problem. The article flags, containing head and deck, generally run horizontally across the page over the body area; sometimes, however, they are allowed to run vertically in a column made up of one primary width combined with the narrow width. Images—and, often, the beginnings of articles or subparagraphs—hang from a series of flow-lines that define nine rows of modules.

Adding to the overall newspaper-like quality of the publication, which affords a certain journalistic credibility, is a distinct system of typographic treatments for each level of information: primary and secondary headlines, primary and secondary decks, subheads, callouts, running text, and captions. Two type families—a sans serif gothic and a modern serif—are

An open, flexible layout structure, compelling photography, and clear, yet texturally dynamic, typographic treatments contribute to the visual accessibility of this humanitarian publication that actively engages its audience.

1

Exklusives Interview
Richard Gerster
zum Solidaritätsfonds

Un monde
Eine Welt
Un mondo

DEZA-Magazin
für Entwicklung
und
Zusammenarbeit

Nummer
5
Dezember
2003

"
Gebt uns
den Neuenburgersee,
mehr nicht
"

DEZA–
Frau in Palästina

75 Mal Südsicht:
Film Festival Fribourg

1

The cover features a large-scale photograph that always bleeds left to right, combined with several typographic elements, whose positions vary. The red circle contains the masthead information in three languages; the white title within indicates in which language a particular edition is produced. The cross-axis typographic lockup of the edition date and subject descriptor references the white cross of the Swiss flag. Although the elements—masthead circle, photograph, featured topic article, and text callout—remain the same in terms of size and treatment, their positions on the cover may vary considerably.

One World Magazine
Studio di Progettazione Grafica I Sabina
Oberholtzer and Renato Tagli I *Cevio, Switzerland*

01

1, 2

The grid, articulated in different ways from spread to spread, allows for clear and consistent presentation of information but adds vitality and movement in its variation. The narrow, multifunctional column adds a syncopated rhythm to the regularity of the primary text columns. In the *Forum* spread (1), it holds for the heading, running vertically up the side; in the other spread, it is used mainly for captions. The newspaper-like flag heads are situated in a band above the body, two rows deep, that also accommodates callouts in large blue dots. The story heads are allowed to run vertically.

Tribune: Richard Gerster zum Solidaritätsfonds

Exklusives Interview
mit den Stars dem neuen PC-Game

Bulgarien:
Schweiz an erster
Stelle bei soforthilfe
und Strukturellen
Aufbau
Seite 22

Globalisierung werändert alles:

Beat Kappeler über neuste Trends in der Entwicklungszusammenarbeit

Frauengruppen in Kenia

Wasser-dasumstrittene Nass

Wasser-dasumstrittene Nass

Forum

24

25

2

Länder und Leute

Mit grossen Schritten-Länder-porträt in Palästina

Schweiz erster
Stelle
bei Soforthilfe
und strukturellem
Aufbau

dolor sit amet, consectetuer adi-piscing elit, sed diam nonummy nibh euismod tincidunt ut laoreet dolore magna aliq uam erat volutpat.

16

17

used in all their weights and widths to impart navigational clarity and to invigorate the pages with typographic color. Flexibility is built into the heads through typeface choice; they may appear in the sans serif (always bold, but regular or condensed width) or in the black weight of the serif.

Maximum distinction is made between running text and other elements via discreet and consistent use of the regular weight serif versus the black condensed serif for subheads and the bold sans serif for captions. The serif of the text face, somewhat visually more active than other possible text face choices because of its extreme stroke contrast and geometric structure, is leaded amply to allow more interline white space. Similarly, the decision to justify the columns helps minimize the text's activity by doing away with the additional distraction provided by a rag. Although the columns align top and bottom in a given story, the text is allowed to run out when it comes to its natural end, adding the possibility of white space to interact with the text and the geometric invasion of photographs into the text areas.

Despite the rigor of the typographic styling, however, Oberholtzer and Tagli were determined to give the publication a friendlier and more accessible feeling. "The overall design needed to be relatively serious," says Sabina Oberholzer, "but it was important to give some sense of the multiethnic subject matter through the layouts, even though the pictures really speak for themselves. We added elements like red dots around folios and blue bars within the text to be more fun and encourage reading; and really, the variety of typefaces was just as much about conveying a sense of differences as it was about making the information clear."

One important aspect of the design is its flexibility to be reproduced in several languages. "The magazine is directed to people working in these programs, Swiss citizens (who speak several languages) as well as program directors in foreign offices." The column structure of the magazine allows each edition to be reproduced in three languages—Swiss German, Italian, and French—without radically altering the type size or destroying the flow of stories across columns. As noted above, text can run out at its natural end—or fill a full set of columns—without the difference being that noticeable; negative space left as a result of the text running out in a shorter language seems natural. The multiple-language factor also had implications for the cover: the masthead title needed to show all three languages yet emphasize the one being used in its particular edition. A system of three titles, differentiated by tint, solved the problem. "Using the red ball signified the world, but with the white type and the masthead lockup, the type also feels like the Swiss flag," Oberholtzer elaborates.

Eine Welt   17 dezember 2004

lor sit amet, con sectetuer adips scing elit , sed diam nonummy nibh euismodu.

Lorem aet dolor magnaper susci pite lobortis nisa ut aliquip ex ea commodo coniti sequat. Duis au tem vel eum iri re dolor in. Lore hendrerit in vul putate velit esse molestie conse quat, vel illum dolore eu feugiat nulla facilisis au vero eros esun.

28

luptatum zzril delenit aug doloretefeugaitnulla facilisi se molestie consequat, vel il eu feugiat nulla facilisis at et accu ms

Frauengruppen in Kenia

odio dignissim qui blandit p luptatum zzril delenit aug doloretefeugaitnulla facilisi ipsum dolor sit amet, cons adipiscing elit, sed diam no nibh euismod tincidunt ut se molestie consequat, vel ill eu feugiat nulla facilisis at niam, quis nostrud exerci ta

3

A lively mix of typefaces adds color and clarity to the various informational components in the layouts. Linear serif text is contrasted by a bold-weight sans serif, as well as an extrabold neoclassical serif in the headlines. The headline type, with its ball serifs and geometric contrast, exhibits visual similarity with details such as the folio dots and heavy blue rules used to mark subheads within columns.

One World Magazine
Studio di Progettazione Grafica | Sabina
Oberholtzer and Renato Tagli | *Cevio, Switzerland*

01

1

1

An extrawide column
at the far left, composed
of a standard text-width
column and a caption-
width column, carries a
large sans-serif headline
and deck configuration.

1

2

Länder und Leute

Annick Tonti

DEZA — Frau in Palästina

Gestern abend wurde
einem grossen fest
die Premiere
des computerspiels

Umstrittenen
Bewässerungsprojekte

Kultur

75 Mal Südsicht: Film festival Fribourg

Exklusives Interview
mit den Stars dem neuen Filme.

Frauengruppen in Kenia

Wasser-dasumstrittene Nass

Work Process

"We started with some very rapid sketches by hand, but began working on the computer with actual text as soon as we could. It was very important to us to see the text move onscreen so we could tell what was happening with it on the grid," says Oberholtzer. "We made a lot of decisions directly as a result of seeing how our type treatments affected the length of text and how much difference in texture they created.

"The computer also allowed us to sketch the covers a lot more quickly," adds Tagli. "The composition of the elements can change depending on what they are—even though there are some constants, like the size of the red circle—and how the photo interacts with them. So we usually just moved the elements around directly onscreen until they began to do something; it's very spontaneous, but we've set up some rules about how big things can be and how they relate to the grid, so it holds together."

3

Detailed, informational
listings are as easily
accommodated by the
structure as full-height
photographic images.
Simple changes in typo-
graphic color—bold
to regular—are used
to create distinction
between informational
components.

3

Wir singen immer noch Kademba aus Senegal

**Wasser-
dasumstrittene Nass**

velit esse modestie consequat, vel illum dolore eu feugiat nulla facilisis
at vero eros et accumsan et iusto
odio dignissim qui blandit praesent
luptatum zzril delenit augue duis
dolore te feugait nulla facilisi.
Lorem ipsum nisl ut aliquip ex ea
commodo consequat. Duis autem
vel eum iriure dolor in hendrerit in
vulputate velit esse molestie consequat, vel illum dolore eu feugiat
nulla facilisis at vero eros et accumsan et iusto odio dignissim qui
blandit praesent luptatum zzril delenit augue duodio dignissim qui
blandit praesent luptatum zzril delenit augue duodio dignissim ve feugiat
nulla facilisi.Lorem ipsum dolor sit
amet, consectetuer adipiscing elit,
sed diam nonummy nibh euismod
tincidunt ut laoreet dolore magna
aliquam erat volupat. Ut wisi
enim ad minim dolor sit amet, consectetuer adi
tis nisl ut aliquip ex ea commodo
consequat. Duis autem vel eum
iriure dolor in hendrerit in vulputate velit esse molestie consequat,
vel illum dolore eu feugiat nulla facilisis at vero eros et accumsan et
iusto odio dignissim qui blandit
praesent luptatum zzril delenit augue duodio dignissim qui blandit
praesent luptatum zzril delenit augue duis dolore te feugait nulla fa-
cilisi.Lorem ipsum dolor sit amet,
consectetuer adipiscing.

**Wasser-
dasumstrittene Nass**

Sed diam nonummy nibh euismod
tincidunt ut laoreet dolore magna
aliquam erat volupat. Ut wisi
enim ad minim veniam, quis nostrud exerci tation ullamcorper suscipit lobortis nisl ut aliquip ex ea
commodo consequat. Lorem ipsum
dolor sit amet, consectetuer adipiscing elit, sed diam nonummy nibh
euismod tincidunt ut laoreet dolore
magna aliquam erat volu.
Ut wisi enim ad minim veniam,
quis nostrud exerci tation ullamcorper suscipit lobortis nisl ut aliquip ex ea commodo consequat.
Ut wisi enim ad minim veniam, quis nostrud exerci tation ullamcorper suscipit lobortistation ullamcorper suscipit lobortis nisl ut aliquip
ex ea commodo consequat.

qui blandit prae-
sent luptatum
zzril delenit augue
duis dolore te
feugait nulla fac.

This spread demonstrates
the tremendous variety
in layout options: images
appear running a full
vertical column, as well
as in a rhythmic, modular
configuration; heads in
horizontal and vertical
format coexist; enormous
quotations, horizontal blue
bars under black-weight
serif subheads add color
and texture.

Entwicklung und Zusammenarbeit Schweiz

**Bulgarien:
Schweiz
an erster Stelle
bei Soforthilfe
und strukturellem
Aufbau**

Lorem ipsum do-
lor sit amet, sed
consectetuer adi-
piscing elit, nibh
sed diam nummy
nibh euismdnot
ut laoreddolo dolo
dolore magn.

Einblick — DEZA

**Bénin
Organizations de producteurs**

Lorem ipsum dolor sit amet, consectetuer adipiscing elit, sed d-
iam nonummy nibh euismod tincidunt ut laoreet dolore magna
aliquam erat volupat.Lorem ipsum dolor sit amet,consectetuer
adipiscing elit, sed diam nonummy nibh euismod tincidunt ut
laoreet dolore magna

**Mali
Foresterie**

Lorem ipsum dolor sit amet,
consectetuer adipiscing elit, sed
diam nonummy nibh euismod
tincidunt ut laoreet dolore magna aliquam erat volupat.Lore-
m ipsum dolor sit amet, consectetuer adipiscing elit, sed diam

**Niger
Gestion des eaux et des sols**

Duisalierat volutpat. Duis aute-
m vel eum iriure dolor in hend
rerit in vulputate velit esse molestie consequat, vel illum dolore
eu feugiat nulla facilisis at vero
eros et accumsan et iusto

**Tchad
Education de base**

eodio dignissim qui blandit
praesent luptatum zzril delenit
augue duis dolore te feugait nulla facilisi.Lorem ipsum dolor sit
amet, consectetuer adipiscing
elit, sed diam nonummy nibh
euismod tincidunt ut laoreet do-

Lorem ipsum dolor sit amet,
consectetuer adipiscing elit, sed
diam nonummy nibh euismod
tincidunt ut laoreet dolore magna aliquam erat volupat.Lore-
m ipsum dolor sit amet, consectetuer adipiscing elit, sed diam
nonummy nibh euismod tincidunt ut laoreet dolore magna

**Afrique du Sud
Formation pour parents.**

Lorem ipsum dolor sit amet,
consectetuer adipiscing elit, sed
diam nonummy nibh euismod
tincidunt ut laoreet dolore magna aliquam erat volupat. Lore-
m ipsum dolor sit amet, consectetuer adipiscing elit, sed diam

**Région du Mekong
Centre pour culture maraichère**

Sed diam nonummy nibh euismod tincidunt ut laoreet dolore
magna aliquam erat volupat.
Ut wisi enim ad minim veniam,
quis nostrud exerci tation ullamcorper suscipit lobortis nisl
ut aliquip ex ea commodo consequat. Duis autem vel eum iriure
dolor in hendrerit in vulputate
velit esse molestie consequat,
vel illum dolore eu feugiat nulla
facilisis at vero eros et accumsan et iusto odio dignissim qui
blandit praesent luptatum zzril
delenit augue duis dolore te feu

**Pakistan
Défendre les femmes**

Lorem ipsum dolor sit amet,
consectetuer adipiscing elit, sed
diam nonummy nibh euismod
tincidunt ut laoreet dolore magna aliquam erat volupat.Lore-
m ipsum dolor sit amet, conse-
tetuer adipiscing elit, sed diam
nonummy nibh euismod.

**Bolivie
Micro - entreprises urbaines**

Dolor in hendrerit in vulputate
velit esse molestie consequat,
vel illum dolore eu feugiat nulla
facilisis at vero eros et accumsan et iusto odio dignissim qui
blandit praesent luptatum zzril
delenit augue duis dolore te fou-
gait nulla facilisi. Lorem ipsum
dolor sit amet,consectetuer adi

**Nicaragua
Coltures vivrières**

Lorem ipsum dolor sit amet,
consectetuer adipiscing elit, sed
diam nonummy nibh euismod
tincidunt ut laoreet dolore magna aliquam erat volupat.Lore-
m ipsum dolor sit amet, consectetuer adipiscing elit, sed diam
nonummy nibh euismod tincidunt ut laoreet dolore magna
Lorem ipsum dolor sit amet,
consectetuer adipiscing elit, sed
diam nonummy nibh euismod
tincidunt ut laoreet dolore magna aliquam erat volupat.Lore-
m ipsum dolor s

**Pérou
Eau assainissement**

Lorem ipsum dolor sit amet,
consectetuer adipiscing elit, sed
diam nonummy nibh euismod
tincidunt ut laoreet dolore magna aliquam erat volupat.Lore-
m ipsum dolor sit amet, conse-
tetuer adipiscing elit, sed diam.

**Cile
Aphie a la démocratie**

Duisalierat volutpat. Duis aute-
m vel eum iriure dolor in hend
rerit in vulputate velit esse molestie consequat, vel illum dolore
eu feugiat nulla facilisis at vero
eros et accumsan et iusto

**Columbia
Education de base**

eodio dignissim qui blandit praesent luptatum zzril delenit augue duis dolore te feugait nulla
facilisi.Lorem ipsum dolor sit

This complex, multipart publication acts as a promotional tool and a customer service device for its creators, Graph Co., Ltd., a brand consulting and printing company based in Hyogo, Japan. Part brochure/magalog, part print order system, the publication brings together traditional editorial structure and printed ephemera to create a branded message for potential clients that also acts as a catalog and ordering sheet for one of the company's print products, a system of promotional cards. In Japan, greeting cards are an important part of social communication, especially during holidays, and businesses often send them to clients and other contacts along with the general public at these times. This blurring of social and corporate messaging is part of the conceptual context that lends this publication some of its friendly, yet functional, character.

02

Hybrid Brochure/Magalog Product Catalog

Graph Co., Ltd. | Hyogo, Japan
Issay Kitagawa, Principal

The publication consists of three major parts that always accompany each other: a stitched, periodical brochure describing Graph's capabilities; a system of greeting cards that Graph offers as a product; and a folded catalog that highlights the greeting cards, explaining the options available for customers and creating a vehicle for placing orders.

The brochure is designed as a "magalog"—a hybrid publication with the editorial structure of a magazine or newsletter that catalogs the company's services. The folded catalog sheet presents a vivid branding message, visible through the transparent glassine envelope used for mailing the entire package, becoming a poster as well as an informational device when opened. The sample cards included in the publication demonstrate Graph's design as well as printing capabilities; as a result of a systematic production process where customer (and in-house) cards are produced, they create an opportunity for Graph to experiment with their own branded cards while providing live samples for customer reference. The mixture of editorial and ephemeral media creates a rich visual experience for Graph's customers and a constantly evolving venue for their self-promotion from edition to edition.

One of Graph's primary goals in creating this publication was to make their customers aware of their dual role as designers and printers—a fact the system highlights in its design and production. The layout of the brochure/magalog is visually arresting, with fluorescent inks and a collage of design work that derives from printers' make-ready sheets; the folded card catalog is a transition from this conceptual message to a finished product, the greeting card product itself. "Often, customers who know Graph is a printing company do not realize it is also a design company, and vice versa," says Issay Kitagawa, Graph's president and founder. "Our aim here is to let customers know that Graph offers both services." The publication form and contents reveal this fact in a direct but conceptual way.

A mixture of editorial and ephemeral material, the components of this publication provide a rich, complex visual experience that is conceptual, informational, and tactile.

Components + Formats

Project Type
Hybrid editorial/ephemeral publication

Components
Periodical brochure/magalog; folded product catalog sheet; product samples (greeting cards); glassine mailing envelope.

Formats
Brochure/magalog A4 page format base, with gatefold and short-sheets inserted; Singer-stitched side binding.
Folded catalog sheet A3, printed two sides in black and custom Graph fluorescent yellow; matte-coated text stock.
Sample cards Mixed stocks and sizes, printed standard process (CMYK) color.

1

Samples of the greeting card system that is the motivating product for this publication. The cards are reprints of designs produced by Graph for various customers. Their presence in the publication is a unique example of product being displayed in a catalog and included for inspection, offering a conceptual transition from the corporate message to the concrete end product for customers to see firsthand. Several illustration and design styles were selected to give the greatest sense of the range of options in the system from which customers can choose.

Build customer awareness of Graph's dual service offering—design and printing

Drive print and design sales through a unique product offering—custom greeting cards

Illustrate the high-quality and cost-effective production methods associated with the cards and, by extension, with Graph as a service entity

Present and clarify the product offering and the variety of options it offers

Instruct customers on choosing card formats, paper stocks, and custom design by Graph

Provide a direct vehicle for ordering cards and other products and design services. Build relationships with customers that may potentially yield more complex design commissions

1

2

3

GRAPH

GRAPH

2, 3

The uncoated stock, stitched side binding, and metallic foil stamp of the brochure/magalog cover combine with the fluorescent ink and typographic simplicity of the foldout catalog to create a simple, but dramatic, visual presence. The cover of the brochure/magalog—a single sheet—can be updated from edition to edition without reprinting a full signature or any other interior content.

Hybrid Brochure/Magalog
Graph Co., Ltd. | Issay Kitagawa, *Hyogo, Japan*

02

1

2

1

The table of contents repeats the fluorescent yellow signature color upon opening the brochure. It is printed on a single sheet and backed up with a corporate profile that can be updated quickly and cost effectively. Color proofing bars and registration marks allude to the company's role as designers and printers.

2, 4

A simple two-column grid organizes text and images in a straightforward structure that is countered by project images, abstract details, and bands of ink.

3

The Singer-stitch binding, unlike a traditional saddle stitch, allows individual sheets, as well as signatures or gatefolds and alternating paper stocks, to be added, removed, or reordered on a regular basis. Here, glossy single pages alternate with the uncoated newsprint base stock; in a second example, the glossy stock on the left is separated from the base newsprint stock on the right by a semi-transparent vellum sheet bound between them.

BROCHURE / MAGALOG The brochure/magalog is a periodical piece composed of individual pages stitched together in a nontraditional thread binding that runs $1/2$" (1.3 cm) in from the spine. Because the stitch, which resembles that of a sewing machine, runs across the format rather than joining spreads at the spine, pages of various sizes (including single sheets) can be bound together. This stitching also means that pages can be removed, reordered, or added to in subsequent editions without having to redesign or reorder the pages within the layout files themselves. Additionally, the designers can experiment with a variety of printing techniques and paper stocks from page to page, unconstrained by the need for signatures. As a production method, the stitching is more cost effective than perfect

binding in a small print run (the other option for achieving these same goals).

The cover design is spare, using only a pearlescent foil stamp of the company logotype in a sans serif that graduates downward in size from letter to letter. The base paper stock is a soft, nearly translucent newsprint; while it holds color well, its tooth and absorbent formation creates a slight ink bleed that lends an interesting preproduction quality to the layouts. This "working-quality" presentation offsets the magalog's corporate message as a capabilities brochure, making it feel both like a newspaper and a prep sheet for a print job. It also allows inserted contrasting paper stocks to stand out, while at the same time showcasing the greeting cards' print quality—rather than competing

Strategic Statements

"First, we wanted to revise our greeting card product," explains Kitagawa. "This included the visual look of the sample cards, the catalog explaining about the cards, and the envelope used to send the sample cards and catalog to the client. We also wanted customers to understand that post cards are not the only way to use a card. A postcard can be used as a flyer or ticket; a name card can be used as a tag. The customer can also change the size in which the card will be cut, although there is an additional fee for cutting. By seeing that the design of the card system and publication are of high quality, customers will think that the quality of printing will also be good. Of course, the aim is to increase the demand for printing and design by GRAPH, whether it's via the card system or bespoke requests and to have customers repeat their orders to us. In terms of presentation, we wanted to keep the visual of the catalog sheet interesting but simple; hence, the use of two colors, while we used bright designs for the sample card items. This would be more visually stimulating to customers. The brochure/magalog becomes an editorial supporting device for us. The initial launch was in October, as Japan has a culture of sending postcards for New Year's greetings, but we'll update everything every three to six months to make improvements and add new material."

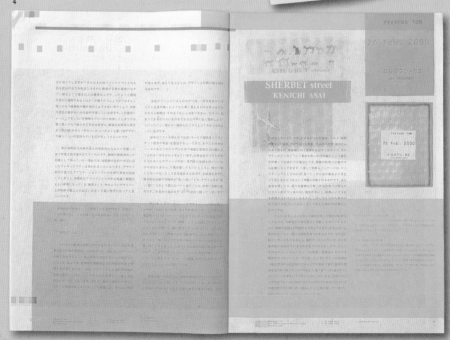

with them—so customers may perceive that their own communications will be of greater concern than those of Graph.

The interior layout mixes a standard, two-column editorial structure with collages of Graph's design projects in process and fluorescent colors that look like separations and process proofs prior to final printing; the make-ready effect is enhanced by press details such as registration marks and press-form color proofing bars. Typography is limited to one typeface—Medium Gothic, a commonly used standard face—for the first portion of the piece (in Japanese) and a typewriter-like face for the English portion, both using only one weight.

Hybrid Brochure / Magalog
Graph Co., Ltd. | Issay Kitagawa, *Hyogo, Japan*

1

1
Yet another spread of the brochure/magalog experiments with paper stock and gloss, instead of matte, printing inks.

2
A gatefold endpage continues the make-ready sheet style established in the brochure/magalog's interior, showing multiple projects and graphic details surprinting as though found on reused prep sheets.

3
A detail of the back cover head and binding, showing print proofing elements, the transparency of the newsprint stock, and the Singer-stitched binding; the thread-end hangs free.

2

3

4

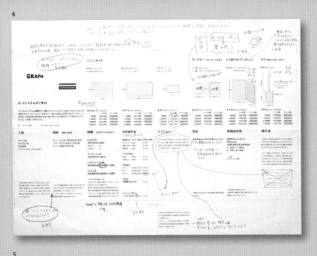

5

GRAPH

4–6
Iterations of the foldout sheet demonstrate the designer's working method, from initial layout idea to final form. Decisions about the placement and sequencing of informational sections and details, which changed from revision to revision, were made by evaluating full-size print-outs and cutting and pasting elements back and forth to see how the flow of content changed. Sketching quickly in this way helps save time but also provides a very direct experience for the designer looking to determine how a layout changes in actuality, rather than simply onscreen.

PRODUCT CATALOG SHEET The foldout catalog sheet is informational and strikingly simple. Considered by Graph to be the focal point of the publication package, supported by the brochure/magalog and samples, its goal is to communicate the concept and quality of the greeting card product, as well as the ease of ordering from within the product's system of options and its inexpensive production. The catalog also fulfills the dual role of branding the publication package, by acting as a de facto cover seen through the glassine mailing envelope and as a conceptual link between the supporting brochure/magalog—which provides context—and the greeting card product. Although it is printed using only two colors to cut cost, visual impact is not lost: the piece uses black and a custom-mixed fluorescent yellow that Graph commissioned from an ink supplier. "It is quite difficult to find a fluorescent yellow of this type," says Kitagawa excitedly.

Folded down, the catalog sheet forms a blast of color with the company's austere logotype, holding the sample cards and purchase order forms as a kind of envelope. Opened, it becomes an instruction manual for customers, showing the various options available for greeting card formats, printing process and pricing. The sheet is structured on an eight-column modular grid with relatively deep gutters between rows. The grid modules are derived from the proportions of the greeting cards and the diagrams that illustrate them, creating an inherently clear visual synchrony between the product offering and the catalog sheet text structure. The sheet is further divided into larger horizontal bands, with headings and important informational components called out by bands of the fluorescent yellow ink. Aside from headers identifying each of these horizontal sections and smaller text accompanying

Special Concerns

"The cost had to be kept to a minimum—especially as the catalog and sample card items would be sent to customers for free—but at the same time, we had to show the high quality of design and printing we offer," says Kitagawa. He elaborates: "We printed the brochure/magalog using leftover paper stocks from other projects, plus a newsprint we use for rough proofing; the cards are ganged up in larger runs to cut costs for customers, so we ran several additional ones in a scheduled run. The cards are proportioned to fit tightly on the sheet and use less paper, too."

6

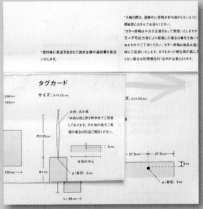

Hybrid Brochure/Magalog
Graph Co., Ltd. | Issay Kitagawa, *Hyogo, Japan*

diagrams, the text overall is set in one size; all of the text is set in the same weight of the same face. The austerity of the typography and the considered use of the grid structure combine to create an informational document that is easy for customers to navigate and that highlights Graph's credibility as functionally concerned, service-oriented designers and printers. The choice of a brilliant white, matte-coated stock for the catalog sheet contrasts the newsprint stock of the brochure/magalog and draws attention to the catalog sheet.

GREETING CARDS Folded into the catalog sheet (which is folded over the brochure/magalog cover) are sample greeting cards, representing the product that drives the overall publication. Their proportions inform all of the components of the system, from the foldout sheet to the brochure/magalog. They are printed in standard process (CMYK) color on a selection of glossy, matte, and mirrored card stocks, offering examples of these options for potential customers. Some of the cards included are also shown in the brochure/magalog, creating an interesting conceptual connection—from catalog presentation of the product to concrete sample.

This intermingling of sample product and actual product echoes the working process qualities of the brochure/magalog, tying the three components of the publication into a complex, yet coherent, whole.

The foldout catalog sheet breaks sections of information into horizontal bands defined by its folds; an eight-column modular grid, proportionally based on the diagrams of the greeting cards, lends additional structure to the text and images.

1

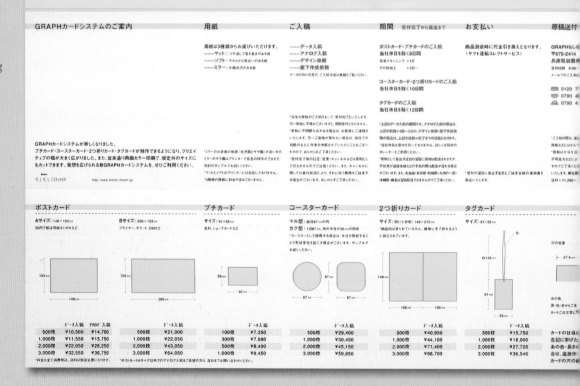

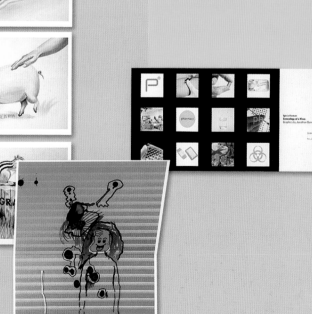

2

A detail of the typography shows the strength and clarity imparted by restraint in the design: one typeface in one weight, at two primary sizes. Arrow details and narrow bands of fluorescent yellow ink add visual interest and enhance the informational aspect of the headers.

3

The greeting cards for multiple customers are printed ganged up on a press sheet to reduce costs and speed up turnaround. Customers may select from a variety of sizes and production options, as well as commission Graph to design the cards for them. In the publication, a mix of formats, illustrative and abstract graphic styles are included to show customers what the potential options are.

Work Process

Issay Kitagawa describes the genesis of the hybrid publication: "We didn't really begin with conceptual sketches. The ideas came out of the actual working process. There were lots and lots of revisions; we have stacks of several inches of printouts of vetoed concepts. Our main concentration was on the catalog sheet; the brochure/magalog was assembled quickly from various sources (other promotional materials).

"The first task," Kitagawa continues, "was to change the catalog to make it more understandable and to show the new range of card items. There was a previous catalog that was split into two separate items: a long, yellow and red information strip and the other blue and orange strip. They were difficult for the customers to read and comprehend, so we decided to merge the information into one sheet. The first version was cut and bound into six pages plus front and back. However, we soon felt that each page slightly stopped the flow of information; customers had to flip from one page of the catalog to another should they want to refer back to a certain section.

"A second version was designed on one sheet of paper, printed both front and back and folded once both horizontally and vertically. By having all the information on just two sides (front and back), all the customer needed to do was to see one or the other page. Also, customers would expect a bound catalog, which would not be as interesting (plus we didn't want it to be confused with the brochure/magalog). However, as there were only four partitions, not enough information could be covered in this layout. So, finally, we designed it on one sheet but folded it twice horizontally and once vertically. Just by changing the way the paper was folded, there were six partitions and more information could be shown. Manual cut and paste of sections was done to see what would be the most clear. During this process, the idea of using an arrow to highlight the content of each section emerged. This arrow would also help customers with the flow of information."

03

La Voz de Galicia
Regional Newspaper

La Voz de Galicia in-house design |
À Coruña, Spain
Jesus Gil Saenz, Art Director

Most newspaper design proceeds along a relatively narrow path of conventions, compared to other kinds of editorial publications, such as magazines, annual reports, or even newsletters. This restraint is due partly to the conservative nature of news publishing and the kind of credibility that the paper must inspire in its readership; any sense of frivolity or impropriety in the presentation, and the paper risks being discredited as a reliable news source. This necessary conservatism is augmented somewhat by a kind of historical sense of the tradition of news publishing, which has its roots in postfeudal Europe around the 1500s.

Reporters, editors, and newspaper typographers take their craft seriously because of this sense of tradition, so dramatic innovations in newspaper structure are few and far between. The seriousness of the tradition has a functional side, related to the issue of credibility: the information being presented must be easily navigated, easily read, easily updated on a regular and rapid basis as stories get pulled or added before press time. On top of these constraints is the often relatively poor quality of newsprint, which precludes excessive ink buildup and necessitates a profound attention to the detail of typeface weight, structure, spacing, and color to ensure clear reproduction. The fact that any newspaper designer or design team is able to accommodate all these concerns and produce a newspaper that is not only informative and reliable, but also engaging and pleasing to look at, is an accomplishment in itself.

Simplicity of organization and lively, accessible typographic detailing help lead readers easily through this Spanish newspaper.

Components+Formats

Newspaper
A3 vertical folded; printed four-color process (CMYK) and single spot black on two paper stocks (one standard newsprint, one pinkish stock for financial news); divided into three major sections: national/international hard news, local news, soft news (sports, dining, entertainment, Sunday supplements).

The regional daily Spanish paper, *La Voz de Galicia*, founded in 1882, has an elegant A3 format, similar to the U.S. tabloid but a bit wider. A decorative masthead, printed in a distinctive red ink across the top of the format, sets off its overall contemporary appearance. The drawing of the masthead's letters is florid; sharp geometric *textura* junctures are punctuated with a number of swirls, ball serifs, and modulated backstrokes that produce a very baroque presentation, evocative of the intensity of Spanish culture and language. The masthead also serves to connect the modern version of the publication to its roots, establishing its credibility by virtue of tradition. Beyond this decorative titling, however, the recent redesign of the newspaper is all business. A quick scan of any page—the front page in particular—makes a stark simplicity of hierarchy quite noticeable. There tends to be one major headline, accompanied by an image; following that, a few paragraphs of text and sometimes a sidebar or lead for a secondary story or section. Unlike the majority of newspapers, *La Voz* eschews filling its pages with competing headlines at all—never mind competing headlines set in multiple sizes, alignments, treatments, weights, and widths. A maximum of two story heads (or one feature head and one feature subhead) appears to exist on any given page. This restraint is evidence of the editorial and graphic design teams working closely together to create a clear and user-friendly system for displaying information so that it doesn't overload the reader.

The paper is structured on a primary grid of five columns, each ten modules high from top to bottom of the body. The margins are relatively tight to the body but wider than the gutter between the columns. This gutter interval serves as a measure for subdividing the five primary

MIÉRCOLES, 20 DE NOVIEMBRE DEL 2002 | A CORUÑA

La Voz de Galicia

NÚMERO 39.526 | AÑO CXX | PRECIO: 1 € | www.lavozdegalicia.es

ESPECTÁCULOS   EL ACTOR NORTEAMERICANO **JAMES COBURN** FALLECE EN LOS ÁNGELES A LOS 74 AÑOS | **47**

El buque se partió en dos a las ocho de la mañana y vertió 10.000 toneladas más de fuel

El «Prestige» se hunde y lanza otra marea negra hacia Galicia

La nueva mancha se dirige a la costa y si el viento continúa impulsándola puede llegar en dos días

Rajoy anuncia que el viernes se declarará la Zona de Emergencia y promete una primera ayuda de 27 millones de euros

El Gobierno defiende su actuación y confía en que la carga se solidifique en el fondo

XURXO LOBATO, ENVIADO ESPECIAL

La proa del petrolero fue la última parte del buque en hundirse, mientras la carga de otros tres tanques teñía de negro el mar

Lugar del hundimiento

Vertido al hundirse: 10.000 toneladas
Zona contaminada
Dirección de la mancha
Fisterra
Corrubedo
A 140 millas de las Cíes
Profundidad: 3.500 metros

✓ **El avance médico más eficaz contra problemas estéticos**

PHOTODERM VASCULIGHT
• Para eliminación de veñas (La 1ª Consulta gratuita) Con depilación total, parcial y duradera.
• Lesiones vasculares: Varices, varículas, cuperosis.
• Lesiones pigmentadas: Léntigos, pecas, cloasma.

Y siempre con la garantía de un médico especialista en Dermatología por la Clínica Universitaria de Navarra controlando el proceso desde el principio al final.
DR. D. OSCAR MOSQUERA PAZ

FOTOREJUVENECIMIENTO FACIAL
• EL IPL Facial: Mejora eficazmente los signos visibles del envejecimiento cutáneo.
• Enrojecimiento de la cara, pequeñas ventas, manchas en la piel, poros dilatados, arrugas finas.

Consúltenos sin compromiso
981 143 021
FLEBOLASER

C.M.I.
NUESTRA SEÑORA DE BELEN
Teniente Coronel Teijeiro, 3.
La Coruña

Marineros de las Rías Baixas pretenden formar una barrera con mil barcos

■ Mientras mariscadores y mejilloneros de las rías de Muros-Noia y Arousa trabajan a marchas forzadas para salvar todo lo que queda antes de la posible llegada de una marea negra, las entidades que agrupan a estos productores han propuesto la creación de una barrera de contención en la entrada de los estuarios compuesta por cerca de un millar de barcos y las barreras anticontaminación. López Veiga visitó a los afectados en O Grove y les aseguró que los bancos y las bateas no corren peligro. | **2 a 13 y 18**

MARÍTIMA

Antonio Couceiro deja el Puerto coruñés para dirigir la concesionaria de Coca Cola | **27**

INCENDIO

Arde parte del tren regional nocturno que une A Coruña y Vigo | **L14**

2

LUNES
23 DE DICIEMBRE DEL 2002

...RA RECUPERAR GALICIA

...l y puede abastecer el 60% de España

...marea negra

...era gallega
...o calidad

CIFRAS

Pescado y marisco «gallegos» no afectados por la marea negra
80%
■ Las empresas gallegas pescan y marisquean en todo el mundo.

Empleo pesquero
115.000
■ Galicia tiene 400 industrias pesqueras y 8.400 barcos.

La industria congeladora aumenta ventas en diciembre

La Voz de Galicia
In-house design staff | Jesus Gil Saenz
À Coruña, Spain

03

columns into twenty-five smaller column widths. These sub-columns can be used to create mixtures of width configurations, introduce additional gutter space between columns of unrelated stories, or insert caption or callout subcolumns—all without disturbing the general simplicity of the wider, five-column super-structure. Because the interval used to create the subcolumns is the same as the natural column gutter, stories running in five columns and those running in six or seven narrower columns all appear to be about the same density, and are separated by the same space. The text appears optimally spaced in several column widths, and rivers are noticeably absent overall. The rhythmic regularity of the columns—whether five, six, eight, or a mixture of these—creates a remarkably serene presentation that allows the headline and deck to stand out even more. Even the insertion of a callout that is wrapped by two columns creates little disturbance in the overall rhythm. Advertising, which appears in regular locations and clearly follows the grid proportions, integrates seamlessly; it often feels like it ought to be there to balance out the pages.

The horizontal power of the modules is felt in banded and boxed elements on the front page, and especially in the interior page spreads. Never articulated literally, however, they become evident in lateral alignments of callouts, picture depths, head-lines, tags, and column heights. A propensity to set headlines in nearly justified configurations enhances the horizontal connec-tion across both individual pages and double-page spreads.

There are five primary levels of typographic differentiation related to hierarchy, and these are subdivided between sections of hard news and soft news—content such as sports, dining, and entertainment. Hard news headlines, for example, are set in Poynter Gothic, a bold, slightly condensed sans serif with a large x-height and tight interletter spacing. A companion serif, Poynter Oldstyle Display, is used for soft news headlines, but at the same size as those for hard news. A second variation of Poynter Oldstyle—less condensed and more loosely set than the Display—is used for body text. The more regular width Poynter Agate (which is also of regular weight) is used within graphics, tables, and as a caption face, often in all caps.

1

2

1, 2

Comparison of these two front pages reveals the strength and flexibility of the grid. Consistent head-line treatments traverse the full width of the page, while lead story images appear in different propor-tions. In the page to the left, the smaller image is accompanied by a vertical column of article callouts. Despite the reversal of headline location and different deck treatments, both pages contain an advertisement (lower left-hand corners), a two-column article lead, and tinted sidebar. Secondary headlines in these areas change size according to their length.

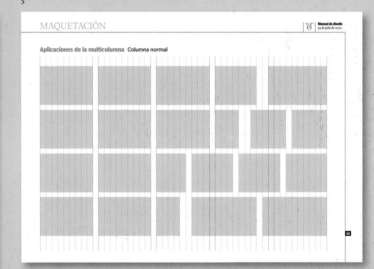

Rich typographic color variation is apparent throughout: clear changes between headline styles, contrasting italic decks and callouts, heavy square bullets, and captions in bold-weight sans serif provide excellent navigational clarity and enrich the textual quality of the pages.

Wider columns are used for feature stories, while narrower columns are used for secondary articles. Blank separator columns and doubled gutters help separate articles at a similar level of importance.

La Voz de Galicia
In-house design staff | Jesus Gil Saenz
À Coruña, Spain

03

1

AÑO 6 | NÚMERO 362 | Coordinación: Jesús Flores | Ángel Varela
6 DE JUNIO DEL 2004

La Voz de Galicia

LOS DOMINGOS
DE LA VOZ

IBIZA CUPRA,
EL NUEVO
DIÉSEL
DEPORTIVO
DE SEAT

18 | Audi-Volkswagen presenta un modelo con aires deportivos, el Cupra, un diésel que varía el aspecto habitual de los Ibiza.

Rianxo, cuna de escritores y marineros

10-11 | Eduardo Chamorro recorre el casco vello de Rianxo, cuna de escritores como Caste-lao o Dieste y tierra de marineros y erianxeiras».

De las 200 lanchas de desembarco que protagonizaron la primera oleada en la playa de Omaha, diez se fueron a pique antes de llegar a la arena

SERVICIO DE GUARDACOSTAS DE EE.UU.

Día-D: 60 años después

Las claves secretas de la batalla que cambió el mundo

2 | Juan Pujol hizo creer a los alemanes que Normandía era el preludio del verdadero desembarco que sería en Calais.

3 | El servicio de inteligencia elaboró mapas sobre la zona de desembarco detallando las curvas de nivel cada diez metros.

Un veterano
paracaidista de
Michigan se desplaza
con soldados
norteamericanos
durante los actos
commemorativos
celebrados esta
semana en
Vierville-sur-Mer.

4-5 | Una visión panorámica de la operación por tierra, mar y aire a través de gráficos.

6 | La sangre que los soldados norteame-ricanos derramaron en las playas de Normandía fue la llave para ocupar Europa.

7 | La mayor parte de la prensa española de la época seguía manteniendo la es-peranza de que triunfaría Hitler.

2

MARTES, 22 DE JUNIO DEL 2004 www.lavozdegalicia.es

RIAZOR
La Voz de Galicia

Un jugador intenta rematar un balón de tijera en el transcurso del campeonato de fútbol playa celebrado el pasado fin de semana en la playa de Riazor

FOTOS: QUEIMADELOS

De la playa al cielo

Más de doscientos equipos contribuyeron a la fiesta del fútbol en el campeonato celebrado en el arenal de Riazor

■ Un año más, el fútbol playa se convirtió en el certamen deportivo por equipos más concurrido del calendario veraniego de la ciudad de A Coruña. Aunque la lluvia hizo su aparición en el último día de competición (el domingo), los precipitaciones no pudieron deslucir el campeonato.

Más de doscientos equipos formalizaron su inscripción en la tercera jornada del cam-peonato de España, cuya final nacional se disputará a finales del mes de julio en Cádiz.

Después de todo un fin de semana para los participan-tes son muchos. No sólo la presencia en la final nacional para el equipo vencedor, sino también premios individuales al máximo goleador, al portero menos batido y a los mejores jugadores del torneo coruñés.

Precisamente, estos jugadores pertenecen a dos de los mejo-res equipos del fin de semana. Junto a clásicos como el Feu-

En este sentido, los nombre propios están encabezados por los futbolistas que participan en el clínic que se celebrará en Cádiz y que además puede otorgar una plaza para la selec-ción española de la modalidad: Javi Álvarez (Bar Carlos) y Dani (Cafetería Manureva).

do, el Bar Carlos de Sada logró protagonismo al imponerse en la final al TB Brokers (4-1), de Vigo. Terminó en la tercera posición el Cafetería Manu-reva, que derrotó al Fuerza 7 en los penaltis tras empatar a cuatro goles.

El mejor portero fue Jorge, del Bar Carlos, y el máximo goleador fue Johnny, del equi-po que resultó campeón en la jornada final.

ENTIDADES
Escuelas deportivas de Irixoa

COMPETICIONES
Principales plantillas del fútbol playa

INICIATIVA
La Copa Umbro, todo un espectáculo

Work Process

This collaborative process took nearly two years of studying the flow of articles among pages and focus-group testing of different structural alternatives.

1, 2

Thoughtful typographic detailing supports all information graphics, charts and tables, and images used in the softer lifestyle and features sec-tions. Double rules, angled rule enclosures, and bullets add informational clarity and visual texture.

Sometimes it is used upper- and lowercase as a secondary deck. The Poynter serif italic appears as callouts and deck paragraphs in all contexts. Two slab serifs, one lighter and extremely condensed, the other a slightly extended extrabold weight, are used for labels that tag sidebars, callouts, and other informationally subordinate text elements. While the type families are very closely related in width and general structure, they offer enough color and textural contrast to keep the details in the pages visually interesting without becoming a self-conscious distraction. The interrelationship of the sizes and densities of the spacing for each kind of typographic treatment in the hierarchy seems incredibly harmonious. Even on pages where there are multiple instances of text styles, the overall presence of the type is light, open, and consistent; important points of interest (set off with the high contrast slab serifs or a thick rule) are startlingly easy to find. Indents in body text are decisive but unobtrusive, and bold square bullets punctuate the lead paragraphs of feature stories.

3–11

Pages from the paper's PDF style guide outline grid structure, text and head treatment, and flow of information in great detail. Any given article may use up to seven treatments to differentiate dateline, byline, callouts, and other supporting information from running text.

4

This page from the PDF style guide details elements that accompany the lead of a generic article, demonstrating the typographic color variation that enables easy navigation and adds visual richness to the presentation. A sectional tag—*Entrevista*—set in the bold sans serif and tinted to appear similar in weight to the accompanying support—*Miguel Díaz Pache*, set in the display oldstyle serif and separated by a narrow vertical rule—provides reference above the head and deck. These are set, respectively, in the display oldstyle and a corresponding italic at radically different sizes.

Educational institutions prosper not just on the tuition they charge students but on donations from graduates and corporations whose executives or workers are recruited heavily from the school. For this reason, universities are prolific publishers of communications that target these audiences: alumni, corporations, and professional groups. This quarterly magazine produced at Dartmouth College is circulated among alumni, helping to foster a sense of posteducational community and create a forum for the institution to publicize its programs, faculty research, and the achievements of its graduates in their respective fields. Part of the conceptual underpinning of this and other such magazines is that it connects alumni to the ongoing evolution of the institution, maintaining their interest and, through the reminder of the academic experience, enticing them to make donations or participate in other ways in the institution's continued success. In this particular case, part of that concept involved positioning the program as an active, dynamic program of inquiry through visual techniques that would avoid a dry, journalistic approach, and reference a sense of technology.

04

Dartmouth Faculty: Scholarship Today Magazine

And Partners, NY | New York City, USA
David Schimmel, Principal

Appealing to an audience consisting primarily of engineers, computer scientists, physicists, social scientists, and so on, the base structure exhibits a solid, informationally friendly hierarchic structure for text. Underlying everything is a heavily compartmentalized grid that permits the configuration of two-, three-, four-, and five-column text bodies and offers the opportunity for one of the first visual features that helps distinguish the character of the publication—regularized spatial intervals, literally compartmentalized by a system of delicate rules. Each compartment is flexible in proportion and can be combined as needed, but each kind of compartment carries only one kind of component.

The feature story title exists in one compartment; its accompanying deck exists in another; in yet another are contained the story's byline and author's credentials. Primary imagery for the story is enclosed in another compartment. The running text begins in the next available compartment. The columns tend to justify at top and bottom lines, enhancing the geometric shaping of the text areas and helping to augment the compartmental quality of the grid.

The rigorous grid of this magazine for a prestigious college, called out in color and linear detail, is both lively and easy to navigate. A mix of custom illustration and photography brings depth and texture to clean layouts.

The net effect is a sense of interlocking parts that repeat in a recognizable structure and sequence but change dynamically from story to story as the length or complexity of the components changes. This systematic quality is particularly resonant with its audience, evoking such images as database architecture, geometry and calculus, fractal theory, particle physics, and related disciplines. "The head and deck configuration have a reference to Web styles," says Schimmel. Indeed, HTML bread-crumb-like text paths—a feature of database-driven Web navigation support—are used as a treatment for running heads, indicating the magazine's name, section, and article title in a manner that recalls the HTML detail in a subtle but recognizable way. "The grid compartment treatment actually translated really

Components + Formats

Printed Magazine
U.S. letter, perfect bound; mixed spot and process colors; spot UV metallic lamination and die-cut cover.

Web supplement
dHTML

Communication Goals

Position the client institution as a dynamic and relevant educational program

Convey a sense of technology and academic rigor through visual details

Engage and appeal to alumni of the client institution

Create a credible editorial forum for academic and professional discussion

1

2

1

The modular nature of the publication's layout—along with its potential for flexibility—is demonstrated first in the cover. Standard locations for a die-cut window that offers a glimpse of the inside and a horizontal strip listing features adhere to the grid; compartments of information around the die cut act as a masthead. The image area left over by these standard components allows for a radically different cover every issue. The spot-UV metallic lamination in the horizontal band and over the title create a textural difference against the other elements.

2

Interlocking bands reference the grid and hold information. In the table of contents, the clarity of this system is evident in the ease with which a reader can immediately find the issue and volume date, a callout for the cover story, and a listing of that issue's contents. Alternating between colored bands and areas enclosed by narrow rules creates strong hierarchic difference and liveliness in the page layout.

Dartmouth Faculty Magazine
And Partners, NY | David Schimmel
New York City, USA

04

Work Process

"We initially presented two concepts to the client," says Schimmel. "The client looked to us to guide them in developing the content and its presentation; we worked back and forth with them in refining the concept they decided to pursue. Because we sought their input at nearly every step of the way, they allowed us to be more adventurous with the creative aspects."

Schimmel and his design team always begin with hand sketches, sometimes cutting and pasting, before beginning to work on the computer. "It's important to establish that connection between what you see in your head and what happens on paper. Plus it's more fun that way," he says. Several rounds of revisions to the interior focused on refining the informational hierarchy of the head and deck but primarily had to do with the content to be included in the first issue being changed. Fortunately, the grid allowed for rapid changes.

"The cover went through the most changes, for mostly political reasons," Schimmel notes.

1

1
Alternating two- and three-column structures between spreads keeps the pacing interesting for readers, while consistent structure—but different color treatment—creates a clear navigational device that includes article head, deck, author's name, and supporting information. The elements in this lockup remain the same in both spreads, but the vivid color in one (left) helps set it apart from the image surrounding it; the more restrained color of the other (right) helps quiet the lockup down against columns of text. The intensity of the color in each also signifies a difference in content— one is a feature article, the other a faculty essay.

1–3
The grid structure—clearly but subtly called out by hairlines—shows its flexibility in organizing images of varying proportions and sizes, as well as allowing for different kinds of content to exist side by side. The sidebar on the left-hand page is signified by a small, red, rectangular flag, set above a headline in a smaller size. Narrow horizontal and larger, squarely proportioned images fit around the grid easily; the article-head lockup on the right-hand page appears unexpectedly to the right but is no less clear as a marker. Grid lines, image proportions, open areas, and tinted panels create a unified but dynamic geometric movement back and forth across the spread.

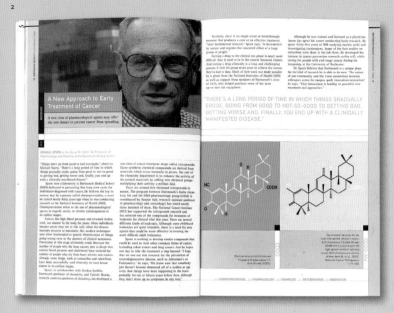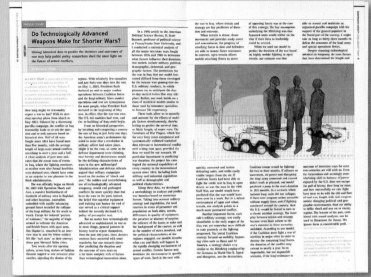

well to the Web version that was launched around the same time as the first publication," Schimmel continues. Within the compartment structure, a primary type family is used for the majority of the typography. Its squared-off curves offer a slightly machinelike quality without being too severe. Additionally, the variation in stroke thickness between the light, medium, and bold weights is not particularly drastic compared to the weight changes among members in other sans-serif families. The result is just enough difference in weight—augmented by thoughtfully considered changes in scale between text components—to indicate informational change and ease reader navigation. A stately, academic reserve prevents even larger-scale type from becoming too clunky or aggressive. The x-height of the primary sans-serif face is relatively large, but the letters are set tightly in text, creating a dense line that the designers have offset with more open leading. Typographic details like colons, bullets, and quantity arrows are used as indicators and decorative nuances to provide a

kind of syntactic connection between text elements and graphic elements such as the grid rules and details in illustrations.

Color and image are important aspects of the magazine's layout and overall feeling. Many of the elements in the layout have color applied to them, especially typographic elements and backgrounds behind text. The color selection is not only a little unusual by academic publication standards—which tend to be either limited in color because of low budgets or full color because of an assumed quality inference—but it operates within a limited palette that is combined in unconventional ways. The decision to limit color interaction sharpens its visual effect; the absence of many colors focuses attention on the colors that are actually present and allows their interaction to become important. In some feature articles, subtle shifts in hue between grid compartments—especially between head and deck compartments or between text-area background and illustration area—offer the same restrained, yet distinguishable, difference between items that the

typographic weights do. In other sections, dramatic changes in hue are balanced by a similarity in the value that causes the colors to vibrate next to each other. Analogous colors of different value are applied as duotones to some photographic images to enhance the images' illustrative qualities.

Commissioned illustrations tend toward the partially abstract and editorial, using simplified drawing techniques and digital collage to impart a diagrammatic quality that feels technological, either by virtue of its geometric or pixel detail, or by its reference to Web-based animations created using vector animation software.

2
Precise detailing—hairline rules separating informational components, double-arrow icons, and a string of important concepts, reminiscent of a webpage bread-crumb trail (lower right-hand page)—lend a mathematical, technological quality to the pages. Strips of information intrude into diagram fields, calling out the grid's architecture and innovatively tagging the diagrams as headers.

Two specimen catalogs for font families produced by Underware, a digital type foundry in The Hague, Netherlands, show the conceptual extremes to which product catalogs—and type catalogs, in particular—can be taken. Of course, designing for an audience of designers is no easy task, but it does afford some freedom in getting the subject to resonate. More so than for other kinds of clients, publication work targeted at graphic designers can stretch boundaries, providing its creator with an opportunity to explore unconventional composition, binding, and image-related ideas.

These two unique catalogs—one for the type family Dolly, designed by Faydherbe/DeVringer of The Hague, the other for the Sauna type family, designed by Sami Kortemäki of Helsinki, Finland—share a conceptual approach that uses humor and narrative storytelling to create a contextual environment for the typefaces they promote; in effect, showing the typefaces in a variety of situations that result from the conceptual nature of the content.

05

Underware Font Catalogs: Dolly and Sauna

Faydherbe/DeVringer | The Hague, Netherlands *Ben Faydherbe and Wout DeVringer*

Sami Kortemäki | Helsinki, Finland

Visually, each catalog is different, reflecting the individual aesthetic approaches of the studios creating them. While a number of prominent type houses deliver specimens of their products in branded vehicles that derive from their corporate identities, the use of different visual approaches for each catalog expresses a powerful branded message about this particular type foundry—namely, that its products and corporate culture are unique, irreverent, and unrestrained by convention.

But another result of this approach is that each typeface is shown in a way that the client feels suits it best, placing the product far above the company identity in importance. In each catalog, the targeted audience of graphic designers is afforded a unique opportunity to see the respective typefaces in a tremendous number of applications, from display to running text, accompanied by a range of imagery and graphic devices, including illustration, photography, and typographic compositions.

In this way, the catalogs convey the possibilities for using the type families they promote and offer a sense of how the faces change, visually and conceptually, in different environments. The thoughtful, narrative approach is a welcome diverson for the busy designer, creating a sense that the client company is friendly and shares identity with this sometimes jaded target audience.

Far from the usual typeface catalogs, these books engage prospective clients— graphic designers—with humorous narrative concepts and inventive layouts in presenting two type families.

Components + Formats

Project Type
Type specimen catalogs

Components
Books with CDs bound in

Formats
Dolly Catalog Perfect-bound softcover book, 5 x 7" (12.7 x 20.3 cm) printed offset lithography in four-color process.
Sauna catalog Singer-stitched, French-folded signatures, printed three match inks and one thermal ink, offset lithography; the paper is a plastic, fiber-based stock that absorbs moisture without curling or shrinkage.

Showcase the potential use of two typefaces in a series of layouts

Resonate with graphic designers in a more inventive way as regards type

Communicate an overall narrative idea as a backdrop for the display of the two typefaces. According to deVringer, "After talking to [the clients about the Dolly catalog], it was clear that they didn't want ordinary typeface catalogs, but something that would be totally unique."

"We wanted to make a book that would entice bookstore visitors to get it and take a bath with it," says Kortemäki of the Sauna catalog. "We transformed the catalog into an object that becomes fully realized in the literal sauna environment.

1

1

Two versions of the Dolly catalog cover, showing the quirky drawing of the typeface's fictitious namesake, a small French bulldog. The mass-produced cover, left, is printed in flat fluorescent ink on regular cover stock; the limited-edition version uses a red velvet paper stock. Both are foil stamped in metallic silver.

2

2

The cover of *Read Naked*, the catalog for Sauna, offers a simple, friendly teaser in the form of the title on a blank pink background, set in a large size and bold weight. The Singer-stitch binding is visible on the jacket's surface.

Underware Font Catalogs
Faydherbe/DeVringer | *The Hague, Netherlands*
Sami Kortemäki | *Helsinki, Finland*

05

1

2

This type specimen is the first showing of the typeface Dolly.
For more information, contact:

Underware
Schouwburgstraat 2
2511 VA Den Haag
The Netherlands
phone: +31-[0]70-4278 117
fax: +31-[0]70-4278 116
email: info@underware.nl

Further information can be found at **www.underware.nl**

This type specimen was published in September 2001 by Underware.

All rights reserved. No part of this book may be reproduced, stored or made
public in any form, electronically, mechanically, by photocopying, recording
or any other way without written permission from Underware.
Copyright © Underware, 2001.
Dolly™ is a registered TradeMark of Underware.

concept & design: Faydherbe / De Vringer (Wout de Vringer), Den Haag
printing: Albani, Den Haag
binding: Boxboom, Den Haag
typeface: Dolly

thanks: Albani Drukkers bv, Françoise Berserik, The Boys, Markus Brilling, Joan-Carles Casasín,
Ben Faydherbe, Fonds voor beeldende kunsten, vormgeving & bouwkunst, Allan Hori,
Edgar Kober, Semi Kim, Robin Kinross, Regina Kiebinger, Anne Knopf, Sami Kortemäki,
Wilbert Leering, Ewan Lentjes, Eike Mevijn, Michael Rock, Susan Sellers, Edwin Smet,
Erik Spiekermann, Guy Tavares, Wout de Vringer, Tessa van der Waals, Lennart Wienecke.

ISBN 90-76984-01-8

Dolly

A BOOK TYPEFACE WITH FLOURISHES

The family consists of four fonts:

Dolly Roman is neutral and useful for long texts.
It has old-style figures.
Dolly Italic is narrower and lighter in colour than
the roman, and so it can be used to emphasize
words within roman text.
Dolly Bold is also useful in emphasizing words
within roman text.
It also works well as a display type.
DOLLY SMALL CAPS are intended for setting whole words
or strings of characters; while roman capitals
are used only for the first letter in a word.
They match the roman in weight and have figures
that line with the x-height.

*These four fonts provide a good basis for most of the problems of
book typography. If you meet a particular problem that can be solved
by adding to or adapting these fonts, then please contact us.*

Underware, Den Haag 2001

1–5
Pages from found sources were scanned and placed at actual size, creating a disconnect between the source and the physical catalog. The scale changes and added fields of background color that distinguish each source result in two effects: the pages become journalistic snapshots of supposed real-world typeface usage, and the spreads have a lyrical, unforced pacing as scale, color, and image treatment change randomly from one spread to the next. The only unifying visual factor is the typeface itself.

1
The catalog's front matter presents the typeface in an academic, centered-axis setting for an introduction and foundry information.

2
This detail shows the font sample CD bound into the interior cover.

DOLLY SPECIMEN CATALOG The catalog for the typeface Dolly draws from exterior sources for its visual environment—spreads from a number of different kinds of books—and unifies them with text built around a fictitious character developed in collaboration between Underware's principal, Akiem Helmling, and Faydherbe/DeVringer, the design studio creating the catalog. This character is a French bulldog named Dolly, given form as an illustration by Edgar Kober, an art-school colleague of Helmling. The cartoonish drawing of Dolly contrasts humorously with the typeface itself—a well-considered text face with classical proportions drawn for good legibility and comfort in extended reading. As displayed in the catalog spreads, the typeface exhibits great flexibility in a range of contexts, responding well to scientific illustrations, photography, and diagrams. At the same time, the typeface maintains friendliness and authority: a large x-height, open counters, and old-style terminals with a brush-drawn character produce text with a casual character yet somewhat academic credibility. The images of the book spreads are placed in the catalog at the size they were originally scanned, regardless of how big or small they were. This disconnect between the scanned pages and the catalog's physical dimensions creates a unique rhythm in the presentation of the typography; sometimes the scanned pages are unexpectedly cropped outside the frame of the catalog spread, while sometimes they are inset at a smaller size with a field of color surrounding them. Each spread—different from the one before, and derived from radically different sources—gives the sense of a series of snapshots of real-world text applications that seems highly objective, honest, and uncontrived. "There were spreads from a dictionary, one from a book about dogs and so on," says Wout DeVringer, the principal designer.

Given that each spread showed pages from a different source book, DeVringer and Helmling decided to develop a thematic thread that could unite the visual content, even if unrelated. They began to imagine who Dolly was and came upon the idea of the strange little dog. "I replaced the

3

4

6

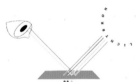

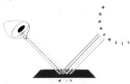

5

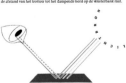

3–5

The casual, yet credible, character of the typeface is shown to great effect in the book-based context of the source environments. Designers are able to see, in a concrete manner, how the text acts in various alignments, in color, at different sizes, and mixed with differently styled images.

3, 4

Manuscript text spreads recalling feld guides alternate between dog-related and non-dog-related content, supporting and contrasting the concept.

2

Spreads with diagrammatic content indicate the typeface's versatility for applications other than running text.

existing text with text set in Dolly," DeVringer continues. "However, now each spread had an original text that was rewritten by friends, colleagues, and even family members. The writing assignment was: write about your (imaginary) dog named Dolly. The amount of text they had to write depended on the word count of the original text and had to match the original spreads exactly!" Reading through the text—which now all follows a consistent subject in contrast to the visual presentation—lends a quirky character to the catalog that speaks to the inventive spirit of its audience. A more conventional exhibit of the typeface's character set follows the narrative section, showing the face at a larger display size in a bookish, almost classical, centered format.

Underware Font Catalogs
Faydherbe/DeVringer | *The Hague, Netherlands*
Sami Kortemäki | *Helsinki, Finland*

05

1

ABCDEFGHIJKLMNOP
QRSTUVWXYZŒÆÇ &
abcdefghijklmnopq
rstuvwxyzœæç
{0123456789}
(fiflß);:[¶]?!*
àáâãåèéëêùúüû
òóöôøõñ
"$£€ƒ¢" «©†@»

For those people who really want, there are special ligatures-fonts
available in all weights, including ligatures like lb, fh, fj & fk.
Phone us for more information or take a look at the website.

Dolly Roman

ABCDEFGHIJKLMNOP
QRSTUVWXYZŒÆÇ &
abcdefghijklmnopq
rstuvwxyzœæç
{0123456789}
(fiflß);:[¶]?!*
àáâãåèéëêùúüû
òóöôøõñ
"$£€ƒ¢" «©†@»

Dolly Italic

2

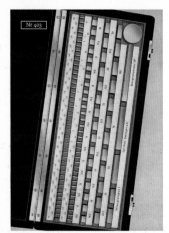

Nr 403

1
Carefully sized, elegantly spaced character sets show the full typeface in its various weights and postures in a straightforward, bookish presentation.

2
An example from the first round of concept spreads, in which DeVringer used random materials, such as receipt, labels, packages, and charts, as a context for the typeface.

Work Process

DeVringer says, "I started the project with the idea of taking all kinds of objects from daily life (receipts, manuals, tickets) and replacing the original text with the same text set in Dolly. I don't really sketch by hand; I go directly to the computer after working out the idea in my head. I thought it looked really great, and Akiem and Bas agreed that this was an unusual approach. After working on it for a couple more weeks and showing them my progress, the project began to move in another direction. Bas thought that using Dolly on all these everyday items didn't really demonstrate the way the face was meant to be used: Dolly was a text typeface that should be used in books!" Adapting the found-object idea, DeVringer scanned reference books as a source, substituting Dolly for the typography; the result demonstrates the face's use in book design.

SAUNA SPECIMEN CATALOG Based on a nearly opposite approach from that used in the Dolly catalog, the *Read Naked* book for the typeface Sauna—orchestrated by Finnish designer Sami Kortemäki, in collaboration with Piet Schreuders and Underware principals Akiem Hemling and Bas Jacobs—is entirely invented, rather than drawing on found layouts. The page designs are customized for the content, a series of essays, anecdotes, and vignettes about the Scandinavian contribution to the world of spas, the sauna. Like its namesake, the Sauna typeface is spare, with overall uniform stroke weights that show subtle modulation outward toward the terminals of their sans-serif stems. Despite the typeface's relative austerity, it presents an expansive character in its large lowercase and slight forward slant—possibly 2 degrees—becoming just the tiniest bit aggressive in its bold and black weights. The face was developed in tandem with the catalog, each building off each other in promoting a conceptual depiction of the sauna experience. As the face was being refined, the designers interviewed people about their sauna stories, developed a documentary essay about Finland's oldest sauna, and collected articles of both a journalistic and humorous nature (one in particular, about the world champion sauna bather, Leo Pusa, is highlighted in the book).

The texts are all treated individually, following a simple two-column grid that is violated on a regular basis as the designers see fit. The spreads were divided among Schreuders, Helmling, Jacobs, and Kortemäki, each working independently and then

3–5

The variety of stories, anecdotes, factual information, and interviews provides a rich source for layout manipulation. Like the Dolly catalog, the one unifying visual element among the spreads is the typeface, and the overall character and rhythm it transmits.

3

Sauna is the most widely used Finnish word. In 142 languages it has the same form – except in Swedish. Not a coincidence, of course. Our word is *bastu*. But yes, Swedish *bastu* is not a real sauna, anyway.

¶ INGRID HOLSTEIN (29), an interior designer in Lund, Sweden

[36]

Henrik Birkvig

DESIGNERS' SECRET SAUNA STORIES

Keep this door closed

4

5

We used to sneak into the hotel down the road for a swim or a sauna and afterwards we all went home commenting on how good our skin felt. They have since added proper locks at the hotel. Carolina D'Avila (22), a beauty queen in Porto Alegre, Brazil.

Underware Font Catalogs
Faydherbe/DeVringer | *The Hague, Netherlands*
Sami Kortemäki | *Helsinki, Finland*

1, 2

The typeface in this catalog is shown to be very flexible in character and application; in these spreads, the face changes from funny to straightforward, depending on context and the structure of its presentation. In the spreads with cartoon illustrations, the modulation in the strokes and their slightly rounded terminals pick up the humorous quality of the line drawings; set in columns of continuous text, the face becomes neutral, almost journalistic.

selecting the spread designs that they agreed were visually and conceptually the strongest. Some of the spreads display more conventional running texts in a straightforward editorial structure—headline, deck, subheads, and so on—while others incorporate image-based typographic compositions with illustrations and photography. One spread, for example, shows a display-sized line of type against a background of tinted inks that represent rising heat and steam levels. Like the Dolly catalog, the variety of typographic applications serves to show the typeface's versatility as well as deliver conceptual messages and engage the audience with humor and narrative.

The designers went a step further, however, in exploring production techniques that transform the book into an object

that is fully realized only within an actual sauna—hence the title, *Read Naked.* First, the paper stock selected is produced from a plastic fiber that absorbs water and dries without distorting its shape. The book is made to be read inside a sauna and withstand the moisture and heat of that environment. Additionally, a number of the text spreads are printed with a thermal ink that becomes visible only when heated above 80°C—in order to fully appreciate the text, the book must be read, yes, naked in the sauna. The revelation of these hidden texts—the secret sauna stories—brings the reader literally and figuratively into the private, suggestive, and steamy experience of this Scandinavian steam bath.

1

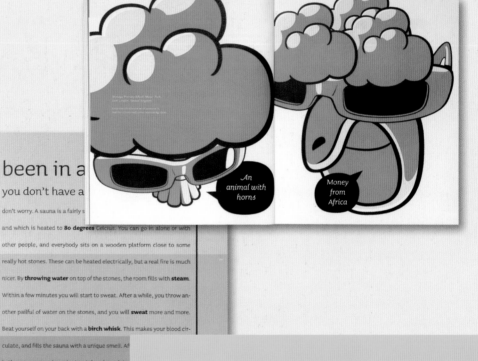

2

Work Process

The development of the typeface and the specimen book itself was simultaneous: a dual concept for development. Initial drawings for the base alphabet and collaboration with writers and designers for the catalog happened in tandem. After three years of extensive refinement to the face, expanding the character set and finessing the digital drawings, the content or the catalog book spreads was distributed among the four designers, coordinated by Kortemäki. The pages were designed independently for the most part, but with some collaboration. After a body of work was produced, the designers and client selected the strongest spreads to include in the final book.

Special Concerns

"From the beginning," Kortemäki explains, "the idea of the book being able to withstand the heat and moisture of a sauna, so that readers could use it in that environment as part of the experience, was a driving force in how the book was conceptualized."

3, 4

The display of character sets follows the narrative section in a two-column structure, set in boxes reversed out to white against a solid flat of ink. Notations regarding weight, usage, and pricing accompany the alphabet specimens in bars of black or white, clearly separated from the specimens and set in smaller text.

SAUNA ROMAN & *ITALIC*

MACHINE
Heat Is *Test*
MEASURING
Blistered Back
MASCULINITY
Fear to Enter *Alone*
Good Sauna Series
LIVE EXPERIENCE
Using Sauna Roman
Stand *Extreme Heat!*

[10]

SAUNA ROMAN & *ITALIC*

BATHING SUPPLIES
Never Been In A Sauna?
NO SEXUAL TOUCHING!
Obscene Remarks *Forbidden*
ON THE VERGE OF PASSING OUT
Display of Trust toward Fellow Bathers

THE ABILITY TO STAND *SUFFERING*
Typographical Standard, *Harmony in Design*
Aim to Please and Satisfy the Patron of Arts

SURPASSED BY *NONE*
Legible Type Appropriate
Body Becomes Machine

AMONGST FIRST-TIME VISITORS
Some can stay there for only a couple of minutes before they feel they cannot breathe and some can't turn their butt on the wooden bench substantially longer

BENEFIT FROM NAKEDNESS
See, Hear, Bodies of All Sizes
In All Stages And Conditions!

PIPELINE TO DOMAINS OF IMAGERY
Youthful flukiness of opium prints wasting life indulging in excursions to dreamland neglecting to take advantage of the opportunities for delight which are to be met in the refreshing realms of scene bathing

CARNAL MANIFESTATIONS
Different letterforms each having their purpose and degree of beauty

---

The SAUNA FAMILY & 10 SAUNA BASICS

REGULAR [THREE WEIGHTS]   **ITALIC** [THREE WEIGHTS]   **ITALIC SWASH** [THREE WEIGHTS]   **SMALL CAPS** [ONE WEIGHT]

1 Ollahan iliman pyyhkeitä. ¶ May I ask you to take your clothes off? – Also a towel.

2 *Elikkä alasti.* ¶ *In other words: reveal your belly.*

7 *Löylyn heitto ainoostaan napoolla.* ¶ *Only use the scoop to thow water, please.*

8 SITÄ EI TRENKÄÄ KOSKAAN KIELTÄÄ. ¶ NEVER SAY "NO" TO SOMEONE TURNING UP THE HEAT.

3 Vaan tulee siirtyä alalauteelle. ¶ No guts to stay? Take a step down.

4 *Akkaan ja kakarootten sekahan.* ¶ *To somewhere between wives and babies.*

9 *Lauteella ei sovi viheltää.* ¶ *Whispering is strictly forbidden.*

5 Eikä muutoonkaan tehdä kiusantekoo. ¶ Behave yourself.

6 *Kuten puhaltelua naapurin selekään.* ¶ *So don't blow air on your fellow's back.*

10 *Puhuta muuta eiku aikuusten aoiaa.* ¶ *Think twice before you speak.*

The Sauna family consists of 18 fonts
The family has three different weights and two kinds of italics for every weight. The lightest weight has also Small Caps. Besides of normal fonts, a set of ligatures is provided to work with the three Swash Italic-fonts. The set of Dingbats gives a little extra to the typographics.

Two italic styles
The italic style is for emphasizing words or sentences within a roman text. Each weight has two kind of italics. The first italic is formal and stable, usable for longer text sections. Swash capitals can be combined with regular italic lowercase characters.

[continued ☞]

Italic Swash is happy and fancy; it's perfect for a display use or pointing out single words within roman text.

Small Caps have the same weight as the Roman. They are intended to set whole words or strings of characters in CAPITALS, while Roman capitals are used only for the First Letter in a word. The Small Caps font has "monospaced" numbers for setting tables. Its monetary and mathematical characters have the same width as its numbers.

[44]   [45]

06

Affymetrix Collateral System

Ruder Finn Design | New York City, USA
Lisa Gabbay, President and Creative Director
Diana Yeo, Senior Designer
Laura Vinchesi, Designer

Components + Formats

Project Type
Print collateral literature system

Components
Templates for product catalog (overall product offering); vertical product family brochures, application notes, technical notes, and data sell sheets; PDF style guides for each publication component.

Format
All print materials formatted for U.S. letter and multiples (tabloid and six-panel gatefold); printed four-color process (CMYK) or two match colors. PDF style guides with internal navigational menu and low-resolution images.

Affymetrix is a manufacturer of scanners, arrays, and software for genomic research. They produce equipment that researchers, pharmacologists, and other life sciences professionals use to acquire and analyze the genetic information of humans and several animal species for various purposes. Their product literature, initially limited in scope, had grown over several years to represent several different lines of product to a wide variety of audiences—academic researchers, medical facilities, pharmaceutical developers, and students—working in a number of fields and having their own specific concerns related to genomic study. Understanding a need to clarify the company's product offerings for easy reference and marketing—to simplify the number and type of publication, yet provide the opportunity to create or customize existing publications on the fly to target specific audiences—Ruder Finn Design undertook the complex task of designing a visual architecture for Affymetrix's product literature.

Complicating the task was the lack of a consistent identity for the client's print materials, despite the fact Ruder Finn had been creating the company's marketing materials and ad campaigns for several years. "We had done all this stuff, but we didn't have a set of rules to follow," says Ruder Finn creative director Lisa Gabbay. "And we didn't know what they would be. We had so much to look at. But we didn't want to limit ourselves in the future, either. So we made the rules up as we went along and kept ourselves pretty open." An existing logo, along with a series of ads and brochures, provided a context for moving forward.

A complicated set of print collateral used to market a complicated subject—genome-based research tools—is clarified and streamlined through color coding, custom art, and a system of production guidelines.

The series of literature components is divided into four major areas by product type: materials for studying DNA, those for studying RNA, instruments that scan and process genetic material, and informatics (software systems) that analyze and catalog data. The four families of products are coded by color, based on a secondary palette developed as part of the overall corporate color system that is derived from the logo itself. The client had become accustomed to very loosely applied color scheming and wanted great variety available for color. As a result, the corporate secondary palette was expanded to allow for this variety but to group versions of colors under very distinct—and visually separate—major colors for each of the families.

Within each family is a descending hierarchy of literature components. At the topmost level, they are more promotional and marketing driven but are also intended to give a larger, system-wide overview of their individual subjects. These brochures are primarily image driven, with a limited amount of text. Each subsequent literature component becomes more focused and more informational; as it does so, the predominance of image and color diminishes. Images are replaced by diagrams or tables, and family color is subordinated to a more sober black-and-white presentation, supported by a neutral warm gray. The color system is delivered through a set of custom-drawn digital artworks that use a grid of square

THE AFFYMETRIX PRODUCT FAMILY >

DNA Expression Analysis

affordable

quality

experience

Artwork for the system uses a textural field of gridded squares in motion, an abstract representation of the gene arrays—photochemical data displays of genetic sequences—that are the client's core product. Differences in presentation of the grid squares indicates, to the trained eyes of the scientific audience, subtle differences in data display specific to different aspects of genomic research. The representation is specific to the company's products, but generic enough to speak on a more conceptual level, rather than showing one kind of genetic data. The family colors are used to customize the base artwork for each set of product literature.

Communication Goals

Convey the dynamic, groundbreaking nature of the client's business

Target both academic and commercial researchers as a potential market for the client's products

Illustrate the complex product system and its uses

Differentiate each product family and its literature subcomponents, creating a sense of organization, reliability, and ease of use

THE AFFYMETRIX PRODUCT FAMILY >

Informatics & Instruments

affordable

quality

10101001010011010010100101011
1101011010010100101010010100101
...

AFFYMETRIX

THE AFFYMETRIX PRODUCT FAMILY >

RNA Expression Analysis

integrated

experience

quality

AFFYMETRIX

A dramatic color system, evolved from the client's existing corporate identity, differentiates four primary families of product: DNA analysis, RNA analysis, instruments, and informatics. At the top level, instruments and informatics are combined into one family brochure for image-based marketing, but are represented by their own brochures at the next level down.

Affymetrix Collateral System
Ruder Finn Design | *New York City, USA*

06

1

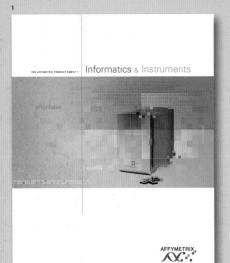

2

Array Products

Title Two Lines lorem ipsum dolor
sitLorem ipsum dolor sit Lorem ipsum

3

RNA Arrays and Reagents

4

1, 2, 4

The three-column grid and its articulation are universal for all documents in the system. Here, the covers for the top- and secondary-level family brochures show a simple use of the grid, while the interiors show a more complex use. The layout for all documents follows this grid.

3, 4

The individual family brochures are less colorful overall, use less-complicated artwork on their covers, and are limited to two match colors inside. The RNA family brochure is shown at lower left.

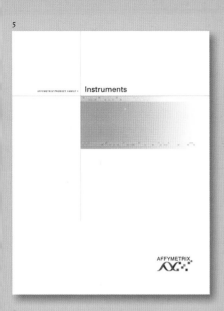

Instruments

AFFYMETRIX

DNA Arrays and Reagents

AFFYMETRIX

Informatics

AFFYMETRIX

5–7

The remaining three family brochure covers follow the decreased image emphasis seen in the RNA brochure cover (3), opposite page.

8–10

The three informational documents that form the backbone of the system—technical note, data sheet, and application note—appear left ot right in order of increasing complexity. This order is made clear through a decreased presence of color, narrowing of textural bands around the titling area, and more concentrated text typography as the document's content becomes progressively more technical, and less driven by branding and conceptual messages.

Technical Note

Location for New Title, Can Take Up 3 Lines If Necessary

Data Sheet

GeneChip® Human Genome U133 Set

Application Notes

Location for New Title, Can Take Up 3 Lines If Necessary

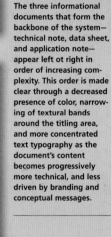

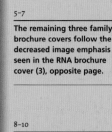

dots, duplicated in each color scheme, to tag each piece in the system. The artwork was distilled from a number of the brochures created earlier by senior designer Diana Yeo; as abstract representations of genetic data called arrays, they are specific to the products developed by Affymetrix, yet nonspecific enough to communicate the idea of gene structure and analysis on a more conceptual level.

Simplifying the entire system is a single three-column grid. The column widths are defined by optimal text setting in three treatments: running text in a regular-weight sans serif; running text in the bold-weight of the same face, but at a smaller size; and a headline running at a larger size in the light weight. The three columns are universal, used to define cover layouts, the insides of brochures, and the fronts and backs of the single-sheet technical and application notes. Similarly, every piece shares two major hanglines that define the location of the document title and the top of the column body. They also share a baseline grid that structures the text, heads, decks, subheads, and captions on the same leading, regardless of size and style. The reason for this rigid text-setting limitation?

The client would be producing the actual materials in-house, guided by documentation—the fewer opportunities for deviation the better. A side benefit, however, was that the system literally designed itself once the guidelines were in place; documents could be produced in a very short period of time, by virtual novices, without fear of inconsistency. One sans-serif type family and one serif—Univers and Garamond Oldstyle, respectively—are used in all of their weights and widths, plus italics, to distinguish informational components. Larger, light-weight heads separate clearly from their smaller, bold

Affymetrix Collateral System
Ruder Finn Design | *New York City, USA*

06

1

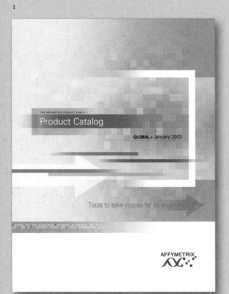

2

3

2

Arrays and Reagents

4	Expression Analysis	5	Catalogue Arrays
			Arabidopsis, C. elegans,
			Drosophila, E. coli 6
			Human 7
			Mouse, P. aeruginosa 8
			Rat 9
			Yeast, Test Arrays 10
		11	Custom Array Programs
			GeneChip Custom Arrays 11
			GeneChip CustomExpress® 12
			Commercial Content Design 13
			Unique Content Design 13
			Made-to-Order 14
		15	GeneChip Reagents
		16	Accessories
17	DNA Analysis and Genotyping	18	Mapping Assays
			HuSNP 18
			New Product1, New-product 2 19
		20	Tag Assays
			GenFlex 20
			New Tag Assay Product 21
22	Health Management	23	p53 Assay
			Probe arrays and Reagents
		23	CYP450 Assay
			Probe arrays and Reagents
		23	Control Oligonucleotides
			Probe arrays and Reagents

CONTENTS

1

The cover of the product catalog uses a composite of the vertical artworks against a more neutral gray field to indicate that it encompasses all of the product offerings.

2

The table of contents in the product catalog uses an expanded, yet simplified, version of the gridded-square artwork.

4

The style guides developed to help in-house or other subcontracted designers implement the template system are distributed as PDF files. Their format is consistent, with a large area defined for display and a narrow column of content listing to the right that acts as an interactive navigation menu. The navigation menu uses a color change to indicate location within the PDF document.

2, 3

Although the three-column grid is still in force, its use in the product catalog changes to accommodate the catalog's specific function—to list products and their corresponding attributes. The three columns have been subdivided into a total of six, with the leftmost used for images and callouts; two sets of two columns are used to carry listings and text; and the last column is used for itemized pricing information.

decks, running on the same leading defined by the baseline grid in proportional size changes. Though the choice of Univers depended mainly on its flexibility, its austere, machinelike qualities also contribute to the system's branding messages of precision and complexity. In contrast, Garamond offers a warmer, more academic credibility to the primary texts.

Each component tends to follow a similar layout as well, becoming more regular as the individual document becomes more specific and technical within its family. The titling area at the top of the document defines not only the family but also the type of document—application note, technical note, data sheet—and the products it describes within the family. Three lines of titling depth are given for headline and deck, if needed. The leftmost column is devoted to an introductory overview, while actual running text begins in the second column. After the first page or cover, headings are relegated to a slim band at the document head, branded with one of the variants of the gridded-square art in the color appropriate to the given family.

A system of detailed guidelines was produced to catalog the document templates and help in-house personnel create new documents as needed. The style guides are distributed within the company as PDF files—a complete publication system themselves. A corporate style guide defines the company's identity framework, including typography and color palettes, as well as their usage in stationery and advertising. The template style guides help personnel through the design process of each type of document, beginning with an overview of color and typography—the brand extension—through the use of the grid, type styles, custom artwork, and formats for diagrams and charts. The PDF files are formatted horizontally with a display area and an interactive content menu to the right so that users may navigate to specific pages as needed.

Work Process

The first task was to define the hierarchic system of the collateral from top down, based on an extensive set of sample materials that had been designed in-house, by the client, and by other consultants. "Dividing the product lines into four major families was the easy part," recalls Gabbay. "But breaking the documents down into specific levels required a lot of brainstorming. We showed five distinct solutions to that problem, in a few presentations over a two-month period; it took a lot of collaboration with the client to make sure the messages at each level—the content itself, the writing, and the visual treatment—were the right ones; each level is targeted to its audience." From the initial approval of the system, three different visual treatments were presented, and the most viable candidate was selected by the client.

The system was then simplified from a typographic standpoint for easy in-house use, each document being built into an electronic template and color keyed to its family. At each level of detail, the clarity of the rules that needed to be enforced for production were evaluated and simplified—the single leading baseline grid is an example of this production streamlining.

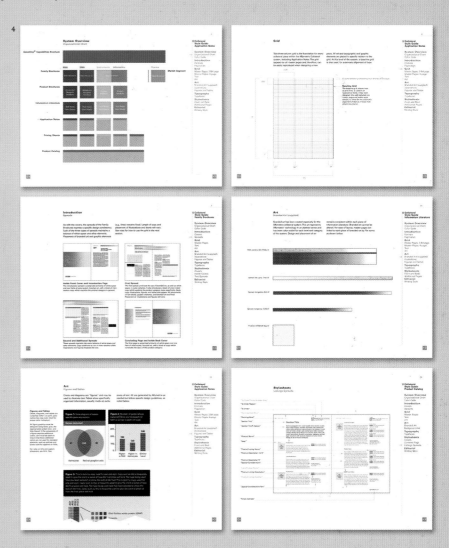

A system of catalogs for Fantoni, an Italian manufacturer of high-quality contract and residential furnishings, dramatically presents the product offering through dynamic photography, austere typographic structure and treatment, elegant detailing, and production. Architects for upscale residential projects and corporate offices often specify the manufacturer's products, and the designers of this catalog system know what makes these people tick. Like designers of many other disciplines, this target audience appreciates understated, decisive, simple objects of exquisite materials; the product catalogs emulate the aesthetics of the furniture. A simple story of structure, pacing, organization, and excellent production values accomplishes this task beautifully and efficiently.

07

Fantoni Catalog System

Designwork SrL | Udine, Italy
Roberto Barrazuol, Art Director

The square formats are a perfect starting point. Their neutrality is a classic modernist statement of objectivity and modularity—both qualities conveyed by the furniture systems they exhibit. Each catalog contains one line of furnishings: either seating, desk systems, lighting, or walls. The given product line is represented on the covers by a composition of large initials, set in Univers 55, a uniform-weight sans serif of regular width that is often associated with modernist design. The typeface is also highly neutral, complementing the presentation of the square.

Although different combinations of initials produce slightly different compositions on the covers, the systematic logic of their placement—in conjunction with the product line's full name and a descriptor on each—offers consistency. The large initials change color depending on the cover stock used for the binding; black, medium gray, light gray, and white cover stocks form the family of paper options against which white, pale gray, industrial yellow, and rich orange-red initials appear. This set of neutral cover tones, easily distinguished from each other when seen together, also serves to link related lines of furnishings. The type colors for the product line initials color-code the product lines and reference color predominant color schemes used for fabrics and material finishes, such as glass, laminates, and metals. Secondary type appears in metallic silver ink. As each catalog tends to be between twenty and fifty pages, the thick cover stock presents an opportunity to perfect bind the covers, giving them a narrow, elegant spine that accommodates a line of type.

In high modernist tradition, restrained typography, carefully sequenced, dramatic photography, and a crisp, simple, modular grid create a forceful architectural framework in which to present a range of upscale contract furnishings for home and office.

Components + Formats

Formats
9" (22.9 cm) square booklets; CMYK (process color) interiors printed on coated stock, perfect bound into uncoated cover-weight stock of four different colors; product signature typography foil stamped on exteriors.

Akustikwall System
Wall Panel System

AW

fantoni

System 1.3ru
Operative Office System

1.3

fantoni

SP System
Operative Sitting System

SP

fantoni

Cherry Collection
Executive Office System

CH

fantoni

Communication Goals

Represent the client's offering of contract furnishing systems as clearly as possible

Create moods with the furniture using dramatic photography

Convey the high quality of the furniture

Establish the product's modernist aesthetic and architectural appeal

Present promotional marketing text in five languages

Illustrate the technical and formal aspects of the furniture for easy specification

1–4
Even given the remarkable simplicity of the cover lay-outs, the tension between consistency and variation is rich and appealing. This rigorous, minimal approach to the catalogs targets the communication to its audience and helps keep the products the focal point. The system of four neutral colors for the covers is equally understated.

Fantoni Catalog System
Designwork SrL | Roberto Barrazuol
Udine, Italy

07

Upon opening the cover, each catalog begins with a full-color image bleeding off a title page, accompanied by a repetition of the titling type from the cover. The matte-coated stock of the interior text pages creates an immediate contrast to the sturdy uncoated stock of the covers. The photography on the title page, like that throughout the system, is richly lit, carefully composed, and thoughtfully cropped in the format. Since the images carry the most information about the furniture, their composition is of paramount importance. Their pacing and alternation, in terms of color feeling, overall value, and tensions between light and dark, drive the sequencing of the images within the catalogs.

The photographs are allowed to fully bleed the open page spreads, butt against each other as single-page formats, and be cropped into more narrow vertical proportions in combination with flat color panels. The images are all resolutely asymmetrical, regardless of their proportion or cropping, and their dynamic composition is a welcome foil for the neutral rigor of the format. It is a very focused and rigorous way of presenting the material. Conceptually, this approach purposely avoids cleverness or associational overlays; it simply lets the subject do the talking in a direct way. The copy that accompanies the images has some promotional

1

2

3

1–3

Opening the covers reveals the same typographic arrangement, but now in the context of a full-color photograph.

Special Concerns

"The message at the basis of Fantoni's communication policy is on a number of parallel reading levels," says Roberto Barrazuol.

"The first level includes the product with all its characteristics; the second includes the ecosustainable industrial approach; the third level concerns a chosen approach to work that enhances well-being and the value of the individual," Barrazuol continues.

"The greatest difficulty we encounter in developing layouts is combining unquestionable commercial needs with the philosophical message that is at the basis of the production, associated with ethical, as well as material, concepts. To this end, the graphic design is conceived as architecture consisting of characters, photographs, colors, and concepts that integrate with each other in the most harmonious proportions and ways," says Barrazuol.

4, 5

Introductory section paragraphs are set in five languages; the text itself in a modern serif, separated by its introductory phrase in a bold sans serif. For variety, the paragraph is sometimes set in a dark color on a light background, in light or metallic ink on a dark background, or across a photograph.

4, 6

Full-color photographs of interiors showcase the furnishings. The compositions of the images—where the elements are placed, angles created by perspective, relationships between textural and flat areas, cooler and warmer areas—show a high degree of involvement on the parts of the art director and photographer. They are very abstract and asymmetrical, acting as a counterpoint to the neutral square format of the catalogs.

Fantoni Catalog System
Designwork SrL | Roberto Barrazuol
Udine, Italy

1

2
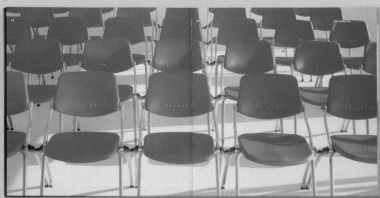

3

4

1–5

A five-column grid organizes conceptual text, in five languages, across multiple spreads. Inset detail images fall on the same grid, which is also used to break individual pages and images for pacing.

5, 6

Like the typography, product and specification diagrams are delicate but strong, reduced to linear form and integrated with the grid.

5
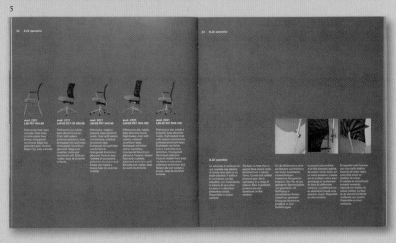

Work Process

"Fantoni communication has a well-established history that has grown over time," explains Roberto Barrazuol, the art director on the project. "For this reason, proposals for new development projects always go through a development process that is consistent and in keeping with previous history, never breaking with it.

"Generally, we submit two proposals, based on the strategic needs we have planned together with the company—typographic/conceptual proposal and a photographic/product proposal. The choice of one or another of these depends on the contingent needs of the final users at whom the communication is aimed. Periodically, we meet with the customer to plan new work and the strategy to be followed. The customer generally gives input and expresses requirements and we suggest strategic solutions to be adopted."

The process generally takes about two to three months, including planning, photo shoot, page makeup, corrections, and printing. Designwork's longstanding relationship with client, suppliers, and printer means an efficient work process and a mitigation of costs.

The organization of the technical specifications on a four-column grid—deviating from the five-column grid—allows adequate space for diagrams and text. The diagrams occupy a home position in their modules, growing up and to the right in scale as needed but always anchored to the module's lower-left corner.

6

qualities to it and even outlines positioning statements about the experience of the furniture in the work or home environment. Ultimately, however, the presentation of the information, in its utter simplicity, makes the text of secondary importance.

In a similarly neutral gesture, the Univers type family is used throughout the catalogs for the majority of the informational—and even some promotional—text. Used in two weights to distinguish between subhead and running text, the Univers is stark, neutral, and hardworking. The type is structured on a five-column grid that permits text to appear in five languages in a single spread, as well as create divisions for colored panels that separate cropped images, position inset detail images, and organize technical diagrams and pages listing specifications. A modern, hairline serif face makes an appearance at section dividers to present brief marketing messages that quietly warm up the total visual neutrality of the remainder of the publications. These marketing messages also appear in five languages. However, rather than being broken up among the five columns of the grid, they are set in a larger size, running together in a single paragraph. The introductory phrase of the marketing statements is set in the bold weight of Univers at a smaller size, sometimes in a contrasting color, to indicate the beginning of the text in its respective language.

Technical specifications for each item in the product line appear at the end of each catalog in several spreads that make full use of the grid. Each item is represented by a small, linear diagram, resting on a baseline created by a hairline rule that separates the columns into rows. The diagrams of each item are presented in relative scale to each other and are shown in multiple configurations or variations as applicable. Text for the specifications is set in Univers, in two weights, at the same text size used throughout for headers, folios, and promotional text.

08

Allegis Capital Quarterly Newsletter

Gorska Design | Minneapolis, USA
Caryl Gorska, Principal

The design of this newsletter distributed by a venture capital firm shows the powerful result of clear organization, a simple structure, and thoughtful typographic detailing. Its reserved, classical quality—rare among newsletter designs—gives voice to the methodical, almost judicial, nature of the client's business and positions them as a credible, reliable resource for capital investment. The client initially briefed the designer that it was looking for a marketing tool that would target investors and start-ups alike; it needed to be conservative but also lively.

At a quick glance, it's clear that a high degree of sensitivity has been brought to bear in addressing the newsletter's typography, the dominant element of its design. One is immediately aware of its open space and a delicate, serene texture, the product of a simple grid structure and few typographic distractions, adorned only by a system of thin rules and the occasional engraved illustration. Even upon entering the typographic space of the cover, readers will note the simplicity and clarity of the hierarchy: a large headline, a slightly smaller deck, the accent of an italic, and smaller detail type called out in a contrasting face and weight.

An unconventional use of engraving, together with a thoughtfully structured layout system and highly crafted typography, conveys the client's authority in financial service with freshness and an appropriately inventive spirit.

"It's a principle I use for every project," says Caryl Gorska, designer and principal of Gorska Design. "Start out trying many things, but as you refine the design, simplify, simplify, simplify. I try to get rid of everything that distracts, [so that] only the essential elements are left." In combination with an unusual solution for imagery, the newsletter's quiet visual sophistication conveys the firm's authority and depth of expertise but also alludes to the freshness and originality of its thinking.

The newsletter is composed of two tabloid sheets, folded and saddle-stitched together, that fold down into eight U.S. letter–sized pages. The first of three featured articles (consistent from issue to issue) begins on the cover directly below the newsletter's masthead in a relatively wide column that is flanked by an image to the left and a narrow column to the right. The title for the first article begins at one of three hanglines that govern the beginnings of new articles. As the text from the cover feature continues inside, it flows into a two-column hierarchic grid that is mirrored from left to right pages across the gutter; outside these two columns, the narrow column seen on the cover appears again. Each column is enclosed by a rule (slightly heavier than hairline), and the rules meet an overall rule border at the margins. A heavier blue rule separates the primary columns from the outer two secondary columns.

Typography in the newsletter is remarkably understated, relying on one serif family for the majority of the text, with a contrasting sans serif—in only one weight—for informational distinctions such as subheads and callouts. The text face is Filosofia, a recently designed variant of older Didone modern serifs, in which the main strokes of the letters abut the serifs

Components + Formats

Format
Tabloid folded to U.S. letter; eight pages, saddle stitched; three spot colors.

VOL. 1 NO. 1 MAY 2004

ALLEGIS CAPITAL QUARTERLY

Venture Capital: Facing—and Navigating—the Perfect Storm

By Robert R. Ackerman Jr., Managing Director

WE'RE UNDERGOING A SEA CHANGE in the venture investment business. That much is well known. But what few people even inside the industry understand are the signs now pointing to a confluence of events that could lead to a perfect storm in our industry. It could be disastrous for those who are not prepared.

One of the biggest factors is that globalization is dramatically changing many of the rules of the game in ways that are just beginning to be fully understood. But what is problematic for the VC industry is that this massive shift is happening at a time when the level of experience in the venture business may be at an all-time low, and much of the venture industry has drifted away from the company-building traditions that made it great. Compounding the problem, add the risk of too much money chasing too few quality opportunities, and a massive shift of capital to late stage startups. Early stage companies, the foundation of our entire entrepreneurial ecosystem, are being neglected. Without deliberate action, this all adds up to a scenario for a bumpy road for venture capitalists and start-up companies and lower returns for investo...

So how can we successfully navigate course under such conditions? Let's loo

Problem 1: Globalization.

The entire business startup paradigm is and globalization means we have to star In addition to innovation and a good ne geographical and cultural consideration startup and its investors may start out a morning and find that the bulk of the er

This trend gained huge momentum whe after the dot-com implosion. The always startups to take advantage of resources i The good news is that this rewards effici huge cultural differences, as well as langu lems, so no one knows if this will truly gen

> "Many VC firms are taking on too many investments in late rounds instead of identifying and funding early stage entrepreneurship."

> "You cannot blithely assume that the firms that have dominated in the past will lead in the future..."

COMPETITIVE ADVANTAGE THROUGH ACTI

Result: Chaos for Everyone.

Every institutional investor, every venture firm, and every entrepreneur, and has to be concerned about the pending storm. The good news is that out of change comes opportunity. Here's how to prepare for it:

Institutional investors need to get off auto-pilot. They simply cannot put all the money into venture capital they would like.

Venture firms must take care to bring in more experienced people as well as bright young go-getters. They need to match the size of their funds to the segment of the industry they are targeting. A seed and early-stage fund should be in the range of $200 million to $300 million. Syndication should make a comeback. This is also the era of trans-Pacific venture capital. The old practice of a U.S. venture firm opening up a branch office in an emerging market, hiring a couple of "local" investment bankers and declaring themselves "open for business" won't work. Every time VCs have tried this in the past, they've had our heads handed to them. U.S. venture capitalists have a lot of expertise to offer these emerging markets, but they also need help in the areas where they are weak. Venture capital is a local business, and VCs need to develop local relationships, partnerships, and networks to help them prepare startups for these new markets.

Entrepreneurs need to choose their venture partners carefully. The rules we end up with are not at all apparent at this point. You cannot blithely assume that the firms that have dominated in the past will lead in the future. You have to make a distinction between the name of the firm and the people behind the door actually doing the work. Look for firms with partners who can bring operational experience, international connections, and the time to put into your firm. A lot of investors and entrepreneurs are putting their faith in very leaky boats. That's not a good place to be when the storm hits.

This is still a vibrant and important industry. We just need to remember and practice more of the fundamental principles on which the venture business was built, and start applying them to the trends of the future, and we can all continue to succeed.

Stand and Deliver

Candid Advice for That First Awkward Pitch with Your VC

By Jean-Louis Gasée, General Partner

MY NAME IS GASÉE and I'm a recovering entrepreneur. I know how it feels to testify in front of a VC jury with one hand on my heart and the other (hopefully) in their pocket. I've suffered the humility of rejection and the almost greater terror of success. And now I hope to transfer the lessons of my experience—and my mistakes—to you, the entrepreneur who enters the Allegis chambers, often with expectation of VC Hell.

I want to address the issues that emerge during a VC-entrepreneur relationship, from courtship through consecration and on to mutually satisfied repose. I want to help you understand our role, what we expect from you, and how, together, we can translate your present subjunctive into a future imperative.

On our first awkward date, you'll pitch your idea. Nothing can prepare you for the experience, except, of course, experience—but there's no reason to settle your maiden voyage in the name of getting one under your belt. So, if I may, let me pass on some advise for your first showing.

Be succinct. Paraphrased from the Web site of a well-known fund: How do you expect to sell your idea if it won't fit on a business card? In my first performance as an entrepreneur, the pitch took over three hours. Years later, having learned this lesson, our entire IPO road show, demonstration included, was 20 to 25 minutes. Fully equipped with hindsight, I think I can explain why it's so difficult to be concise, so hard to mention only the most important ideas: What you do as an entrepreneur is personal, it's your creation, drawing on your experience and your skills. How can you explain yourself in a half hour? Your anxiety over omitting the small but ingenious detail will confound your attempt to be understood. In your first presentation, you will probably need to edit yourself, perhaps ruthlessly. But don't worry about cutting away

"We want to know how you think, what moves you..."

details. If we're intrigued by the outline, we'll beg for more. So make us beg! (But a quick caveat: Let's not confuse a concise, ringing statement with a viable business proposition. "I'm going to be the eBay of BzB." Catchy, but no market.)

If it's too broad, try a different dimension. If you can't see how you can distill your novel into a pamphlet—if the business card is too small, or your handwriting is too big—try approaching the problem from a different direction. Tell us how you see the world "Before You" and the world "After You," what difference you'll make, what fundamental problem you'll solve.

Don't overestimate your audience's intelligence. By that I don't mean to imply that VCs are slow or even technically untrained. But your knowledge of your product is based on months, or years, or even a lifetime of internalized understanding. Don't assume that that which is second nature to you

will be immediately apparent to the VC. We want you to make us feel smarter at the end of your first presentation, not confused and browbeaten.

Nobody's Perfect. We don't expect you to be in command of all the implications of your proposal. You can rely on us to extract ideas and directions from your Rev 1.0 story that you hadn't anticipated. It's not a problem at this stage. The first service we provide is working with you to debug your story.

Rational is good, but passionate is better. Some of us do like to visit the sausage factory, if only for the nostalgia. We want to understand how you think and, just as important, how you emote, what moves you, what your biases are, your frustrations even. We have to look rational in our decisions, but part of the equation includes passion. Not pathological, of course, but driven and energized—it's a necessary (but not sufficient) condition to be fundable.

Neatness Doesn't Count. Nothing impresses us more than chalk talk. You stand up, go to the white board and tell us your story, extemporaneously. This leaves a more lasting impression than a view of the back of your tilted head as you read verbatim from your PowerPoint slides. I'll even go as far as suggesting that a "perfect" presentation looks suspect.

Know your point, and your point is funding. I was once prepped for a deposition by Lois Abrams, an attorney at Brown and Bain. Her most important recommendation: Pause before you open your mouth and remind yourself what your story is. As an entrepreneur, you're in the witness box for one reason. To convince us that you'll provide fertile ground for a portion of the money that we're sworn to sow. As crude as it might sound, keep in mind that you, too, have a hand reaching for our pockets. We expect entrepreneurs to be proud of their work, and it makes our decision easier when that pride is couched, occasionally, at least, in terms more relevant to our capital investment concerns.

One final measure of calibration. As VCs we don't deign to meet with you—we need to meet with you. Investors put their money into our hands in exchange for our promise to used it—intelligently and quickly. And after it's implanted, we're impelled to help you by getting out of your way when you're rolling and giving you a shove when you're stuck. But first, let's get you in the door.

> "We have to look rational in our decisions, but part of the equation includes passion."

2

Communication Goals

Target investors and start-up companies

Convey authority and originality

Be classic but lively and sophisticated

Communicate in a simple, legible, accessible way that respects the reader.

Produce quickly and inexpensively

1, 2

Sensitive typographic detailing, simple decorative devices, and the use of engraving for imagery creates an overall coherent visual language that is delicate and textural, as well as confident and somewhat witty. Clear changes in size, spacing, and weight establish a hierarchy that is easy to navigate.

Allegis Capital Quarterly
Gorska Design | Caryl Gorska | *Minneapolis, USA*

08

without a transition, or bracket. In this particular typeface, the extreme contrast between thicks and thins that characterize Didone faces (such as Bodoni) has been softened; the thin strokes are proportionally just a bit heavier. The face is also slightly condensed but sets relatively loosely; these two aspects counteract the overactive visual quality of older Didone faces in text. Coupled with an ample leading and optimal paragraph width in both the cover's single column and the interior's two-column structure, the cadence of the running text is fluid and confident.

Additionally, the text is set at a comfortable and consistent size throughout. Italic setting makes a sporadic appearance for bylines and secondary-level informational tags. The designer uses several larger sizes of the roman text face for article headlines and decks, intuitively adjusting their scales depending on the lengths and complexity of these components. The size difference between text and these upper-level components is clear and easy to navigate, especially since the only competition comes from the sans-serif subheads, captions, and callouts. The sans serif, a slightly condensed gothic, visually corresponds to the width of the serif text face. Used as a subhead, it is set in black ink, and its size appears to have been adjusted downward

1

The simple, mirrored column grid creates a focus inward toward the text. Outer callout columns add negative space, framing the primary content; the callouts lead the reader into the text. Combined with a straightforward hierarchy of sizes and clear beginning points for articles, the structure makes the content very accessible—readers know what to look at first, second, and last.

1, 2

Subheads in the sans-serif gothic sometimes cap a paragraph (1); at other times, they are used in-line as a lead (2). The strong contrast between the subheads and the text type adds color and tension to the page.

2

Occasionally, sidebars accompany the feature articles. Setting them against a lightly tinted background while maintaining the running text size, weight, and leading separates them from the article without being too distracting.

slightly so that its contrast with the serif text around it is a bit less severe than if it had been set at the same size. When it is used in callouts, it is set larger, but in a medium-value blue that softens it even further. Captions for images, also set in the sans serif, are set in the blue ink as well. A square end-slug appears at the termination of articles to signify their ending.

Adding textural richness to the pages are elegant, antique engravings—a smart and unique solution to budgetary constraints that yields a refreshing and distinct character to the publication. "I realized," says Gorska, "that although the type and grid were working, the newsletter lacked a cohesive style. I knew that the art, or lack thereof, was the problem . . . and without an art budget I had been relying on a mishmash of stock photogra-

phy, screen shots, and graphics." The writing in the newsletter makes use of visual metaphors to enliven the potentially dry financial and technical ideas being presented. The designer found inspiration in the first issue's cover story headline, "The Perfect Storm": "That made me think of old engravings of ships in stormy seas," Gorska continues. The client approved the use of such engravings for all the newsletter's art, working closely with the designer to create appropriate visual metaphors. The copyright-free artwork not only solves the budgetary constraint but also adds both a traditional quality and humorous sophistication to the newsletter, promoting its communication goals.

3–7

Comparing typographic variations side-by-side allowed the designer to evaluate the visual effect of the changes being made. One version (3, 4) uses an all-caps setting for titles, and rules of the same weight; the second version (5–7) shows a simpler headline in upper- and lowercase and a bolder rule separating the narrow callout column. The bolder rule is more lively against the text and helps balance the upward thrust of the illustrated column to the left.

8

The designer's pasteboard shows working cover and interior side by side, along with a number of test components waiting to be dropped into layouts.

3

4

5

6

7

8

Work Process

Gorska entered the project after the editorial had been planned and a rough draft already existed ("Which made my job much easier!" she jokes). She had worked with the managing editor before, and as a result of their collaboration, the project was completed within a two-week timeframe.

The designer began by reading the newsletter's content and other marketing materials that had been produced previously. Her sketching for editorial work is done primarily digitally, rather than by hand, because of the importance of seeing the type in action. "It's easy to change grids, resize art and type, or start over," she says. Although she usually starts working with a spread, in this case she sketched covers first, as the covers would have all the features of the interior typography—head, subhead, text, pullquotes, as well as the added masthead and issue number.

"At first, I tried to match Allegis' marketing materials using sans-serif fonts—but this seemed more brochurelike than newslettery, so I switched to Filosofia." As the cover structure began to reveal itself, Gorska began to sketch the interior in tandem to see how the design would play out inside. "I put the cover and spread layout side-by-side in a single file so I can work on them simultaneously and see how changes affect each."

09

Werte/Schlott Gruppe
2003 Annual Report

Strichpunkt | Stuttgart, Germany
Melanie Schiffer, Principal

"The most basic function of an annual report is to communicate values," state the principals of Strichpunkt, a design consulting firm based in Stuttgart, Germany. Those values include tangible information such as financial performance—revenues and expenditures, assets and holdings—but also include intangible values, such as the ethics and commitment of a company's employees, the personality of the corporate culture, its vision, and its energy. These, after all, are really what attract new investors and connect with shareholders. The values (*Werte*) of the Schlott Gruppe—one of Europe's largest printing companies—are cleverly delivered in this annual report. Although subdued and classical in its overall presentation, the thick, hard-bound volume employs a variety of subtle details, mixed with a dose of contemporary humor, to convey the attitude, commitment, fiscal achievements, and personality of the company. Not surprisingly, one of the outstanding qualities of the publication is its high-end production value.

The case-bound book, with its sewn binding, textured endpapers, heavy, uncoated stock, and embossed detailing, speaks volumes about the company's mastery of its craft. A massive amount of information—including nearly 200 pages of financial information—is contained within its pages, conveying a sense of thoroughness in management, as well as transparency and openness where its investors are concerned. A short section of humorous images, lavishly produced in full color on a glossy stock, helps shift gears, giving insight into the company's internal energy and philosophy.

The report comes bound in a deep, cool, hard gray cover. It is a hefty object with significant physical presence—at more than 1 inch (2.5 cm) in thickness, it far outweighs most annual reports, both literally and figuratively. The cover information appears in a mixture of embossing and imprinting with opaque inks, limited to typography and linear typographic detailing. Imagery throughout is limited to a few portraits in the first section, a discussion of philosophy by management, and to the short photographic section that separates it from the financial disclosure that makes up more than half of the report. The designers have set the majority of the text in Sabon, an old-style serif that is stately and organic, mixing it with two secondary faces and structuring it in a manuscript block that nonetheless is quite modern in its appearance.

The exquisitely bound book houses a substantial annual report for one of Europe's largest printing companies. Classical, well-crafted typography combines with contemporary layout, detailing, and quirky photography to communicate the client's values.

One of the most interesting qualities of the report is this visual dialogue between the classical and the contemporary. By using oldstyle typography and a potentially conservative structure but treating this base in somewhat unconventional ways, the designers communicate the company's prestige and sense of history while achieving a look that conveys elegance, craft, originality, and a contemporary outlook. The manuscript block, for example, is hung low on the pages, creating an enormous head margin that is spatially extravagant but functional on occasion as a place for supporting information—small photographs, charts, and tables. This margin is defined by delicate dashed rules that, along with decorative tick marks, small folios, and a cool, subdued color scheme, create a rich

Components + Formats

Format

6" x 8" (15.2 x 20.3 cm) vertical, case-bound book with embossing and opaque inks; Smyth-sewn binding with headband; interior text sections printed two colors; image section printed process (CMYK) color with spot varnish and bump plates.

Provide an extensive financial document, thoroughly narrating the growth and performance of the company

Convey the corporate culture of openness, transparency, individuality, honesty, and humor

Communicate the company's high level of service and commitment through materials and finishing

1

Werte.

GESCHÄFTSBERICHT 2002/2003

2

GESCHÄFTSBERICHT SCHLOTT GRUPPE AG

2002/03

Werte.

3

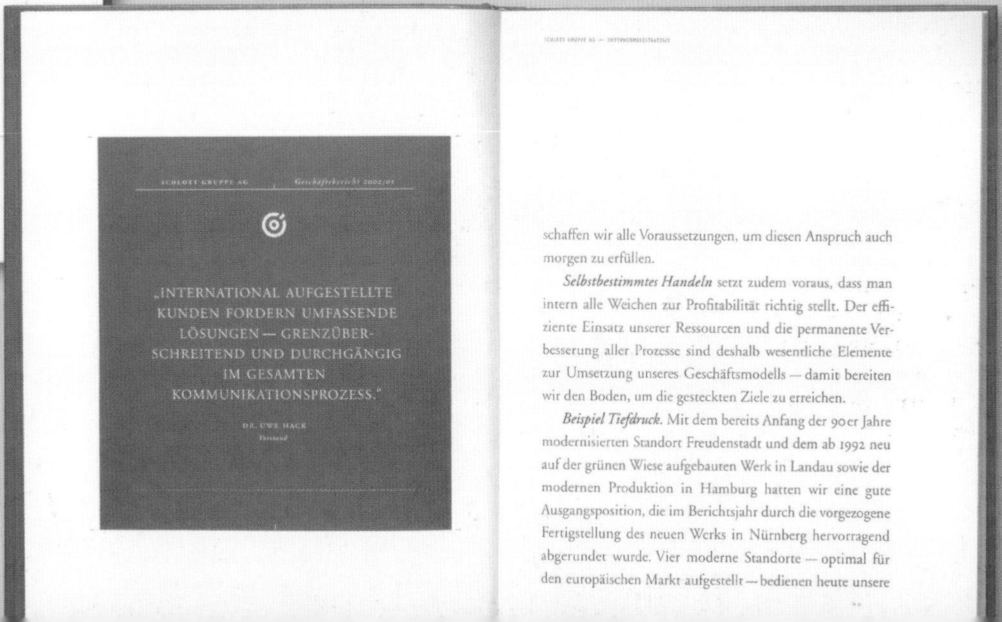

1

With no image and little typography on the cover, the material presence of the report comes to the fore. The cover stock is uncoated and deeply embossed with the company name and the title, *Werte* (*Values*). This treatment of the title, against the cool gray stock, imparts a feeling of permanence and authority. The book's intimate size and friendly proportions offset this austere formality.

2, 3

The half title and section frontispieces use a classical, centered-axis aligment for text against expanses of white space to create a light, elegant feeling.

SCHLOTT GRUPPE AG — *Geschäftsbericht 2002/03*

„INTERNATIONAL AUFGESTELLTE
KUNDEN FORDERN UMFASSENDE
LÖSUNGEN — GRENZÜBER-
SCHREITEND UND DURCHGÄNGIG
IM GESAMTEN
KOMMUNIKATIONSPROZESS."

DR. UWE HACK
Vorstand

schaffen wir alle Voraussetzungen, um diesen Anspruch auch morgen zu erfüllen.

Selbstbestimmtes Handeln setzt zudem voraus, dass man intern alle Weichen zur Profitabilität richtig stellt. Der effiziente Einsatz unserer Ressourcen und die permanente Verbesserung aller Prozesse sind deshalb wesentliche Elemente zur Umsetzung unseres Geschäftsmodells — damit bereiten wir den Boden, um die gesteckten Ziele zu erreichen.

Beispiel Tiefdruck. Mit dem bereits Anfang der 90er Jahre modernisierten Standort Freudenstadt und dem ab 1992 neu auf der grünen Wiese aufgebauten Werk in Landau sowie der modernen Produktion in Hamburg hatten wir eine gute Ausgangsposition, die im Berichtsjahr durch die vorgezogene Fertigstellung des neuen Werks in Nürnberg hervorragend abgerundet wurde. Vier moderne Standorte — optimal für den europäischen Markt aufgestellt — bedienen heute unsere

Very few images are used outside the Values section. In this case, duotoned portraits of executives are shown occupying the lower part of the head margin.

and modern experience. Text sizes are varied in different sections; in the first, text runs at a friendly, almost display size, while in the financial section it is reduced to a more conventional text size. Cool blue and silver text detailing creates a sophisticated, machined quality that speaks of precision and mastery. Within the major sections, subsections are distinguished by a centered configuration of title type, enclosed in silver metallic fields or delicate ruled boxes that echo the structure of the cover. Informational components within these areas are richly separated by weight, case, and size; all-capital setting for some elements is very formal, contrasting with rhythmic changes introduced by italic and roman lowercase setting. The designers have opted for nonlining, oldstyle numerals throughout, further adding to the elegant, crafted look of the report.

In the Values section, which is printed in full color on a glossy, coated paper stock, key values symbolizing the attitudes and philosophies of the company and its employees are accompanied by quirky images of objects that correspond to the concepts being discussed. Personality, for example, is symbolized by the underwear of a sales force member. "After all," says Strichpunkt, "you feel the most comfortable with something that is familiar to you." It is this kind of odd association that drives the images in this section, which range from tins of mincemeat to fuzzy teddy bears, in an almost childlike show-and-tell of what makes the company tick. The images are stunningly photographed, silhouetted, and varnished. The cool metallic and neutral grays and blue of the typography persist, offering a crisp contrast to the lush color of the photography. In this section, one of the accent typefaces, a condensed sans serif, is used for callouts, while the serif recedes to a secondary role for image titles and the structural details of the page, such as folios and running head.

The third section, the financial disclosure, is a pleasure to behold . Despite its intensity and thoroughness, the exquisite detailing of the typography, tabular data, and diagrams makes the section comfortable to read for extended periods and simply enjoyable as an object. Text and tables are contained within the dropped manuscript block, spanning the width of the page, while more richly colored charts and graphs appear above, detailed and clearly deposed with typography that exhibits fine hierarchic distinctions among components. The text is set smaller than would normally be optimal, but generous leading compensates for the small text size. The sans-serif gothic makes an appearance in captions, table headers, and charts and graphs, while a second accent face—a subtle slab serif—is used for subheads and section running heads. The table columns throughout the section divide the manuscript column width as needed, based on comfortable spacing for the longest figures in the table. Dashed and solid rules of varying weights and tonalities help separate figures within rows. Major sections of the financial matter are opened with a flat field of ink; subsections within are distinguished with open boxes drawn by rules and less formal typography.

1

2

3

02: *transparent*

fig. 2-4

GUT, WENN MAN GENAU WEISS, WORAN MAN IST
UND WAS ES BRINGT.

Jörg Raasch, 27 | schlinz GmbH, Freudenstadt
fig. 2-4

p. 36

02

Die Basis langfristigen unternehmerischen Erfolgs heißt Vertrauen.
Deshalb begegnen wir Kunden, Mitarbeitern und Partnern stets offen und ehrlich.

03: *aufrichtig*

fig. 3-3

ES GIBT DINGE, DIE SIND
EINFACH VERTRAUENSSACHE.

Bernd Ross, Vorstandsvorsitzender | schinz gruppe AG, Freudenstadt
fig. 3-3

p. 37

03

3, 4

The glossy, vividly colored photographic section provides a dramatic contrast to the surrounding text sections. Images are arranged in the center, following the generally centered logic of the typography throughout. The "value" at the top is set toward the left of each page, while the supporting callout text, in a condensed sans serif, is allowed to move about the format as needed. The images are spot varnished to help them lift off the pages.

1

The manuscript block—a basic editorial structure based on Renaissance texts—is given a contemporary presentation by altering its spatial relationship to the page format. The deep head margin, mostly free of content in the first section, is relatively informal in comparison with margin proportions in conventional manuscript layout. The large text size in the first section's spreads (shown here) is also somewhat unconventional.

2

Typographic detailing is restrained but distinct. Within the paragraph, callouts within text are distinguished by a subtle color shift.

4

04: *persönlich*

fig. 4-4

AM WOHLSTEN FÜHLT MAN SICH, WENN EINEM
ETWAS VERTRAUT IST.

Thomas Kirschen, Verkauf | subanschuck GmbH, Plauen
fig. 4-4

p. 44

04

Jede Geschäftsbeziehung ist einzigartig. Deshalb setzen wir alles daran,
für jede Herausforderung eine einzigartige Lösung zu finden.

05: *individuell*

fig. 5-4

DER UNTERSCHIED ZWISCHEN „PASST" UND „PASST GENAU"
KANN SEHR WOHLTUEND SEIN.

Christian Schwarz, Letterchup | müller dietz GmbH, Schwandorf
fig. 5-4

p. 45

05

Schlott Gruppe Annual Report
Strichpunkt | *Stuttgart, Germany*

09

1

2

1, 2

Each text section begins with a treated title block, constrained by the proportions of the main text column. Variation in the treatment of the text (sometimes uppercase, sometimes roman or italic, reversing out or printing a second color) and of the area itself (as a field of ink or a delicately ruled box) adds a bit of surprise and helps evolve the detailed logic of the typographic system.

2

The classical manuscript block is broken for tabular data in the financial section; combined with extremely precise rule treatments and a sans serif used for captions and diagrammatic text, the traditional layout is nonetheless contemporary.

Work Process

"As we do mostly, we presented just one concept," says Strichpunkt designer Melanie Schiffer. "This was refined in many intensive sessions with the Schlott Gruppe CEO, who was personally involved in finding items that would fit to the values of the company. The challenge was to find exciting items to represent abstract values as stated by employees, as well as being interesting in a visual way."

Schiffer continues, "We decided to represent the core values of the company with objects, rather than people (having done a portrait-based report the year before) e.g., a clear soup, an ice scratcher, an anuarium and the contents listing of an instant food package for the value 'transparency.' From initial 'scribbles,' and the initial presentation, the process took a few weeks to complete, including the shooting of custom photography."

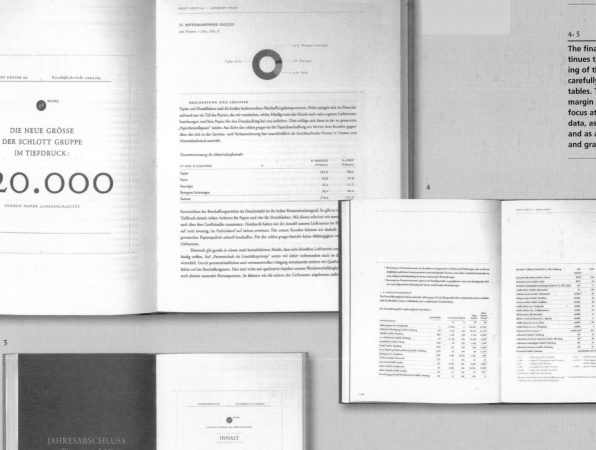

3

Extra ink colors—a deeper blue; a warm, greenish gray; and a rich, reddish brown—are used to enliven the charts and graphs in the financial section. The colors are roughly the same value and somewhat desaturated, in keeping with the subtlety of the text treatments.

4, 5

The financial section continues the exquisite detailing of the typography in carefully sized and spaced tables. The large head margin acts alternately to focus attention on the data, as a resting space, and as a place for charts and graphs.

10

Bar Apéritif Magazine

Creuna Design | Oslo, Norway
Stein Øvre, Art Director; Frøde Slotnes, Designer
Aase E. Jacobsen and Jan Amundsen, Editors

This glossy trade publication is distributed exclusively to professionals and buyers in the bar and restaurant industry. Orchestrated by Creuna Design, based in Oslo, Norway, the magazine provides information on drink mixing, personalities in the business, profiles of bars and restaurants, and articles on spirit distilleries and producers, along with liquor reviews and historical and cultural content surrounding the products. The magazine is produced four times a year, with each issue devoted to one or two kinds of liquor and related themes. Given the constantly evolving aesthetics and experience of the bar scene, the magazine's designers aim to deliver a unique visual experience in each issue while providing visually branded continuity through typography, color, and other details. "The design templates are subject to a continuous evolution," comments art director Stein Øvre.

From a conceptual standpoint, the design of these details—typography, color, graphic elements—draws on the rich environment of bars and restaurants: objects such as glasses, bottles, liquor labels, and interior design motifs common to bars. One of the most important visual aspects of the magazine is its typography, which uses two custom-designed fonts by Øvre's colleague, Frøde Slotnes. The masthead used on the magazine's cover shares formal qualities with Bar Fontana, a primary headline face used throughout for titling. The drawing of this typeface derives from the form of bottles and glasses, showing a thin, bubblelike character in its uniform stroke weight and angular, yet rounded, shoulders. The typeface's counters are extremely open, lending a fragile transparency to headlines. "It's supposed to have a liquid feel to it," says Øvre. Alternate characters allow for some variation in title setting.

The companion face, Cleanfax, was developed by Slotnes as an experiment in form in 1994. The drawing is based on the automatically generated headers that fax machines print at the top of incoming messages. "I liked the clean, pixelated quality of these headers," says Slotnes. Cleanfax exhibits similar proportions to Bar Fontana—open counters, uniform stroke weight, and an emphasis on vertical presentation, with slightly uplifted midline—but contrasts the latter's glassy feel with angled joints. Cleanfax was originally used for initials and some numbers, but with successive issues of the magazine, it has emerged as a more active player in heads and decks, adding to the magazine's typographic branding. A very neutral sans-serif text face—Berthold Akzidenz Grotesk Light—is used for body text as a foil to the idiosyncratic display faces. "I use Akzidenz the same way many people use Helvetica," comments Øvre. "It's been my default typeface for some time." As neutral as Akzidenz is, its open counters, slightly squared shoulders, and thin strokes provide visual continuity with the branded display faces.

The magazine is structured on a grid of four columns with relatively even head, foot, and side margins. Images and text occupy the height of the body columns, rarely intruding in their pristine negative space. Sometimes these margins are left white; in other instances, they are filled with solid color from the magazine's limited palette. The strong horizontal

In this quarterly trade magazine for professionals working in the hospitality industry, dynamic color photography, lush color, and a constantly changing abstract graphic language deliver energy and style.

Components + Formats

Project Type
Trade magazine [nonconsumer]

Format
A4, printed four-color process (CMYK)
on gloss-coated stock, perfect bound

Communication Goals

Bring the energy and fun of the hospitality industry, and the experience of socializing in bars, into the layouts

Engage professionals in the bar and restaurant sector with a smart, constantly evolving source of relevant information; to position the magazine as a must-read resource by keeping the graphic presentation evolving constantly

As art director Stein Øvre puts it, "Design elements inspired by fruit, bar interiors, bottles, glasses, and fixtures are all part of the 'mix,' like a good drink that produces an uplifting state!"

1, 2

Covers for the magazine maintain a consistent format, with tremendous presence given to the *Bar* masthead in a band of neutral gray intended to minimize any conflict with the lush, colorful images that fill the lower four-fifths of the format.

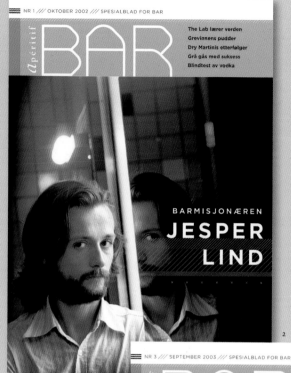

3

"Play" images that the art director sketches before even seeing the content follow a general graphic language of textures, curls, and linear motifs that characterize every issue. Their abstract formal qualities derive from the fruits, bottles, glasses, and bar room fixtures, as well as from the brittle, idiosyncratic linear display typography used for headlines. Most of these experiments happen independent of the page spread structure, while others are direct investigations into possible layout solutions.

Bar Apéritif Magazine
Creuna Design | Stein Øvre, Frøde Slotnes
Oslo, Norway

1–3

Recurring departments in the front section generally run on single pages, opposite advertising. The horizontal bands created by keeping the head and foot margins generally clear of material help separate the editorial content from the ads. In the department pages, one of the default branding colors—or sometimes a "guest" color in a given issue—fills the margins to distinguish them further from the features in the well.

2, 4

A vibrant mix of silhouetted images and changing type weights and sizes keeps the department pages lively issue after issue; one light sans-serif face for text provides consistency, contrasted by the display faces and bolder subheads.

1

2

3

4

character of the resulting layouts helps clearly define the editorial content and distinguish it from advertising, which is among the primary content in the magazine. The foot margin contains folios, running feet, and section markers (set in Cleanfax) that also help separate the editorial and advertising. Text is primarily set justified, although listed information, decks, and callouts are set flush left/ragged right, usually at a larger size. The heavy weight of Gotham Bold also makes an appearance in subheads—most often in vivid color—and adds a welcome weight and contrast to the slick, austere, and brittle quality of the text and display faces. Regular departments, featured in every issue, focus on reviews of liquor and new establishments, along with news items of interest to the audience. The departments precede the feature well, set off by the use of color banding in the head and foot margins that is consistent in their pagination within a given issue.

Color and texture play dominant roles in presenting the content. Most of the photographs are lush, glossy depictions of drinks, bottles, fruit, and interiors, selected by the editors and generally left to speak for themselves. A restrained system of

default branding colors—strong "cocktail" colors that include a pink, a bright orange-red, and the three process primaries, as well as black, white, an olive, and a neutral gray reminiscent of metal fixtures—appears in every issue. Selected accent colors accompany articles as needed, playing against the default colors to add flexibility while retaining the branded consistency of the default color scheme. "We chose the process colors—solid cyan, magenta, and yellow—as part of the mix because they print as solids; we use a lot of thin, linear graphic treatments (as well as very thin type) throughout the magazine and needed colors that wouldn't need to break in tints so they would reproduce well in these treatments," explains Øvre.

Aside from typography, color, and flashy photographs, another distinguishing visual element is the use of textural and graphic devices throughout the magazine. In keeping with the linear character of the typography, these textures are often made up of lines—bands of diagonal rules set close together in bright colors that impart a buzzing, energetic quality to margins, edges of photographs, and backgrounds. The textures often interact with the images and headlines, creating an optical transition

between representational image and the background white or colored context of the spreads. However, other kinds of linear treatment—illustrations, circular and wedge motifs such as chunks of fruit, and found textures, such as those that might be encountered on a bar's floor, wall paneling, or stools—are included on a regular basis. The variety of these additional textures helps keep each issue of the magazine distinct and fresh—an important goal for the design team in maintaining an up-to-the-minute publication for the fast-paced and stylish hospitality industry.

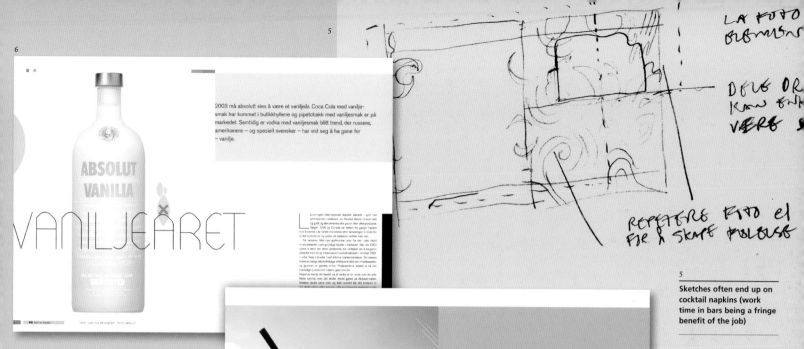

6

2003 må absolutt sies å være et vaniljeår. Coca Cola med vanilje-smak har kommet i butikkhyllene og pipetobakk med vaniljesmak er på markedet. Samtidig er vodka med vaniljesmak blitt trend, de russere, amerikanere – og spesielt svensker – har vist seg å ha gane for – vanilje.

VANILJEÅRET

LA FOTO
BLAMBAB

DELE OR
KAN EN
VÆRE S

REPETERE FOTO el
FOR Å SKATE POBLUSS

Sketches often end up on cocktail napkins (work time in bars being a fringe benefit of the job)

7

Det er et utrolig skue å se utover et agave felt i solnedgang. Det oransjerede sollyset blander seg med det grønnblå skinnet fra agaveplanten. Det bølgende landskapet i Jalisco med massive fjell i bakgrunnen danner en flott ramme. Herfra kommer tequila, Mexicos sjel.

MEXICOS SJEL

Produksjon

TEQUILA   TEKST BJØRN TORE AASTORP RUUD

5–8

The feature spreads in every issue—and even within the same issue—differ radically in presentation, following cues from the article content. Interviews with bar and restaurant personalities maintain a more reserved editorial approach, structuring text in a question-and-answer format that follows the column structure in a simpler way. Articles about featured spirits, meanwhile, take on more character and dramatic color, as well as pronounced graphic treatments, to convey the energy and context of the information.

8

THE LAB

LÆRER

VERDEN

The Lab i Soho er folkets favorittbar.
Hit kommer bartendere fra hele verden for
å hente inspirasjon. Men hva skal til for å
lage en cocktailbar som gjestene alltid
vil vende tilbake til? Mannen bak The Lab
har tydeligvis funnet svaret.

Manage og trend

Bar Apéritif Magazine

Creuna Design | Stein Øvre, Frøde Slotnes
Oslo, Norway

10

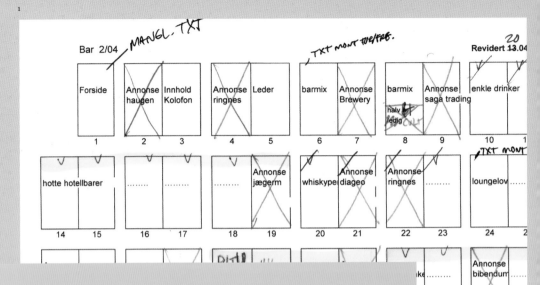

Work Process

Øvre says, "My role is art directing and design-ing. The magazine doesn't have a photo editor, and Creuna Design doesn't participate in the photo shoots; we get the images from the editors, who also supply us with the text for the articles. But we do decide, sometimes in collaboration with the editors, which pictures to use." Each issue of the magazine is designed in a two-week period, with roughly 80 percent of the content arriving at the beginning of this phase. Øvre begins sketching (sometimes on cocktail napkins) even before specific content arrives.

"I start by sketching abstract ideas, some-times in off hours outside work. The sketches are related to the magazine's established look, but I'm also testing new ideas . . . just play, really, without thinking about what articles the designs might be used for. Many of these sketches don't end up in the final publication,

although sometimes they show up later on or in other projects. I use this method for other projects as well, so some ideas for other projects may show up in *Bar*."

After initial meetings with editors, during which the pictures are selected, Øvre and other designers review his earlier sketches to see whether anything connects with the content. "Sometimes, the connection is natural," says Øvre. "Other times, it's interesting to just place photos and graphic elements together to see what happens, kind of like mixing a new drink you've never tried before. This often sparks a creative period where we experiment directly with the content and then we find we're heading somewhere." By the end of the first week, the majority of the layouts are roughed together. From there, the process becomes one of refining and polishing the layouts during the second

week, up until the files are delivered to the printer. On occasion, new content will appear during the second week, adding to the mix at the last minute. The quick pace helps keep the layouts spontaneous, forcing Øvre and his team to act instinctively and have fun.

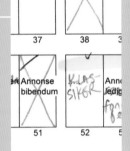

1, 2

Rough pagination for a particular issue (1) follows a simple listing of feature and departmental content (2). Seeing the entire lay-out in a concise, graphic form allows the design team, in collaboration with the editors, a chance to move content around, plan for the locations of ads (whose positions are contracted for and, hence, can not be moved), and get a sense of the pacing among spreads.

Simplicity and spontaneity are key; the short timeframe for design and production plays an important role in the magazine, so the editorial structure and basic elements, developed before the launch, become a kind of toolbox that Øvre and his team can use efficiently to work through layouts. "And always," Øvre says, "I'm concerned with making each issue better than the last."

3

4

10-11 FASTDRINKS

3–5

Early sketches for an article on fast drinks lead rapidly from pencil renderings to digital collage and finally into finished spread. In this sequence, the essential energy of the spread and its graphic elements are clearly visible in the minimal line drawing on the napkin.

A toolbox of elements keeps the fast-paced design process on track, ensuring visual consistency among issues but also a great deal of flexibility in arranging the parts.

A vibrant scheme of default colors appears in every issue, complemented by accent colors added to play off article photography.

The simple four-column grid allows for rapid and consistent layout development. The gray area defines the body for text and photographs, keeping the head and foot margins free.

The linear strokes and open counters of the austere masthead letters refer to bottles and glasses.

Two custom typefaces—Bar Fontana (top) and Cleanfax (bottom) carry the weight of the heads and decks throughout the magazine. Slight differences in roundness and angularity among their strokes create contrast and tension, while their uniform widths and high counter emphasis unify them visually. A neutral sans-serif text face balances their stylized qualities.

5

6, 7

Other kinds of elements—in this case, illustrative, rather than purely abstract—also play a role in the overall visual language of the magazine. Here, graphic translations of cultural forms lend a specific visual context to the article, about nightlife in Bombay, India, while preserving the linear idea of other treatments.

6

7

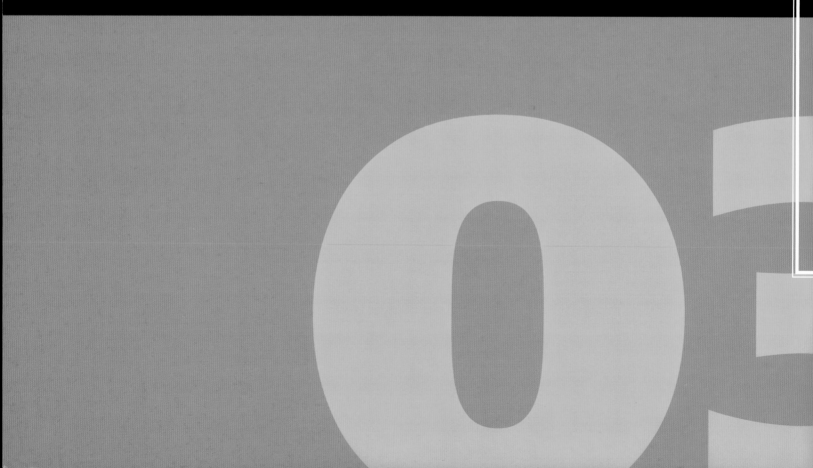

Publications in Action

A Showcase of Real-World Projects

Literature systems, newsletters, magazines, newspapers, catalogs, annual reports: publications abound in every country of the world, fulfilling a need among audiences for information of every kind. The more people there are, the more messages are created for them, and the more they come to rely on the stream of media created by authors and designers, companies and cultural groups to tell them what's happening and when, where they can find help for relevant concerns, or what other people are doing that they might want to do too. Every publication tells a story, no matter how small or large that story is, or whether two people see it or two million. What follows is a selection of these stories—as conceived, planned, organized, and styled—given form by graphic designers on behalf of the people who like to read them.

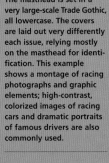

1

The masthead is set in a
very large-scale Trade Gothic,
all lowercase. The covers
are laid out very differently
each issue, relying mostly
on the masthead for identification. This example
shows a montage of racing
photographs and graphic
elements; high-contrast,
colorized images of racing
cars and dramatic portraits
of famous drivers are also
commonly used.

Magazines

Periodical Publications, From Glossy Consumer Rags
to Cultural and Institutional Organs

2, 3

The table of contents
changes proportion and
orientation in each issue,
sometimes running as a
vertical column, and at

Ruedas y Tuercas
El Comercio | *Lima, Peru*

01

An aggressively laid-out automotive magazine produced by Peru's largest publisher emphasizes photography to promote the energy and charismatic personalities of racing. The publication uses a conventional three-column grid—sometimes violated for special features—to organize somewhat minimal text around an array of journalistic images. The designers operate around the grid freely, shifting text around mostly full- and three-quarter bleed photos of racing teams, rallies and races, portraits of celebrity drivers, and promotional shots of highlighted makes and models. The typography is, for the most part, of secondary concern in terms of styling: text is set in a light sans serif, tabular configurations of automotive specs are fit into small spaces toward the outer edges of the grid, and titling and subhead details consist of weight changes and, sometimes, a slight size change. Bitmap and other accent faces make an occasional appearance to bring texture and a mechanical feel in small doses. Overall, readers are encouraged to steer around text and take in the dramatic driving scenes and flashy detail shots of car interiors and finishes.

4, 5, 7

Most spreads feature one full-bleed image or two large images in close juxtaposition, with a minimal paragraph of text supporting them. Typographic styling is secondary to selection, sequencing, and cropping of images.

5–7

Some editions are treated with their own overall style; this review of major rallies for a particular season configures montaged photographs with dotted textural screens and linear elements in a compartmented, gridlike presentation. The complexity of the configurations changes depending on the nature of the spread—simpler driver or team profiles (2, 3) contrast more textural section dividers (4).

Greater South Sound Home and Garden

Premier Media Group | *Lakewood (WA), USA*

02

Vivid images and classic editorial typography contribute to the rich, visual quality of this lifestyle magazine that focuses on entertaining, home décor, and daily living in the Pacific Northwest area of the United States. The photography exploits the region's strong northern light, imparting a recognizably golden contrast to table top, beach, and domestic scenes. Since the lifestyle experience in this area is the primary concept, the magazine keeps its focus on the images; full-bleed color pages enhance the already dramatic presentation, even with subjects that are relatively mundane. Special care in the cropping and positioning of photographs and typographic headline treatments ensures spatially dynamic yet serene layouts. The type is structured on a compound two- and three-column grid with generous head margin, focusing attention inward to the body and provid-

ing an elegant sense of separation from the format edges. Feature stories are differentiated from supplemental content with a full-spread opener and prominent use of the two-column structure. Supplemental stories generally run on three columns. Given the variety and importance of the photographs, the designers simplify the type system toward one primary family—an elegant English sans serif in several weights that are used to differentiate heads, subheads, and captions—with details such as drop caps, headlines, and callouts accented in a mix of scripts and serifs. Within sections of informational material, such as recipes or listings, bold and regular weights of the sans-serif text clarify each of the components.

1

2

1

Gill Sans, an English sans serif, is used throughout as a primary family. While it is most often present as text, it is often used at a large size in combination with images for feature openings. Simple typographic detailing—here, an accent script face—adds texture and movement to counter the consistent sans-serif text.

1, 3, 5

Feature openings start with full-bleed photographs or a combination of page-bleed image paired with page-bleed color. The palette used in the magazine consists of vivid purples, burgundies, mossy greens, and other rich jewel tones that complement the saturated color of the photographs.

2

The magazine's covers feature a full-bleed photograph with lush color, interesting cropping, and a few flagged story titles to draw in readers. The masthead is large, spanning the width of the format, and set all uppercase in a medium-weight sans serif. An expressive ampersand adds texture and energy.

putting down roots
choosing and caring for landscape trees

BY PAMELA KOCH
PHOTOGRAPHY BY MELISSA MUNSON AND THOMASINE ROSS

A graceful Japanese maple punctuates the Chase Garden's lovely alpine meadow in spring.

When it comes to home landscaping, trees provide much more than vertical appeal. They soften stark edges and make houses feel like homes. Well-placed trees reduce the need for air conditioning in the summer and heat in the winter by providing shade and windbreaks. Trees also remove air pollutants, produce the oxygen we breathe, and combat global warming by removing carbon dioxide from the air and lowering our usage of fossil fuels.

Natural environments and details within setup shots like this tabletop help reinforce the sense of the locale that is the publication's focus.

coastal cookout
Host a Beach Party in Your Backyard

When the sun finally makes its appearance, it's time to celebrate—Pacific Northwest style! Throw a backyard beach party with a nautical theme and delectable seafood dishes, and pay homage to Washington's beautiful coast and rich maritime history.

BY LINDA HAMINSKY, EMILY WINARD,
AND STACIE MARGOLISON | PHOTOGRAPHY BY JEFF HOBSON

the invitations

Keep the invitations simple. Using Word or a similar word-processing program, set the document's size to four inches wide and six inches high. Create a thin copy-stock border; use the same color for the invitation's wording, which should be in a sans-serif font such as Arial. Using strong gray, pale, a small sea star to the top left corner. Wrap a thin ribbon of sea ribbon around the invitation two or three times, knotting it on the backside and cutting off any extra length. Because the sea star is bulky and fragile, it could break when going through the post office's machines if placed in a standard envelope. To ensure it passes in and intact, place the invitation in an envelope and then place the envelope in a bubble mailer, available at any post office or mail center.

the decor

Choose a color scheme that echoes the Pacific Northwest's coast. Use sea-blue napkins, yellow votive candles, cobalt blue-tinted water glasses, and a bright pastel tablecloth. Create a soft turquoise of crumpled linen. A crisp white tablecloth creates a blank canvas against which a simple table arrangement could go far in other changes. If you can't find place plates, substitute plain white dishes that match the blues. Borrow echoing the glass plates. The blue glass exhibits since another purpose. The setting sun's light reflects off the glass, creating a wonderful mosaic glow on the table. Use blue glass to mimic a cool blue grosgrain ribbon around yellow napkins and affix a pearl sea star. Mason jars help filled with lightly scented sea glass and seashells double as place cards. Use simple ribbons that they don't fly away when the wind kicks up. In lieu of flower place two or three hurricane lanterns down the table's center. Fill with light-colored sand (available in most pet stores), blue votive candles, sea-dollars, sea stars, and a handful of polished ocean glass.

H2O

FEATURES

FROM SIMPLE TO GRAND,

FROM URBAN INDUSTRIAL

TO LUSH OASIS, FOURTEEN

FANTASTIC WATER FEATURES.

The tidy of rachel Harrmeconstant's made-rustic waterscene appear to float on the top of the beautiful country's to pool. The spirit, elegant lines of his design perfectly complement the surrounding architecture. (phone: rainbow-nw@comcast.net or 206.555.5812.)

WHAT IS THE MOST VERSATILE AND CAPTIVATING ELEMENT IN THE LANDSCAPE?
Water. Easily lending itself to dramatic effects or scenes of serenity, water has no equal for variety and beauty. And water's allure is not only visual: from roaring torrents to the smallest trickle, water can evoke moods from peaceful to stimulating. Whether you have a tiny balcony at a modern apartment or a large yard surrounding a vintage Victorian, there is a water feature to fit your style and your budget.

A consistent approach to art directing photography helps give the magazine a coherent, branded feeling. Most images exhibit intense color, usually a result of directional lighting, whether natural or created in the studio. In this feature opening, the light in the background environment takes on a golden, high-contrast quality that helps separate the dog into the foreground. Subject matter in most of the photographs is relatively simple, uncluttered, and carefully composed to bring out abstract movement and shape.

Move!
Ruder Finn Design | *New York City, USA*

Visually dynamic layouts combining illustration, photography, and montage with expressive type treatments communicate the mission and philosophy of a public relations firm in this promotional magazine. Each issue begins with a collage of images from the interior—photographs from client projects and feature story opening illustrations—assembled into a composition that graphically conveys the magazine's title. A clean, three-column grid that justifies text within columns, as well as at the head and foot margins, provides an architectural structure against which the variation in image content and typographic treatments are allowed to play. The articles in every issue are different: contributed by executives in the firm, they explore client-management methods, strategies, and successful case studies, as well as issues of social or political concern to the company, which takes pride in being an advocate for cultural institutions alongside its work for global pharmaceutical companies and the United Nations.

Images for article-opening spreads are distilled into immediately accessible symbolic compositions, mixing abstraction and realism to convey primary concepts as quickly and clearly as possible. Each article is then styled to follow its particular opening image while presenting primary text, heads, decks, and captions in a rounded, geometric sans serif in its entire family of weights. Additional typefaces are used solely as accents or as part of composite illustrations. In keeping with the overall energy of the title concept, color is used boldly in simple analogous and complementary relationships.

1, 2

Two typographic treatments visually reinforce the concept of the masthead. The italicized *e* creates a literal motion (from standing upright to lurching forward), while the exclamation point creates an abstract motion—a verbal emphasis or loudness and a visual disconnect in space, coming forward because of its scale change in relation to the word.

1, 2

The covers offer an encapsulation of the stories inside by combining their illustrations in dynamic compositions. Each issue uses a vivid background color as a base, against which the selected illustrations are combined in a montage. Each cover attempts a new configuration for this composite—for example, a spiral, a series of diagonals, warped bands, or staggered bars.

3

A clean structure for the contents page operates independently of the three-column grid. Page numbers are set to the left of their article listing for easy reference, and color is used to call out the article titles against the decks and bylines. Selected images from inside are montaged around the page to intrigue the reader.

4

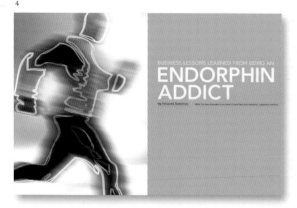

BUSINESS LESSONS LEARNED FROM BEING AN
ENDORPHIN ADDICT
by Howard Schimmel

5

PROFIT or PRINCIPLE
by Jessica Bertoe

6

WHAT WILL BABY WANT NEXT?
MEETING THE HEALTH NEEDS OF BABY BOOMERS
by Ken Rabin

7

CAFÉ PHILO
by Emmanuel Edouardias

8

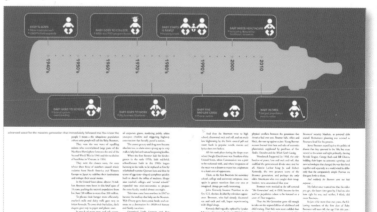

All the type is set in a geo-metric sans-serif family, using mostly one weight throughout. Subheads, callouts, and captions use the bold weight, with size and color changes helping to distinguish them.

4–7

Article opening spreads always begin with a full-bleed image (or image set against a colored field), which is distilled into semiabstract, conceptual symbols that are designed to be read quickly and impart as much meaning as possible in a direct way. Dramatic color and unex-pected illustrative details provide richness. The article title, always upper-case at a large size, is contrasted by the lead line, set much smaller in mixed case and strung across the spread. The lead line runs off the opening spread and resumes on the spread following, creating a clear jump and a direct entry point into the running text.

8

Tightly controlled justifica-tion of columns at the head and foot—as well as justified text within columns—creates a severe, architectural quality that separates images cleanly from the text. Pacing is varied by shifting images within spreads from top to bottom and from left to right, as well as by varying their proportions and the scale of elements within them.

Sleaze Nation
Scott King | *London, United Kingdom*

Opposing trends in editorial design yield textural, kinetic publications with many levels of detail . . . or minimal, unfussy approaches such as that seen here. In direct contrast to its title, this magazine is about as visually unsleazy as it could be. One sans-serif typeface carries the publication, composed very cleanly and decisively among photographs that are graphically bold and dynamically arranged. Simple pacing strategies—single page white, single page bleed, full-bleed spread, repeat—lead the reader through features but stay out of the way. No particularly unusual typographic devices or illustrative conceits are present. The understatement seems to have the effect of making the publication seem exclusive, targeting hip, high-end individuals despite the demographic implied in the title. Oceans of white space surround sans-serif headlines and decks set in one weight; short amounts of text are set against enormous images. The simplicity of the layouts creates a bloodcurdling chill of attitude. This chill is offset by the provocative quality of the photographs, which are given a great deal of space. Some are portraits of unusual personalities, relying on their charisma to carry the image and confront the reader; other images are utterly banal and, in their lack of character, add to the aloof, disaffected quality of the layouts themselves. The cold posture affected by the magazine may resonate with its audience, tired of busy, overworked layouts from other recent trends—as well as of popular magazines trying to cram helpful information into every available space—and looking for something clean with which to identify.

1

3

2

Sonic Youth

y

1, 3

Cover images and typography are about as cold and neutral as can be—absolutely deadpan. The images are flatly lit, devoid of contrast and emotional character; the typography of the masthead is equally banal. But somehow these treatments reek of "cool." It may be that the ladies' home magazine on the adjacent shelf is very slick and pretty; the extreme contrast to context creates subculture exclusion.

Flirty Harry

Although Blondie are back in the studio, these days Debbie Harry is more into acting. You'll soon be seeing her in the new gay porn flick The Fluffer. We share a sofa with New York's Downtown Queen.
Text Stuart Turnbull Photography Terry Richardson

Debbie Harry's presence permeates pop eternally, sublimely, segueing a well-rooted-in-the-underground stance with the commercial demands of the brash pop zeitgeist.

US universities run major courses that deconstruct the Madonna phenomenon while out in the real world the best cheekbones and lips in pop continue to house a sage-like grin that knows exactly where it's been and where it's going - namely anywhere that Harry can tickle people's preconceptions.

However, Harry, we have a problem with using the name 'Deborah' here. Our rational aversion to the full pronunciation of the moniker is on account of an unfortunate exposure to the 1970 T-Rex hit Deborah (not written with Harry in mind), on which Marc Bolan falsettos the misguided couplet, "Ooh, Deborah / You look like a Zebra." This combined with the fact she always was 'Debbie' in our mind's eye ushered a certain confusion when the machinations of a solo career and the independence-driven decision to reclaim the full length of her own name caused 'Debbie' to go 'Deborah'.

Out of respect for the lady, however, we shall here introduce her as Deborah Harry, a woman we encounter mid-morning one Thursday in New York City, while down Britain's alleyways scores of teenagers can still be found strolling in Blondie T-shirts, 1978 style.

But it's 2001?

"Hey. Well, wow, that's great. That's good to know. Yeah," enthuses the woman whose iconic visage continues to be screen-printed onto cloth. What's she up to now though?

"I'm doing great and feeling really good these days. Knock wood," she laughs, heartily. "How you doin'?... We're working on a new record," explains the Sunday Girl. "So it'll be interesting to see how that goes. It's always nice to make music."

Acting provides another favourite platform.

"I recently did a Sarah Kane play, Crave, at the Axis in Greenwich Village, I had a wonderful theatre ➤

050 SLEAZENATION.COM

SLEAZENATION.COM 051

SLEAZENATION.COM 073

Text Steven MacKinney
Photography Stefan Ruiz

PORN TO ROCK

THE WORLD OF PORN IS CHANGING, AND AS A RESULT SOME OF ITS MAIN STARS ARE PURSUING A BIT OF 'CAREER DIVERSIFICATION'. SLEAZE TAKES A LOOK AT THE SITUATION IN GENERAL AND SPEAKS TO HEATHER HUNTER (PICTURED - RATHER WELL, WE THINK) IN PARTICULAR.

Strange that: Pornography used to be purchased at low-grade bookstores on the wrong side of the tracks, transported to your house via an unmarked paper bag. Porn was dirty, the models in the magazines an anomaly, nameless bodies living so far away from mainstream society they didn't really exist. Desperate men and women needing money so badly they'd forego their dignity and betray their family to be photographed doing unspeakable acts. You knew they couldn't enjoy their 'line of work'; their facial expressions always asking, 'where's the cheque?' amidst the double-penetration and shag-carpeted floors of some generic wood-paneled basement ➤

064 SLEAZENATION.COM

SLEAZENATION.COM 065

2, 4, 5

The designer has a sense for scale and impact, shown in the strong juxtaposition of medium-sized headline; small byline; clean, justified columns; and asymmetrically cropped, high-contrast image—studies in typographic color and rhythms of black and white.

5

The potentially shocking nude is rendered non-sexual in the cold context of the white feature lead page and its enormous headline type. Rather than being "in" the image, the reader observes the image clinically, separated from the context of the layout by the stark division of the page down the gutter.

ECOS
InPraxis Kozept + Gestaltung | *Munich, Germany*

05

1

A travelogue-like photo-graphic treatment in the table of contents contributes to readers' excitement about the cultural and scenic aspects of the regions whose language they are learning.

2

The masthead, set all uppercase in a strong serif face, dominates the covers in conjunction with a full-bleed image. Cover images are interestingly cropped and lushly colored; secondary typography for teasers and leads is set in Trade Gothic.

3, 4

The flexible structure is constantly violated by callouts, sidebars, and insets in energetic layouts reminiscent of travel and lifestyle magazines. Circular cutouts, colored boxes, floating rules with captions, and other devices carry supporting information in a mixture of type styles and sizes. Color-coded graphic inclusions at the upper corners denote the current section—the golden orange indicates this spread is part of the *Secciones*.

A near-total immersion magazine for native German speakers uses conventions of travel and lifestyle magazines to appeal to its audience of readers learning the Spanish language. The majority of the magazine is set in Spanish to allow learners to experience the language full-on. Photography plays a key role in connecting content to meaning; images are selected not only for their romantic and illustrative qualities—aimed at conveying the emotional and cultural aspects of regions where Spanish is spoken—but also for their potential as contextual markers, almost translating on their behalf. Three sections are denoted in the table of contents: Secciones (editorial sections or departments);

Guía (the Guide, an "out-and-about" listing of the latest in Spanish CDs, film, books, and such); and a major editorial section. The feature stories are prominently exhibited with page numbers in a horizontal image band. Each section is listed below and distinctly color coded. Clever information design, however, extends beyond mere coloration to include linguistic coding and iconography that gives readers supporting content in their native language—German—in a seamless, behind-the-scenes approach. Editorial listings in the table of contents, for example, include the German translation directly underneath that of the Spanish, but in a much smaller size. Beginners can use the German to direct

them toward articles of interest, while more advanced readers can ignore them altogether. A system of icons is explained in Spanish, making readers connect the meaning of the symbol in Spanish with their intuitive understanding of the pictorial symbol. For additional support, notations in the contents and in text direct readers to supplemental online material. For the most part, text is set in a slightly condensed serif with moderate contrast; heads, decks, callouts, subheads, captions, and diagrammatic type appear in the Trade Gothic family.

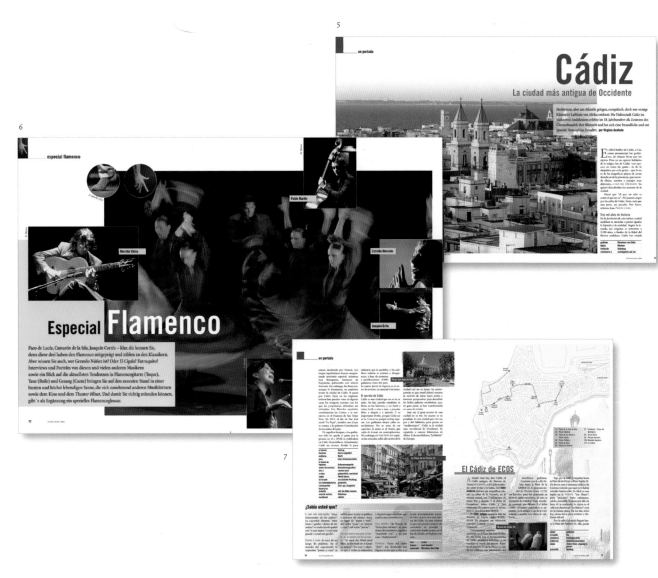

5

Decks are set in German to allow initial entry and establish context for readers to work through translation as they go. Every article includes a standard callout—generally in a tinted or colored box and indicated by a tabbed configuration of words—that lists vocabulary words and their meanings in German, each separated by a dotted horizontal rule.

5, 6

In the feature story openers, a large image (or collaged grouping of several images) dominates the spread. The typography for feature titles tends to be very active, giving way to more staid treatments in following spreads while images remain relatively active in their arrangement.

6, 7

Floating captions in colored bars add movement, interacting with both image and text areas. They often carry informational markers that connect the caption text to other images, maps, or diagrams.

Cantatto
Designwork SrL | *Udine, Italy*

06

A quarterly publication for a theater group makes use of bold type treatments and intriguing, evocative performance photographs to attract audiences and communicate with its membership of contemporary theater lovers. The small-format magazine—roughly 6" x 8" (15.2 x 20.3 cm)—is printed in process color on an uncoated stock, giving it an intimate, personal feel. In contrast, the typography throughout, set in a combination of slab serif and sans-serif gothic faces, is wildly articulated in a system of large sizes, albeit on a four-column modular grid. The tension between the small-format space and large, highly active text is engagingly theatrical in its own right, with treatments of size and style distributed among text components in varied ways. Titles and callouts are allowed to cross the gutter, as well as overlay photo-

graphs, unifying the page spreads in their composition and creating a dialogue of movement and texture between images and type. While heads, decks, and subheads shift around in treatment, the text generally appears in smaller sizes and is more closely related to the grid structure. The majority of the magazine highlights specific performances—both past and future—within a given season, along with profiles of actors, writers, and directors. A calendar and other supporting information is found toward the back, also structured more informationally on the grid; large-scale typographic elements call out specifics and continue the dynamic visual logic of the editorial spreads.

1, 2

In these spreads, varied treatment of editorial headlines, decks, subheads, and callouts—different sizes, different typefaces, and staggered alignments—pay homage to the grid underneath but interact with the photography as the callouts do on the cover. The large title in one spread (1), crossing the gutter, counters the upward motion of the figure with its aggressive horizontal emphasis.

1

2

3

1, 6

Photographs are composed as single- or double-page bleeds, depending on their subject and composition. Varying the image proportions helps introduce additional rhythm to the spreads and changes the illusory spatial depth of the typography. Here, the type becomes part of the image, floating in and around the figure at various levels.

3

The relatively sedate table of contents, arranged informationally on the grid, provides no clue as to the dynamic typography to come.

4

Full-bleed images provide a field for content callouts that reference the grid structure within. One feature is given prominence in larger-sized type. The callouts move up and down within their columns in response to the composition of the images behind them. A typographically concise masthead, set in a condensed sans serif against a colored box, includes the issue number as part of its structure.

5

Informational spreads, such as this one, return the text to a more restrained presentation, hanging from different flowlines with each issue to accommodate the presence of inset photographs or large numerals.

Nordic Reach
Flat | Petter Ringbom | *New York City, USA*

07

An eminently stylish magazine devoted to Scandinavian design and culture at large, *Nordic Reach* employs a standard editorial grid—two- and three-column compound—in remarkably unconventional ways. By inventively mixing the irregular outlines of silhouetted images with abstract geometric textures and shapes, enclosing paragraphs in boxes of color, and shifting material around the grid unexpectedly, the designers create an almost organic movement through editorial space. Stunning photography of Scandinavian landscapes, architecture, and fashions (sometimes mixed together) show a high degree of art direction, appearing unnaturally vibrant, theatrical, and almost mannered in their presentation. This operatic quality extends to images of objects, their silhouetted forms often lit to accentuate their sculptural aspects. Portrait images run from naturalistic to highly posed compositions. Linking this variety of imagery together is a system of decorative abstract details pulled from Scandinavian textiles, carving, and printing. The spatial drama created by the interaction of real and abstract space, flat decoration, and vivid photography conveys the intensity and physicality of Scandinavian people, their connection to art in daily life, and their history as energetic conquerors . . . once of land, now of style.

1

RENAISSANCE ART
for RENAISSANCE PEOPLE

Norwegian artist Vebjørn Sand is not only inspired by Renaissance and Baroque painters such as Leonardo da Vinci and Rembrandt, he is proud to be one himself.

Based in New York for the last four years, Sand, 37, received a classical art education at the National Academy of Art in Oslo, the Academy of Art in Prague and the Art Students League of New York. He is also as interested in mathematics and philosophy as he is in painting.

In his home country, Sand is something of an art celebrity, best known for public art projects such as his outdoor exhibition in 1997 of paintings from two expeditions to Antarctica. The exhibition, with the myth-inspired name Trollslottet (Troll Palace, from a Nordic fairy tale), attracted more than 150,000 visitors in three months, the largest audience ever for a living artist in Norway.

His second project, the Kepler Star (named after astronomer Johannes Kepler), was constructed near Oslo Airport. His third project, the world-renowned Leonardo Bridge, is based on a bridge originally created in 1502 as a tiny drawing by Leonardo da Vinci. Now, 500 years later, da Vinci's vision has been realized, as a pedestrian bridge across highway E18 in Ås outside Oslo. There are long-term plans to build similar bridges around the world with possible projects in the United States, Italy and even Turkey, where Da Vinci originally intended to build the design.

The stereo in Sand's Manhattan studio played baroque music during our visit. On easels at the far end of the room sat a painting reminiscent of 19th-century Swedish artist Anders Zorn and another using Renaissance imagery. Sand talked about his experiences painting in Antarctica.

Norway had annexed a huge area known as Queen Maud Land of Antarctica by the end of the 1930s, he explained. The country had an active whaling industry there and Roald Amundsen's expedition to the South Pole had taken place in 1911, creating a great deal of interest among Norwegians in the sub-continent. This interest continues and inspired two expeditions in the mid-1990s to the Norwegian territory. He was invited along to record his visual impressions of the experience.

"Our intention was to be the first to reach Norway's highest peak in Antarctica, Jøkulkyrkja (3148 meters)," Sand said. "We skied cross-country and climbed. In the old days, the big expeditions always brought a painter. For instance, Amundsen's British competitor Robert Scott's ill-fated expedition of 1912 had Edward Wilson, whom

NORDIC REACH | No. 9 VOLUME XVII

2

2

NORDIC**REACH**
A QUARTERLY OF SCANDINAVIAN CULTURE, NUMBER 9, VOLUME XVII

what
women
want

THE NEW NORDIC MAN: DESIGN, DENMARK, IKEA'S FOUNDER IN RARE INTERVIEW.

1

Feature stories, especially those focused on personalities, reflect a more formal editorial approach, beginning with head and deck set centered over two justified columns. The formal structure is often contrasted by decorative illustrative motifs. Portraiture in such stories is almost regal in its presentation; even the "naturalistic" portraits are noticeably affected by their lighting and composition.

2

Surreally stylish photographs are given prominence on the covers, separated from the masthead area by a band of color. The masthead's typographic austerity— all-uppercase setting of a neutral sans serif in one weight—contrasts the intricate detail and figurative subject of the images, while the band plays off their dominant color. In selecting images in which odd details or unusual settings conflict with the pristine clarity of the photograph— as in the image of the woman suggestively eating a heart-shaped piece of chocolate—the art directors introduce irreverent associations, skewing the image away from mere representation. The inclusion of a little mystery intrigues and titillates.

Two type families are used interchangeably for all text components, although specific informational tags, such as a section's running head, remain consistently treated in small-size uppercase setting. The serif type family appears mostly in running text, although it is also used in callouts and for formal, austere title setting. The sans serif is slightly condensed and exhibits characteristics of historical serif texts, such as ligatures, that link it not only to the serif but also to the sense of cultural continuum conveyed through the contemporary application of images and text to a very traditional structure.

3, 4, 6

Spreads alternately mix two- and three-column grids, sometimes from page to page. The more horizontal emphasis of the wider columns contrasts the vertical motion of the narrower columns; these structural changes allow the designers to explore more fully the ambiguous spatial qualities of images and abstractions.

5–7

Editorial department sections are laid out using a more systematic, grid-based approach. Pages in this section tend to adhere to the three-column structure, using reversed-out boxes to support text, and other geometric treatments such as horizontal bans of color, to support text and visually relate the pages.

Nationaal Archief
UNA (Amsterdam) Designers | *Amsterdam, Netherlands*

This magazine, produced for the Dutch Nationaal Archief, highlights materials in the collections and promotes awareness of the archive as a resource for research, exhibitions, and education. Unlike many magazines for municipal museums or archives, which tend to be very conservative, this one is designed in a contemporary idiom, using only sans-serif type, set flush left, in asymmetrical arrangements on a tight twelve-column modular grid. Providing a public institution of such historical importance as the Archief—which houses 1,000 years of Dutch political and social history in documents, maps, photographs, registries, and drawings—a forward visual presentation creates a powerful connection with the public, who are more apt to be interested in institutions that appear relevant to their everyday lives. Interestingly, the clean geometry of the compositional and typographic elements contrasts sharply with many of the documents being shown, highlighting their individual characters and period resonance. Neutral informational markers for sections, which run as footers near the folios at the bottom of the pages, provide subtle and consistent navigation, while allowing the headlines and decks for features to interact with specific imagery and

1

1
The structure of the table of contents is consistent from issue to issue. An image cropping at left, colophon, and complete contents listing, as well as introductory statement from the director, run sequentially left to right above a black band that houses supporting material—image caption, contents head (*Inhoud*) with folio, and director's byline and photo. The geometry of the band, rules, and columns, as well as the informational distinction provided by simple weight and scale changes, are both visible along this band at the bottom of the page.

2
A systematic organization of cover material can be seen in these three examples. While the black masthead band at the bottom—which includes a remarkably small logotype—remains consistent, the vertical division of image and color, as well as headline size, varies from issue to issue. The power of discreet typographic elements to clarify information is clear even here: of the four columns of text in the black band, three are clearly related as content features by a white hairline rule.

bands of color as seems appropriate. The grid is most often used in a three-column configuration, although four columns is also common; the true precision of the grid becomes evident on a rare basis in smaller intervals that separate captions and insets along the foot and in the table of contents. Sensitive, direct, and often inventive typesetting—with clear distinctions among hierarchic components—lends credibility and ease of use to the stately, yet inviting, publication.

3, 4

Complex arrangements of large-scale feature heads, deck paragraphs, colorful blocks, and transparent colored overlays speak to the subtle direction that the grid provides—rigorous unity, but also more options for how elements interact in layouts.

The title type in these spreads, for example, rests on a lower baseline that crosses the boundary between image and band; large images may appear to slide behind text.

5

Type in the Vitrine section, which focuses on a specific document, runs vertically in five columns traveling up the outer edges of the format. The rotation of the type—and its reversal out of vivid red bars that distinguish this section—enhances the quality of the document being enclosed in a case for viewing.

3

4

5

3–5

Each section—Nieuws, Actueel, Vitrine—begins with a footer at lower left of the left-hand page; captions for all images follow at this flowline under a rule. Note the asymmetrical location of the folios on left and right pages.

Down Low
Eggers + Diaper | Berlin, Germany

The design of this magazine challenges assumptions about the systematic nature of, and requirement for consistency in, publications by continually changing every visual aspect of its layout from page to page and from issue to issue. Contrary to standard practice, the designers have tossed aside conventional ideas about brand recognition in aid of a more important concept—communicating the ever-changing, eclectic energy of hip-hop music and resonating with the wildly diverse subculture that goes with it. Every issue—and, more surprisingly, every article—is approached with a clean slate in terms of layout, typography, and image; everything goes. Like the musical genre it represents, the magazine becomes a DJ's mix of design influences and type styles, sampled images and textural electronic abstractions. Page spreads are just as likely to be poetic, highly active decon-structions of language in twenty typefaces and sizes as they are slick, grid-based layouts that borrow from avant-garde corporate design or hand-generated collages. Even folios and the table of contents change. In one sense, this undefined mix of stylistic explorations is a highly branded system of randomness, easily distinguished from competing publications because it is so obviously different all the time. And it is as much an opportunity for its designers to reinvent on a continuous basis as it is an appropriate, targeted experience that readers can experience anew every issue.

1, 2

Violating a cardinal rule for masthead design, these two covers show radically different type treatments and arrangements for the magazine's title. The consistency of difference, however, in itself becomes a kind of branding—readers' expectations of finding a new kind of visual presentation in each issue positions the magazine against its competition.

1

2

3

4

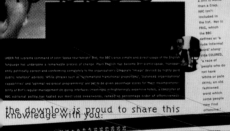

3, 5

Careful attention is paid to the effects of typographic color changes so that, despite the frenetic texture of the layout, the text is still accessible. The designers use weight and scale change to create entry points for the reader within the overall composition; readers may opt to begin the text at different points, assembling the complete sequence themselves.

4, 6

The magazine's fluid design approach allows spreads such as these—one a dynamic texture of body copy and callouts, the other a heavily grid-based column layout—to coexist, and even follow each other, within the same issue. Conceptually, the variety of formal approaches is similar to music sampling or mixing.

Literature Systems

Corporate and Nonprofit Branding Systems:
Brochure Families, Mailers, and Serial Literature

1

1

The conceptual simplicity
of the cover panels makes
great use of the gallery's
location on the water as
a metaphor for film. Each
edition of the calendar
mailer shows the same
scene, changing with the
seasons. The color and
layout decisions are made
by nature.

Hafen 2
U9 Visuelle Allianz | *Offenbach, Germany*

10

Clever layout and folding of a poster format create a series of mailers or take-away brochures for a gallery and film center in Offenbach, Germany. The large poster format organizes a calendar of screenings and other events—the primary content of the poster/mailer—into a modular structure of toned rectangles. Since the number of events changes each mailing, every arrangement of informational modules is different. Furthermore, an oversized rectangle with seasonal or event-related content is arranged playfully around the regularly spaced ones, and its color changes each issue. Within each module, a simple hierarchic system of weight and size changes for the information is enhanced by a color break between elements in black ink and white knockout. The typography, in general, is minimal in treatment: one sans serif face, primarily in bold weight, is used throughout. Size and color changes lend some contrast. The module proportions are defined by the measurements of the panels when the poster is folded. Folding the poster in half and then into a series of accordion panels results in a narrow, envelope-shaped format that presents a photographic image on top and address information on the bottom. Although image changes with every edition of the mailer, it is noticeably a repeated scene of the river outside the gallery's location in Offenbach. The scenes are photographed at the time of a given mailing; the winter ones, for example, show the banks devoid of leaves, while others show greenery and summer boats. In essence, the snapshot on the outside of the mailer becomes the frame of a long, slow film that changes over time.

2

Simply moving the block rectangles around the modular structure creates dramatic change from mailer to mailer. The arrangement is based on calendar sequencing, so the rhythm of blocks and negative spaces has some basis in the informational structure.

3

A promotional field of color violates the neutral modularity of the grid in each edition.

4

Hierarchic distinctions within the gray modules are created through value relationships of the type to the background.

New York City DA's Office
C. Harvey Graphic Design | *New York City, USA*

11

This literature system for a New York City government agency demonstrates the clarity afforded by a simple structure and production values. A single cover image, well-considered interior illustrations, and user-friendly typography distinguish the system. This no-nonsense approach is appropriate for the sober nature of the client, its execution yielding an elegant and useful communication system that respects the reader. Two format proportions are used for different publications in the system. A narrow vertical format is used for informational service and resource pamphlets, appearing as two- or three-panel folded flats, or as a narrow saddle-stitched booklet with eight pages or more. A wider format is used for extensive informational texts. A universal mustard-yellow ink provides consistency, while secondary colors from a contrasting palette allow the designer flexibility

and effectively differentiate the brochures from each other. Type, legible in both the gold and all the secondary colors, is distributed among informational components to clarify typographic hierarchy: text and images appear in the second ink color, while callouts and heads appear in the gold ink. Images are reproduced only in the secondary color. A clear system of typographic treatments differentiates hierarchical components and flows consistently across a simple hierarchical two-column grid. The degree of concern given to the typography becomes apparent in the column width (selected for optimal character fit and rag) and the myriad textual treatments (acronyms, custom punctuation styles, hanging bullets, and ligatures).

1

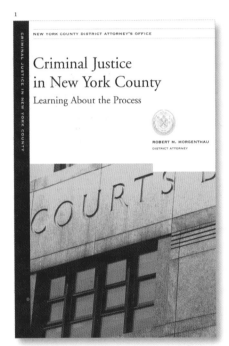

2

1–5

Three type families interact to produce a variety of texture. An oldstyle serif is used mainly for text; a slightly condensed sans serif provides contrast but shares proportions with the serif. Copperplate Gothic, set all caps for detailed heads, offers additional contrast in width and also brings an appropriate sobriety and historical note to the communication.

2

The covers, though different in proportion, adhere to the same basic structure. Large, crisp title type contrasts with the detail type and the muted contrast of the images; the images themselves contrast with the geometric shapes that enclose them, restated in the horizontal bands in the head margins of the interiors. The images themselves are intriguing in their cropping and composition, despite being recognizable; the potentially sinister aspects of public law are subtly conveyed through this intrigue.

3

ROBERT M. MORGENTHAU
DISTRICT ATTORNEY

The Office of the District Attorney of the County of New York has the responsibility and authority to investigate and prosecute crimes in the borough of Manhattan. In each case we bring before the court, our office represents "The People of the State of New York." As the elected District Attorney of Manhattan since 1975, I have committed myself to upholding the laws of the State of New York without fear or favor and to making sure that justice is done in every case. In continuing the office's tradition of making the criminal justice system accessible to the residents of New York, we have created this brochure. This guide and legal glossary is designed to explain and clarify the criminal justice process in New York County.

Sincerely,

Robert M. Morgenthau

In the majority of cases, an arrest is the first stage in the criminal justice process.

THE POLICE AND THE ARREST

What is the function of the police?
The police investigate crimes and arrest individuals who are suspected of committing crimes.

What is a lawful arrest?
Most criminal actions begin when a person is taken into police custody. An arrest is lawful when the police officer has probable cause to believe that the person being arrested has committed a particular offense.

What happens when someone is arrested?
Once the defendant is in custody, he may be identified by the victim or witnesses, and he may make a statement to the police. He will always be searched, and the officers are entitled to seize any contraband or evidence found during the search. Evidence includes the proceeds of the crime, any tools used to commit the crime, distinctive clothing, or other evidence that helps to connect the defendant with the victim or the scene of the crime. The arresting officer takes

4

THE NEW YORK CITY CRIMINAL COURT

Almost all Manhattan cases are arraigned in the Criminal Court of the City of New York. After arraignment, the Criminal Court handles only misdemeanors and violations. The Supreme Court of the State of New York handles felony cases.

What is the function of the Courts?
The Courts are charged with ensuring the fair application of the law. Judges preside over all legal proceedings in court.

Almost all Manhattan cases — felonies, misdemeanors, and violations — are arraigned in the Criminal Court of the City of New York.

Arraignment Parts are staffed in Criminal Court seven days a week, 365 days a year. During busy times, an Arraignment Part is open through the night. After arraignment, Criminal Court handles only misdemeanors and violations. The Supreme Court of the State of New York handles felony cases. (Note: in New York State, the highest appellate court is the Court of Appeals, not, as one might expect from the name, the Supreme Court.)

What is an arraignment?
In New York City, defendants are usually brought before a judge of the Criminal Court of the City of New York for arraignment within twenty-four hours of arrest. Once the case has been docketed by the Court and the complaint and the defendant's criminal history are ready, the defendant is produced for arraignment in Criminal Court.

At arraignment in Criminal Court, the defendant is informed of the charges against him and a bail determination is made. He is also given various notices, including: whether the case will be considered by a Grand Jury; whether he made statements to the police; and whether there was an identification by witnesses. If the defendant cannot afford an attorney, one is appointed prior to the arraignment.

THE NEW YORK CITY CRIMINAL COURT (continued)

At arraignment, the defendant is brought before a judge and informed of the charges against him or her. In Manhattan, defendants are usually arraigned in less than 24 hours.

If the defendant is charged with a violation or a misdemeanor, he may plead guilty at arraignment. In a few cases, a defendant charged with a felony is offered a misdemeanor plea at arraignment. Many defendants plead guilty at arraignment, though guilty pleas also can be entered at later stages in the case. The defendant can plead guilty to all of the charges in the complaint, or to a lesser charge when offered by the Assistant District Attorney. A defendant cannot plead guilty to a felony at arraignment. If a defendant pleads guilty, the judge delivers the sentence.

What is Bail and How is it Set?
Bail is collateral, in the form of cash or bond, that must be posted by the defendant to ensure that he or she returns to court on a future date.

If appropriate, the ADA in the Arraignment Part will request that bail be set and give reasons for the bail conditions requested. Once the defense counsel responds, the court will set the bail amount. If the defendant posts the amount of money required to make bail, he or she will be released. A defendant can also be released on his own recognizance ("ROR'd") if the court feels that bail is unnecessary. If the case is particularly serious, the court may remand the defendant, who is then held in custody without bail.

COURTS

continued on next page

5

ROBERT M. MORGENTHAU
DISTRICT ATTORNEY

Dear Friends,
In 1987, I created the Northern Manhattan Office to provide the residents north of 96th Street with easy access to the resources of the District Attorney's Office. By addressing problems relating to domestic violence, criminal trespass, drugs, elder abuse, and fraud, this office has become a vital link between community residents and law enforcement officials. This brochure will explain the resources available through this office. The staff of the Northern Manhattan Office is here to help you.

Sincerely,

Robert M. Morgenthau

INTRODUCTION

How can the Northern Manhattan Office help me?

If you are a crime victim, a concerned citizen, or a member of a community organization, the staff of the Northern Manhattan Office can help you by:

• Conducting interviews with crime victims or witnesses;

• Meeting with victims, witnesses and their families to assess their social, emotional, and financial needs;

• Talking to you or your group about a local crime concern and working with you and the police department to develop a solution;

• Receiving complaints from the public about matters that may be criminal in nature, such as fraud and elder abuse;

• Explaining the court process and orders of protection; and

• Providing you with referrals to community agencies that can offer you additional direct services.

AVAILABLE SERVICES

The Domestic Violence Project
Domestic Violence Coordinators meet with victims of domestic violence in a safe and supportive environment. Victims learn about their available choices, orders of protection, and the difference between Family Court and Criminal Court. Should criminal prosecution be necessary, victims will speak to an Assistant District Attorney. The coordinators will also provide referrals to services for domestic violence victims within the community. Children are welcome in the office.

Community Affairs Unit
The unit provides assistance to block associations, tenant groups, and other organizations seeking to solve neighborhood crime problems, such as drugs and criminal trespassing. The Unit also offers educational programs for individuals, schools and organizations that want to learn more about the criminal justice system.

Special Prosecutions Bureau
Residents can write, call, or visit this office to make a complaint about matters that may be criminal in nature, such as fraud and elder abuse. All complaints are confidential.

Witness Aid Services Unit (WASU)
The unit provides a variety of social services, counseling services, and court-related services designed to meet the needs of crime victims and witnesses who have cases in the District Attorney's Office.

3

Careful use of two colors of ink creates unity in the system and clarifies the informational structure. The primary gold identity color defines major headlines and subheads. The secondary colors in the palette have been carefully selected for their similar value; some are more intense, but all will reproduce legibly at small sizes.

3–5

Solid bands of color mark the primary text column and section heads. A pale tint of the primary color indicates the narrow column used for support information.

4, 5

The grid is consistent between the narrow and wide formats; the primary text column in both is the same. In the wider format, the left margin is considered to be a second column that contains supporting information and images.

Museo Ascona
Studio di Prottegazione Grafica | *Cevio, Switzerland*

12

A flexible system of long, accordion-folded formats and a single, gothic sans-serif type family provides a consistent visual underpinning for a museum's exhibition announcements and schedules. Every edition in the series has a front and a back side. Folded down, the format is handy for carrying around in a pocket, and the panel left showing as a cover identifies the museum and a given exhibition. The front sides are given to expansive uses of images, shapes, fields of color, and primary informational text—the exhibition title and its dates, promotional and descriptive copy, information about related lectures, opening events, or supplemental shows. The designers use this long horizontal panel as a place to organize information—which is always different—to correspond directly to whatever images and shapes they use to give the exhibition a visual identity.

Usually, the composition of images shown directly affects the layout of the typography, so that while the single type family is consistent, the structure is always different. Shapes and colors used on the front side often derive from the exhibition and its promotional posters, usually designed by the same team. The reverse side of the format is given to supplemental information—exhibited artist's biography, additional scheduling information—usually running in three languages. The text is set all one size, in two columns per panel fold, while each language is set in a horizontal band, separated by hairline rules.

1

The designers often employ abstract geometric shapes in combination with photographic images. Here, the surprint of color in the shapes—and in the areas where the color does not print—creates interesting spatial ambiguities that may allude to the ambiguity of the featured artist's works.

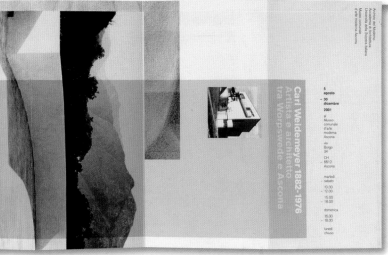

1, 4

The long format and its multiple panels allow for a great deal of flexibility in laying out material for a given exhibition. Sometimes, the panels are used to break the space and separate different text components (1), while at other times, the full width is used as an uninterrupted field for composing images and text (4).

2–4

Text on the promotional side may be simple (2, 4) or highly complex (3). The type is allowed to follow the image for cues to its layout, mimicking or contrasting compositional elements. Because of the consistent use of only one typeface for all the publications, the variation required to accommodate different typographic necessities doesn't compromise brand (identity) recognition.

5

The informational (reverse) sides of the pieces often reproduce text in several languages. Here, a biography of the featured artist is set in Italian, German, and English, separated by hairline rules. Notice how the text length varies among the different languages; the solution to the problems of fitting and structuring the layout to accommodate variations in informational complexity requires accounting for the worst possible scenario—the longest. The presentation of the text needs to look decisive and intentional whether it runs long or short. The grid also accommodates supporting images when desired.

Gilbert Paper
Worksight | Scott and Emily Santoro |
New York City, USA

13

These two paper promotions explore regional Americana as a vehicle for showcasing a manufacturer's products. Each uses vernacular imagery and typography derived from its respective subject to create conceptual and visual backdrops in which the target audience—graphic designers—can see content in action and its integration with various paper stocks. The messages created by the subject matter are layered, branding the manufacturer as an American company interested in preserving cultural history and communicating with designers whose personal experiences may relate to the regions selected for exploration. By giving the promotions actual content—rather than presenting the paper stocks in a conventional swatchbook with dry specification text—the designer further engages the audience and allows a kind of real-world application to drive the use

of the paper stocks in appropriate and easily understood ways. Though each brochure draws its imagery and typography from its respective regional subject, an overall visual logic is evident. Several horizontal intervals are used repeatedly for text alignments; type sizes and styles change consistently; and dramatic integrations of photography, illustration, type that jumps and slides around in arcs and angles, and abstract geometric and textural forms. Textured stocks and vellum flysheets, along with a variety of printing processes, add dimension.

1

2

4

1, 2, 6

Each booklet focuses on a region important to American cultural history. These two examples explore the American West and Coney Island, an amusement park and beach resort in Brooklyn, New York.

Historical references are delivered primarily through typeface selection, color, and organization.

3

3, 4

Changing paper stocks enables designers to see how different ink processes and color combinations feel on the papers being shown. The translucent stock provides an opportunity to mix information on the front and rear layers of the sheet with the opaque surfaces with which it interacts.

5

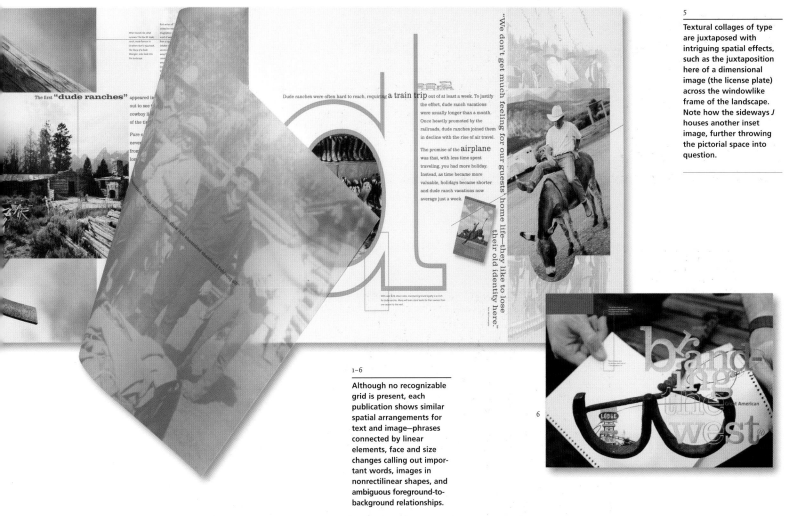

5

Textural collages of type are juxtaposed with intriguing spatial effects, such as the juxtaposition here of a dimensional image (the license plate) across the windowlike frame of the landscape. Note how the sideways *J* houses another inset image, further throwing the pictorial space into question.

1–6

Although no recognizable grid is present, each publication shows similar spatial arrangements for text and image—phrases connected by linear elements, face and size changes calling out important words, images in nonrectilinear shapes, and ambiguous foreground-to-background relationships.

6

Baltic

Blue River Design | *Newcastle-upon-Tyne, United Kingdom*

The multiple formats in this system of exhibition and event announcements for an art museum are unified structurally by a single column width and text size for running text, and a single larger size for titling. The two different formats, for example, both use the same column width, but the wider one distributes text in two columns, while the narrow, accordion-fold format uses a single column on each panel. One size governs the titling on the covers of both formats as well, creating an interesting opportunity to rotate the title on the narrow format so that it reads vertically. The type is similarly constrained in style, with a condensed gothic in uppercase for titling, and a rounder grotesk in two weights used for subheads, text, and captions. An equally simple color scheme—made up predominantly of black ink printed on white stock, with process cyan and magenta used for covers and accents—adds to the system's decisively uncomplicated presentation. The result is a series of highly recognizable, yet stylistically neutral, publications that allow images of the featured exhibitions to exist without conflicting with the system or with each other.

1

2

3

4

5

1, 2, 4, 5

Covers of the collateral feature a bold, condensed sans-serif gothic for titling. The stark contrast of the branding typeface against solid backgrounds is a simple but memorable language for the system.

2, 3

Mixed use of two- and three-column structures allows for a range of content in a neutral and flexible environment.

O'Neill Printing
Rule29 Design | *Elburn (IL), USA*

15

An interrelated system of icons, images, and marketing concepts provides the basis for a printer's family of branded promotional literature, including a system of postcards and brochures. Four base concepts—ink, paper, people, and craft—are assigned a custom icon, a selection of photographic images, and sets of body copy that vary in length and depth. Using the components from this "kit of parts" in different combinations on materials that will reach their audience at different times and in different contexts breaks up the communication into concise messages that can be used over time.

One major benefit of this approach is that it affords the company the opportunity to contact prospects continually on a periodic basis, each time building on previous communications and keeping the company "top of mind." The series of postcards, for example, can be mailed to cold contacts to create opportunities for dialogue; they are brief, inexpensive to produce, and nonrepetitive. The smaller brochure can be used as a more involved entrée after the sequence of cards is exhausted, or as a leave-behind for current clients after meetings or during the course of a particular project; it brings together several of the message components in a similarly concise, but slightly more involved way, becoming somewhat editorial. The larger brochure is a more in-depth capabilities document; its involved design and production techniques—multiple paper stocks, printing processes, gatefolds, and die cuts provide a demonstration of the company's core competency with a harder sell and flashier visual language. Consistent use of three complementary type families, along with the icon drawings and a simple color palette, unifies the various pieces.

1

1

A system of concise, inexpensive postcards is used as an entrée to developing business from cold contacts, as well as a periodic reminder of the printing company's expertise and approach. The postcards' small size permits them to be printed ganged up and in volume, offsetting the expected cost of four-color printing, which is used to carry photographic images that support the icons assigned to each concept.

2

2–4

The capabilities brochure expands on the typographic base, adding print-process registration marks, color bars, rules, and other graphic elements in a more abstract combination with photography.

3

4

Jewish Museum Berlin
Eggers + Diaper | *Berlin, Germany*

A simple, yet lively, abstract visual language helps unify a museum's diverse array of publications. As is often the case with cultural institutions of this kind, creating informational and promotional material that is both adequately branded, continually refreshing, and appropriately tailored—on both a visual and conceptual level—to radically different subjects presents a unique challenge. To solve this problem in an engaging way that allows for flexibility and evolution over time, the designers of this literature system have defined a visual language of horizontal banding—manifested primarily in a series of colored strips, but in format selection as well—that derives from the border treatment of the tallit. This abstracted representation of a highly recognizable and meaningful symbol not only adds conceptual depth but also offers endless possibility for variation across publications. The form can be hinted at subtly by a long horizontal format, or it can be made explicit. Additionally, the geometric nature of the band can be used as a device for housing typographic elements such as headers or captions, for separating informational components, and for clarifying complex information structures such as calendars, maps, or schedules. The use of

1

2

3

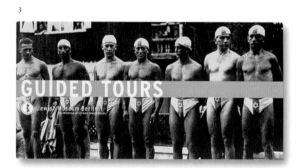

4

1–3

In the foldout monthly informational brochures, the identifying horizontal proportion is again in evidence; the cover panel comfortably holds abbreviated edition dates, as well as a background image. Unfolded, the piece becomes vertical, but the horizontal strip asserts itself as an informational device, highlighting exhibitions and events of particular importance. A tabular gridded structure distinguishes dates, times, and subject listings. The colored square on the last panel becomes horizontal in relation to the vertically oriented signature.

5

color in the banding helps carry brand into publications that may otherwise be lacking in color. Applying this visual language in all these ways creates a rich and varied experience for museum goers. Of course, this strong visual concept is not the sole visual identifier for the publications. A specific palette of colors, along with a house type family—a condensed sans serif with unusual terminals—articulated in a highly informational way over tabular and modular grid structures, all contribute to the system's accessibility and character.

7–10

Well-considered informational diagrams and vellum flysheets, with opaque abstract elements distilled from the photographs they overlay, add informational depth and visual interest to this elegant brochure promoting the museum's functional spaces. The translucent vellum, because of its long, horizontal proportion, becomes an interactive version of the branding language.

6

7

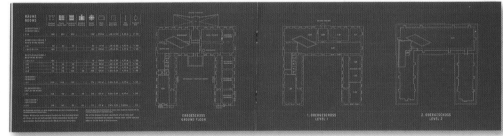

8

9

10

3–6

The covers of three collateral pieces, while very different in format and color, are visually branded with literal or proportional reference to the horizontal strips of color that define the system. In the stepped brochure (5), the horizontal band becomes a codng device for content.

6

By reorienting the colored strips to the vertical edges of this stepped-format brochure, the designers are able to accommodate its specific spatial requirements for content, yet maintain its brand association. As an added bonus, the now-vertical strips become navigation tools, helping separate content from page to page. The cross-cut image, in its entirety, is another horizontal band.

rundherum

Büro für Zukunftsfragen
Wir fördern Engagement.
Wir bringen Menschen zusammen.
Und Themen. Für eine Nachhaltige Entwicklung.

Wir können auch anders.

Autofreier Tag 2004
Wir können auch anders

Am 22. September 2004 findet der diesjährige Autofreie
wird die europäische Woche der Mobilität abgehalten.
und Verkehrssicherheit." In den letzten Jahren war vorarlberg.at
beteiligten sich letztes Jahr 36 Vorarlberger Städte und G
und die Eigeninitiative vor Ort zurückzuführen ist. Um an
Schulen, Kindergärten, Unternehmen sowie Einzelne aufg

Nähere Informationen:
Die Koordinierung des Autofreien
Tages übernimmt wie gewohnt das
Büro für Zukunftsfragen im Amt
der Vorarlberger Landesregierung.
Wenn Sie sich dafür interessieren,
wenden Sie sich einfach an uns!

Autofreier Tag:
Wir können auch anders
22. September 2004

Ansprechpartner:
Büro für Zukunftsfragen
Karla Tschofen
T +43 (0)5574/511-20800
karla.tschofen@vorarlberg.at
www.vorarlberg.at/zukunft

Sanfte Mobilität ko
Der jährliche Autofreie Tag so
sie von der Gemeinde erhalten,
öffentlichen Verkehrsmittel oder
zu gehen oder mit dem Fahrrad z

Wie Sie sich beteiligen
Nutzen Sie als Gemeinde diesen S
was vor Ort zur Vermeidung von Ver
das Angebot vor Ort besser kennen z
Aufmerksamkeit der Medien an diese

Welche Art von Aktionen - Unsere Vorschläge
. Ausgewählte Plätze und Straßen - zumindest für diesen Tag - als autofreie Zone ausweisen
. Fuß- und Radwege und den öffentlichen Verkehr mit Festen, Aktionen usw. ins Rampenlicht rücken
. auf bestehende Nahversorger aufmerksam machen, die den Verzicht aufs Auto erleichtern
. Schulaktionen im Rahmen der Grüne Meilen-Kampagne durchführen
Weitere Beispiele aus den Gemeinden sowie Institutionen, die Sie bei Ihren Aktionen unterstützen,
finden Sie unter www.vorarlberg.at/zukunft. Bisher haben sich bereits 26 Gemeinden angemeldet!

Das diesjährige Thema: Kinder
Heuer fällt der Autofreie Tag auf einen Mittwoch und steht unter dem Motto „Kinder und Verkehrs-
sicherheit". Sichere Straßen für Kinder und Jugendliche stehen daher im Mittelpunkt. Weitere
Informationen erhalten Sie auf der Homepage des Klimabündnisses (http://www.klimabuendnis.at).
Natürlich steht Ihnen auch das Büro für Zukunftsfragen gerne für Auskünfte zur Verfügung.

rundherum

Wir fördern Engagement.
Wir bringen Menschen zusammen.
Und Themen. Für eine Nachhaltige Entwicklung.

Wir können auch anders.

Kinder in die Mitte nehmen -
Miteinander der Generationen

...ertung...
...vag wahr, um
...en zu lassen. Die besondere
...unterstützen

und herum

Geschicklichkeits -
Spiel - Nachhaltigkeit
begeisterte
Messebesucher

Nachhaltigkeit als die Kunst, mehrere Bereiche auszu-
balancieren - Diese Erfahrung konnten viele Besucher
der Dornbirner Herbstmesse am eigenen Leib machen.
Unser Geschicklichkeits - Spiel - Nachhaltigkeit, ein
lebensgroß nachgebautes „Kugelspiel" machte das
möglich: Im Team sollten vier Kugeln versenkt werden,
und zwar je eine im Bereich Umwelt, Soziales, Wirt
schaft und Globale Verantwortung. Spielerisch wurde
dabei gezeigt, dass der Weg zur Nachhaltigkeit nicht
immer leicht ist. Denn: Nachhaltigkeit ist erreicht, wenn
alle vier Bereiche - also Umwelt, Gesellschaft und
Soziales, Wirtschaft und Beschäftigung sowie Globale
Verantwortung - im Einklang sind.

Nähere Infos: Büro für Zukunftsfragen, Bertram
Meusburger, T 05574 511 20612, bertram.meusburger @
vorarlberg.at

Newsletters

Monthly and Quarterly Small-Format News Organs
from Corporations and Cultural Institutions

Rund Herum
Sägenvier Designkommunikation |
Sigi Ramoser | *Dornbirn, Austria*

17

In this uncomplicated newsletter, a two-column grid and horizontal breaking of information yield clean, informational, and lively compositions. The simplicity of the structure permits quick, cost-effective layout without sacrificing visual power or contrast; these qualities are actually built into the system. Each edition is an A3 folded down to an A4 format, producing a cover and one interior spread. This format is folded once again for mailing. The cover, thus divided in half, presents identifying masthead information, an image that bleeds left to right, and the title of the feature article above the fold. The image is changed each edition, while masthead information remains consistent. The feature story begins below the fold and continues inside. A dark horizontal band holds the identifying information on the cover and makes a transition into the interior spread,

providing continuity and a simple, decisive beginning to a progression of intervals from the top to the bottom of the page—small, medium, and large. The text is set in various configurations on five columns, hanging from a flowline but finishing out at varied depths from column to column. All of the type is presented in one neutral sans serif, with size change and weight differences adding texture and providing navigation through the hierarchy. Images appear cropped within rectangles, or silhouetted to interact with the column structure, as deemed appropriate. A calendar and event information is provided on the back page.

3

1
Taking advantage of the interrelated proportion of DIN format sizes, the full-size newsletter folds in half to achieve a standard mailing size. The fold acts as a separator between masthead information above and feature introduction below.

2, 3
The rigorous hangline of the text is countered by intuitive placement of inset and silhouetted images; sometimes the text itself leaves the grid when the designer feels this will improve the interaction of elements within the layout, as appears to happen with the left-most paragraph on the second page spread (3).

Andersen *Viewpoint / Proviews*
OrangeSeed Design | Minneapolis, USA

Two complementary newsletters help a manufacturer of windows and doors reach contract and retail buyers in the construction industry with product and marketing information that promotes their business. Geared toward construction professionals, the newsletters are designed to appeal to their hands-on, no-nonsense need for clear information. At the same time, they deliver branding messages through color and type selection and also appeal to tertiary audiences—do-it-yourself home construction consumers and, potentially, architects who may specify the products for contractors hired to build. Elegant spatial layout, colorful photographs, sensitive typographic styling, and abstract details speak to more visually conscious prospects. A compound three- and four-column grid organizes running text and callouts, and secondary product display areas, respectively. The structure is consistent between both newsletters; their covers vary the grid slightly by using the second and third columns of the text area, while reserving the left column as a margin for colophon or callout information. In both cases, the newsletter mastheads are set in a condensed sans-serif face that is treated minimally to customize it and relate it to the brand typographic system.

1

2

3

1, 4

On the cover, a narrower left-hand column is used for supporting information, such as a colophon or content listing. The narrow column emphasizes the left alignment of the second, regular-width column with the masthead and marks this column as the beginning of the primary text.

2, 3

Overall, color is kept neutral and warm, with black and a secondary color for accents. Tinting different areas, as in this spread, allows the text setting of each to remain the same; the change in contrast between type and background separates the different areas.

3

The need to be clear and direct suggests simplifying type treatments in a limited space. Here, for example, a number of different kinds of information are being presented, but they all follow a similar internal logic: two type families, with text set in a serif and subheads set in the bold sans serif. Supporting callouts are set in one face, using two weights.

Throughout, the same sans serif, in a family of weights, creates easy-to-navigate columns of text while differentiating subheads and captions. Narrow rules help define spatial zones among the columns, and strong geometric inclusions help communicate the architectural nature of the subject with a minimum of fuss.

4, 5

As these covers show, a clear column structure can provide both consistency and flexibility in layout. The placement and size of photographs can change, but their relationship to the grid unifies them with the type structure.

6

The compound use of a three-column (upper area) and four-column (lower area) structure can be seen here. Changing grid structures within a page for a specific purpose, such as clarifying the difference between two sets of content, is a powerful means of helping readers navigate and changing the visual rhythm within the page.

4

5

6

ASKO Schönberg
UNA (Amsterdam) Designers | *Amsterdam, Netherlands*

This vigorous, yet elegant, newsletter for a music ensemble communicates the energetic nature of the organization first via format—a narrow, two-square tall folded sheet roughly 18" (45.7 cm) high—emblazoned on its cover with a block of vivid color and an asymmetric configuration of letters spelling out the group's name. The seasonal publication delivers performance schedules and highlights soloists and composers featured in the current repertoire, distributed over two or three signatures as needed. The signatures simply fold together without binding. Each signature is printed in black plus three other spot colors, which change every issue. A compound two- and three-column grid on left-biased asymmetrical margins balances text at various sizes against full-bleed images and expressive type configura-

tions that allude to musical composition. The designers make full use of the structure, shifting calendar information around the three-column grid and editorial content over both column sets, paying careful attention to the shapes of the text in relation to the often asymmetrical, unusually cropped photographs. Negative space is an important player in the layouts, helping create movement among the elements. Despite the lively arrangement of material, the information remains accessible and legible; equal care is taken in crafting typographic distinctions within detailed content such as the performance schedule.

1

2

1, 2

When the publication is folded for distribution, the front "cover" displays a square field of saturated color. A constantly changing arrangement of the musical ensemble's name reverses out white and dances across the square format. Fully open, an editorial statement about the season fills the lower half. This text is set in a bold sans serif whose size changes with each issue so that it extends consistently from the fold to the foot margin. The season indicator, in black, is consistently set at a larger size compared to the group's signature at the top, reversing white and flushing left to the format edge.

Asko Ensemble Schönberg Ensemble

a s K o
Sch ö n
b er g

1/2003

Het zijn gouden tijden voor duizendpoten als Fred Frith. Van jongs af gewend zich op verschillende muzikale terreinen te bewegen, kreeg hij jarenlang het verwijt te horen dat hij zijn talenten versnipperde. Tegenwoordig wordt er met enige jaloezie gekeken naar een muzikant als Frith: multi-instrumentalist (behalve gitaar speelt hij onder andere piano, viool, contrabas en slagwerk), improvisator en componist, met voelsprieten in de Newyorkse *downtown scene*, de moderne klassieke muziek, de jazz, de elektronische en de popmuziek, die bovendien muziek schreef voor theater, dans, film en video-installaties.
De van oorsprong Engelse Frith dankt zijn reputatie als experimenteel musicus aan de groep *Henry Cow* die hij in 1968 samen met Tim Hodgkinson oprichtte. Het repertoire omvatte complexe composities, liedjes, tapebewerkingen en vrije improvisaties. De band, die tien jaar bestond, was voor Frith de start van een even grillige als kleurrijke carrière. Zelf spreekt hij liever niet van 'een carrière'. 'Het enige dat mij interesseert, is dat ik de ruimte krijg om samen met inspirerende, creatieve mensen mijn ideeën te ontwikkelen.' Toch is er wel degelijk een rode draad aan te wijzen in zijn muzikale loopbaan: improvisatie. Sinds de lp *Guitar Solos* uit 1974 heeft hij zich ontwikkeld tot een musicus die de eigenschappen en mogelijkheden van improvisatie tot op het bot heeft onderzocht. Dat hij de afgelopen jaren steeds vaker componeert voor ensembles die hoofdzakelijk bestaan uit klassiek getrainde musici – zoals Ensemble Modern en het Asko Ensemble – doet daar niets aan af. Sterker nog, misschien is dat improvisatietalent wel zijn troef. Zelf zegt hij: 'Een goede improvisator is uit de aard der zaak een goede luisteraar en dat kan erg behulpzaam zijn bij het aanvatten van andere muzikale vormen.' *Weatherwise or Otherwise*, met de componist op gitaar, levert daarvan het bewijs. Jacqueline Oskamp

2, 3

Editorial text generally is set in the bold sans serif, with size changes indicating subheads and other hierarchic changes. The serif is used for supporting date and time information in captions accompanying the articles.

3, 4

Unusual cropping, unexpected scale, and asymmetrical compositional decisions push the photographic subjects around the format, increasing the ambiguous, shifting spatial depth of the elements in the layouts.

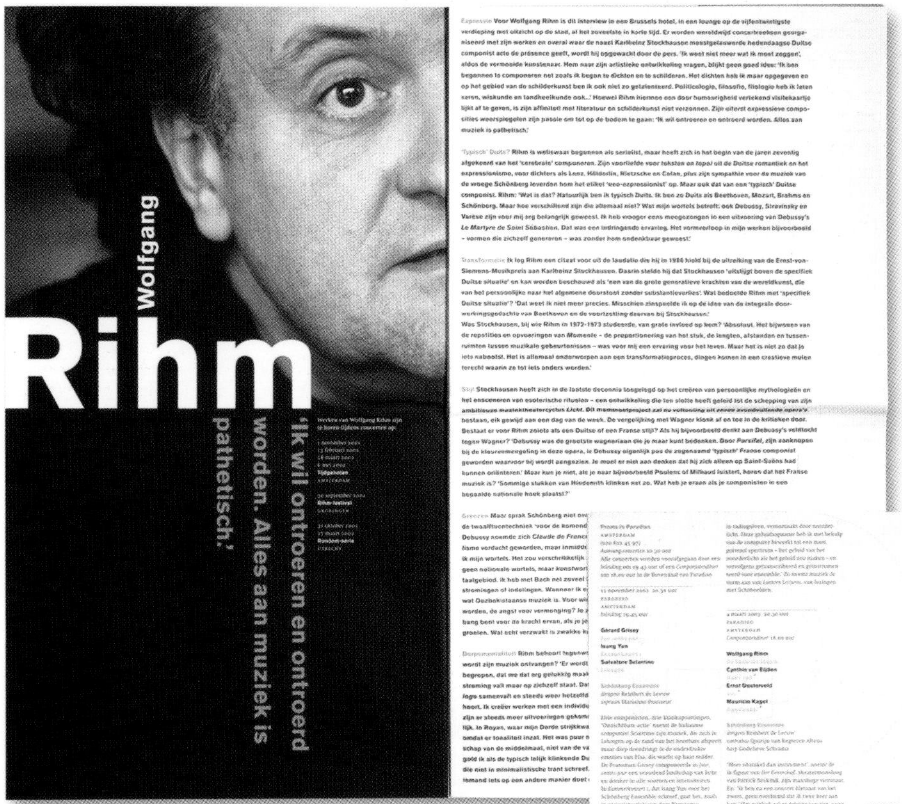

Wolfgang Rihm

'Ik wil ontroeren en ontroerd worden. Alles aan muziek is pathetisch.'

orA Kel

Stilte van het

The calendar is carefully typeset for readers looking for specific information. Sans-serif and serif typefaces are mixed to create pronounced textural differences, and each informational component within a given listing—date, venue, concert time, composer and work, and featured performers—is given its own distinct typographic treatment.

Soundings
Conquest Design | Arlington (MA), USA

20

This quarterly newsletter for an educational institution covers a broad range of subjects, from economics to dance, writing to social sciences. Its neutral visual styling helps avoid the potential confusion of attempting to represent every one of these subjects equally or even accurately; the communication here becomes one of academic credibility and interest to people associated with the school. Neutrality carries associations of objectivity and inquiry—qualities that can be ascribed to an institution of higher learning. Given the intellectual pedigree of the university of which the school is a part, this kind of objective, credible presentation is of paramount importance to the client. As a result, the designer treats information respectfully, ensuring clear hierarchic distinction through size and weight changes, and using color for accents and informational enhancement within the typography but only rarely within images. Every issue exhibits two standard ink colors—a warm neutral ink and a black—along with a third color that changes seasonally. Text generally runs in black, although callouts and headlines may be set in color or reversed out from colored bands. The structure is a relatively precise eight-column modular grid in which four-module-wide and three-module-wide columns of text shift back and forth, creating apparent vertical overlaps between columns and margins that shift subtly left and right. These shifts also allow callouts, captions, and images to hang from column alignments or be indented dramatically. Images adhere to the column widths but are free to expand vertically as needed.

1

2

3

FALL 2004
soundings

MIT SCHOOL OF HUMANITIES, ARTS, AND SOCIAL SCIENCES

SPRING 2004
soundings

Professor Esther Duflo discusses process evaluation, and the intersection of economics and development.

FALL 2003
soundings

Message from Dean Khoury

1–3
The newsletter folds in half to self-mail without an envelope, saving on postal expense. The cover, on one side of the fold, features a full-bleed photograph, masthead, and teaser caption; the mailing side, along with space for addressee, includes a follow-up caption related to the one on the cover and an editorial message from the school's dean. On the outside, horizontal banding and linear details add texture and clarity.

4

5

A serif is used primarily for text, while a sans serif is used for titling, sub-heads, and captions. In this spread, which presents an interview with a faculty member, the informational clarity afforded by typographic simplicity is evident. The questions are called out in bold sans serif, and tinted gradations set off related but informationally distinct material, such as the sidebar at the lower right. The use of shifted columns on the more precise underlying grid is also visible.

5

7

4, 5

Because the newsletter's focus is on text, rather than image, the decision to call out a lot of text in the third (variable) color accomplishes a number of ends. First, it introduces color to the textual grayness of the pages. Second, it helps differentiate and focus attention on informational components. Finally, it gives a specific coloring to each issue.

4, 6

Active, as well as more reserved, layouts are accommodated by the grid structure, which remains clear. Mixing the weights of the sans-serif family to call out informational details within captions or sub-components adds texture and vitality to the conservative structure.

6

7

Careful attention to spacing details—such as the difference in spaces above and below the rule between paragraphs in this listing—helps readers access information more quickly, imparting a sense of precision and concern for the reader. This kind of respect from a designer helps a publication connect with its audience.

18 First Place
Stereotype Design | *New York City, USA*

21

This newsletter for the Museum of Jewish Heritage organizes an ever-changing selection of editorial content on a five-column grid. Its slightly squared tabloid format lends it a newspaper-like presence and establishes ample ground for vigorous typography at larger sizes. While a number of pages are given to more conventional newsletter fare—updates on fund-raising campaigns, donor events, and the like—every issue features essays from noted contributors and articles focused on curated exhibitions or material in the museum's archives. The former generally structures text on two-column configurations derived from the five-column grid underneath, with heads set large in black-weight sans-serif type, in a contrasting color. The body copy runs in a serif face. Heads are in a consistent size throughout, clearly distinguished in size and spacing from callouts that appear in the same face, but smaller and more densely leaded. Image captions appear in the bold-weight sans serif. Within the more engaging editorial spreads, heads and decks take on a more spirited presen-

tation, appearing very large and all uppercase in the same sans serif. The grid is articulated more dramatically; some text components run across three columns, while others continue in the two-column structure. Text components are composed in these pages with larger images—some inset, some bleeding or interacting with blocks of color. Although the typeface selection is limited to two families, the use of an oldstyle serif in justified text columns, contrasted by large, uppercase setting of headlines in sans serif—especially in conjunction with historical photographs from the Museum's collections—subtly recalls the design aesthetic of the early- to mid-twentieth-century Europe. In doing so, the publication purposely evokes memories of this turbulent period in the Jewish experience among its mature readership, resonating with its audience at a deep emotional level despite the generally neutral presentation of the content.

1

Each issue's cover features a different historical photograph, printed in black and white, against which the stationary masthead remains consistent. The right-angle rotation of the masthead's elements locks it almost architecturally to the upper-left corner of the format.

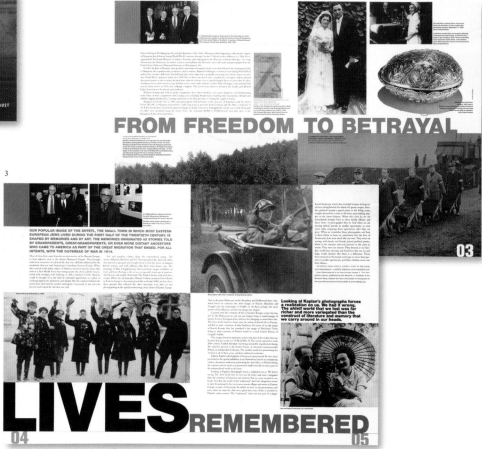

2, 3

A clear system of weights and sizes helps separate informational components in the hierarchy and adds texture to the pages. Scale change becomes more image oriented in the editorial features; here, headlines and callouts spread across the gutter, poke in and out of the column structure, and appear in multiple sizes. Combined with rule details, blocks of color, and historical photographs, the typefaces and their arrangement contribute to an association with design from turbulent periods in recent Jewish memory.

3

The newsletter is sometimes printed in four-color process, but adheres to a restrained palette; this limitation keeps the color feeling in line with those printed using two colors.

2, 3

Big type is not reserved strictly for headlines: the folios, set in a bold, condensed sans serif, act as anchors for the spreads.

News & Events
Allemann, Almquist + Jones | *Philadelphia, USA*

22

The six-panel tabloid newsletter for a science museum makes extravagant use of color, illustrative and abstract montage, expressive typographic detailing, and diagrammatic science imagery to convey the energy and wonder of the museum's event offerings, especially those geared toward children. The dynamic asymmetry and color of the museum's annual reports (see page 206) is taken even further. Information is structured on a single column in each panel and given generous margins to avoid cropping when the newsletter is folded down to mailing size. The column structure is violated when additional movement and spatial ambiguity is desired. The back panel accommodates postal requirements, including indicia and space for addresses; the front of the folded publication becomes a bold cover with the branded Events logotype. Much of the typographic variation in headings, callouts, and expressive treatments follows from this wordmark as a way of conceptually linking the idea of the "events" with the content in the newsletter. As each successive panel is opened, the format changes in proportion as well as size. The composition of these typographic and image "events" unfolds in a kind of kinetic story, independent of the actual verbal content, which can then be opened up as a poster.

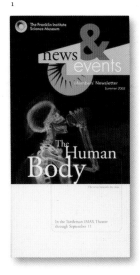

1, 2

A dynamic lockup of serif and sans-serif elements in the masthead creates a consistent counterpoint to changing exhibit images.

3, 4

Fully opened (3), the newsletter is transformed into a poster. The designers consider the interaction of individual panels (4), as well as the complete format, in composing photographs, textures, type treatments, and abstract shapes.

3

4

A textural system of colored dots customizes stock photography (on the cover) and provides a simple branding statement within the interior, subtly restating the circular identity symbol of the corporate signature. The pattern of dots also subtly conveys associations of system, integration, networking, computer readouts, biology, and similar ideas related to the company's business, health care management solutions.

2004 · MILLIMAN REPORT

Annual Reports

Image- and Message-Driven Financial Statements
and Organizational Status Reports

Milliman
Kendall Ross | *Seattle (WA), USA*

The designers of this annual report have used an editorial, brochurelike structure to lead investors and prospects through a discussion of various business activities and achievements. Unlike many annual reports, organized into three distinct sections—image, management, and financials—this booklet spreads important information among numerous spreads, each focusing on an area of interest elaborated upon in a series of smaller articles, much like a magazine. The executive's letter to shareholders—in the first spread seen after opening the report—feels very much like a letter from a magazine's editor, instead of the formal, investor-focused document in the management sections of conventional annuals, which typically presents just a lot of spin. The brochurelike spreads run text across three of four columns, grouping these columns inward to mirror each other from the left- to right-hand pages. In doing so, the outer columns are free for margins in which tinted sidebars are placed, augmenting the sense of the editorial influence that characterizes the layouts. Each major concept is introduced in one to two paragraph decks, set all uppercase, with the designers appropriately adding space to help readability. Continuing, short stories about specific business, research, and financial activity run in the relatively narrow columns, separated by bold, uppercase subheads. Imagery focuses on people, with tightly cropped head shots; the remaining image material is composed of a system of colored dots that add texture and subtle branding to the publication. With the financial data treated as a plain document bound in, the report does double duty as a business update and as a capabilities brochure that conveys a direct, unpretentious message about the company's activities and personnel.

An editorial structure lends a magazine-like accessibility to the report. The Chairman's letter, up front, seems more like that from an editor. Stories about operational and financial activity run continuously from the beginning of a spread to its end and are organized around a particular concept, such as health.

2, 3

The introductory decks, set all uppercase, have been conscientiously set with greater letter- and wordspacing to improve legibility, as well as with markedly more open leading to offset the wider paragraph measure.

2

Sidebars in the outer columns use a large-scale initial as a subject reference, reversed out to white from the neutral warm gray tint that contains the callout information. The text in the sidebar is set bold with generous leading; tinted bullets hang outside the margin, creating entry points to the short paragraphs and following the visual logic of the dot grid used throughout.

4

A full-bleed spacer spread provides punctuation between the message section and the financials.

El Commercio

Empresa Editora el Commercio | Claudia Burga-
Cisneros | *Lima, Peru*

24

An editorial organization of content and imaginative, graphical display of financial information distinguishes this annual report from Peru's largest newspaper publisher. The report is divided into two separate formats. The first is an A4 booklet with groups of short articles that highlight journalistic accomplishments and the newspaper's connection to the community. Each of these sections, which follows a consistent structure, is separated by a spread exhibiting financial data in a composition of linear and circular graphic elements, used as charts and graphs. To avoid a static visual repetition, these spreads change in color with each occurrence, making them more engaging each time they are encountered. The typography in these sections uses dramatic scale change to lend additional visual liveliness to the potentially dry data. Similar linear and graphic treatments accompany

the more straightforward editorial typography of the story sections, helping connect this data to real-life scenarios. The stories are detailed in justified columns of serif text on a two-column grid with ample margins and subdued, duotoned black-and-white portraits of a journalistic nature. Complementary sans-serif typesetting appears in subheads, captions, and notations accompanying the chart details. The editorialized booklet is accompanied by a single-color financial booklet in a smaller format—printed on white uncoated stock—that includes management discussion of business activity and tabular data structured on a hierarchic two-column grid. Subsections are separated by a system of rules of various weights.

1

2

3

1

The smaller financial booklet presents tabular and supporting data in a hierarchic two-column structure. Text and tables generally run in the wider column, with more complex tables of figures expanded to fill the full margin width. Horizontal rules help delineate rows within tables and separate tabular data and sections from each other.

2, 3

Full-bleed fields of cool metallic blue-gray ink suffuse the covers of the booklets in this two-format report. The larger format carries the editorial and image-oriented message section, along with financial highlights delivered in graphic compositions; the smaller contains the in-depth financial data. Fluorescent orange and flat blue inks call out titling information.

4

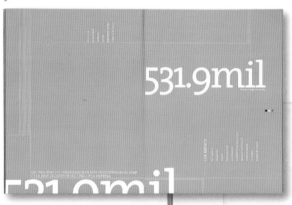

4, 5

The graphical spreads that present financial highlights act as dividers for the editorial subsections. Each one allows one of the three major ink colors to dominate: first the fluorescent orange, then the metallic blue, and finally the deeper flat blue ink.

6

Linear details used in the colored highlight divider spreads appear again as more restrained details within the editorial sections, which provide black-and-white images as a focus against the typography. The journalistic quality alludes to the business function of the client as a newspaper publisher.

5

6

● ● REDACCIÓN

EL 2002 FUE PARA EL ÁREA de Redacción de El Comercio una etapa de desafíos profesionales sumamente complejos dirigidos a hacer frente –junto con otras áreas involucradas– al reto de incrementar la venta de ejemplares del Diario.

En este esfuerzo ha sido esencial la ejecución del Plan de Mejoras, que ha permitido hacer frente a la continua pérdida de poder adquisitivo de la población, así como al incremento de la oferta de diarios en la capital. Por otro lado, la mayor oferta en los otros medios (cable, internet, TV abierta y radio, etc.) de programas informativos también ha sido un reto importante a sortear.

Por ello ha sido un logro importante alcanzar un incremento en la venta de ejemplares de 3,21% con respecto al año anterior. En cuanto a la lectoría, nuestro promedio diario de lectores se incrementó de 518,5 miles a 531,9 miles. Cabe destacar que mantenemos nuestro liderazgo con una ventaja amplia en los segmentos más solicitados por los anunciadores.

El desarrollo de una agenda propia, noticias que nos acercan al lector, más opinión, campañas, investigaciones, amenidad, crónicas de interés humano, mesas redondas, han sido parte del esfuerzo desplegado para mantener nuestro liderazgo como decano de la prensa peruana.

Tras dos años de planificado esfuerzo, la sección Economía y Negocios logró el objetivo de posicionarse como el medio de referencia en su campo. Fue importante para ello el incremento de secciones especializadas, la publicación de los rankings empresariales y la introducción de comentarios editoriales bajo la columna Opinión.

La sección Luces continuó en el 2002 cumpliendo a cabalidad la necesidad de brindar entretenimiento y por ende siendo uno de los los más importantes motores de la lectoría del Diario.

En Deporte Total se aumentó notoriamente la información polideportiva referida a diferentes disciplinas ajenas al fútbol. La cobertura del campeonato mundial de fútbol Corea-Japón logró distinguir a DT del resto de productos deportivos incrementando considerablemente su lectoría y ventas.

3,21%

// AUMENTO LA CIRCULACIÓN DE EL COMERCIO EN RELACIÓN AL AÑO ANTERIOR

// ANA MARÍA MOREYRA

ARTESANA //

EDAD 59 AÑOS // LECTORA DE EL COMERCIO

10, 11

VF Corporation
And Partners | David Schimmel
New York City, USA

VF Corporation is the parent company for a number of high-profile retail clothing brands, each with its own visual identity and target demographic. In pursuing a stylistically neutral, yet elegant and conceptual, annual report for the client, the designers have avoided potential cross-branding confusion and created a serene and credible corporate communication that embodies the nature of the brands. The parent company is clearly the subject of the report, and its hierarchic position as brand owner is clear. The individual retail brands are highlighted through lifestyle photographs in the message section. The images, distilled from each subbrand's advertising, communicate a subtle variety of secondary and tertiary messages, depending on their respective target demographic. This variety is augmented by their juxtaposition but unified by conceptual messages, set in a stylistically neutral yellow band, running above them across the spreads at the head margin. The writing plays with concepts in opposition, the left page line creating a context for the line on the right page. The images are organized on a square grid that is subdivided as needed, page by page. A second section details the strategic and financial highlights by brand category; the square grid from the

1

Styling Life

VF CORPORATION 2003 ANNUAL REPORT

1

On the cover, a complex, textural full-bleed image of a crowd—perhaps the recipients of the brand message (the consumer public)—forms a backdrop to the geometric white and yellow bands that carry the report title type. The narrower yellow band is a defining formal treatment that binds the report together.

2

VF Corporation 2003 Annual Report

65,755 fans
128 football players
90 hot dog vendors
73 ushers
28 janitors
12 line judges and referees

1 guy shaking in his jeans about to propose on the Jumbotron.

(BOTTOM LEFT TO RIGHT) HORACE SMALL, LEE DUNGAREES, RIDERS

3

VF Corporation 2003 Annual Report

There will come a day when I'll be a responsible adult with 2.5 kids and a mortgage.

21

first section is expanded to include the upper and lower margin areas for a two-column structure that is enclosed, top and bottom, by consistent color banding and a clear hierarchic structure in text. The financial data is similarly structured on two columns that are further subdivided into six columns for tabular data, based on the longest figure set in any given table. A rich, desaturated brown ink differentiates this section from the previous two.

1, 2, 3

Stark, non-brand-specific treatment of type and color keeps the individual brands being represented subordinate to that of the parent corporation. Specific branding messages are hinted at through the selection of photographs and details of their subject matter—for example, on the jeans labels.

2, 3

The image section defines a simple system of call and response from left to right page for the copy, which runs in a narrow horizontal yellow bar above the image area. The relationship of the text on the left page to the image below it, and to the text that follows on the right page, creates unexpected and subtly witty branding messages.

4, 5

Modular three-column and two-column configurations appear in the financial section, organizing images of key personnel and financial data. The text in the financial section is printed in one color, with weight and size change in the text separating informational components and helping to introduce contrast into the dense typographic texture.

5

25

...ut until then, searching for the perfect cappuccino with free biscotti is enough for me.

(CLOCKWISE FROM TOP LEFT) GEMMA, WRANGLER (EUROPE), LEE (EUROPE)

4

(CLOCKWISE FROM LEFT) EARL JEAN, NAUTICA BLUE, NAUTICA

4

In the second section, discussion of activity within brand categories is systematized in a two-column structure with a wide upper margin used to list individual brands in a given category. The number of brands in a category may differ dramatically; by creating a large, fixed area for the brand listing (two appear in this area here), the designers are able to maintain the column structure and its hangline in each category.

Adris Gruppa
Bruketa & Zinic | *Zagreb, Croatia*

26

A narrow vertical format, case-bound in white cloth, creates a strong and graceful vehicle for this business venture's annual report. The company conducts business in several industries, among them tobacco and tourism. The international scope and financial vitality of the operations are quickly conveyed in an abstract presentation that focuses on key phrases drawn from the CEO's letter to the shareholders, placed in the context of crisp photographic images depicting sea, sky, shore, ship, and shelter. The images become metaphors for the various sectors in which the company is engaged, as well as for the aspirations described in the concise selections of text. The text throughout is set in Didot, the French counterpart to Bodoni's modern serif of the same time period. Its extreme contrast and modulated strokes provide rich texture, and it is used at relatively large sizes in the report, even for the blocks of text that appear as insets centered within the photographs. The central location of these blocks, given the height of the format, augments the sense of space depicted in the images, pulling the eye inward while the sky, sea, and sails soar upward and outward. This sense of focus helps convey the company's determination and vision as it expands its holdings and financial reach in foreign markets. In the financial section, tabular data and charts are similarly focused toward the central horizon of the format, separated from top and bottom by enormous margins of white paper. Large headings here, as throughout the report, appear in the Didot, set upper- and lower-case in warm gray ink.

1

2

1

The gauzy, white cloth covering the report's case binding softens the solid presence of the booklike structure and, in the context of the company's focus in tourism and similar shipping or travel-based industries, may signify sailcloth or other nautical references as a physical metaphor. The company's name is foil stamped in silver across the upper third of the cover.

2, 6

Cloudscapes, sails, beaches, and agricultural land—environments where the company's business directs it—deliver worldly messages of vision, movement, and growth. Inset blocks of type offer a geometric contrast to the soaring movement of the images, creating inward pull while the format appears to expand outward.

Letter to the
Shareholders

3

Cons
Inco
State
as at
Dece
2003

3, 4, 5

Delicate illustrations, charts, and tabular settings introduce additional linear texture to complement that of the typography.

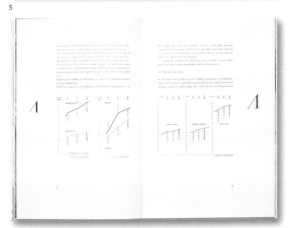

dated

ent

ar

Consolidated Balance Sheet - December

Assets in mn. OOEs for the Financial Year Jan 1 to Dec 31	2001	2002	2003
I. Non-current assets			
1 Intangible assets	14,150	15,173	27,236
2 Tangible assets	1,427,369	1,156,012	1,417,310
3 Investments	84,739	88,245	89,668
4 Non-current receivables	181,216	533,151	135,877
Total non-current assets	1,742,774	1,092,578	1,670,091
II. Current assets			
1 Cash and cash equivalents	39,957	72,962	76,651
2 Trade debtors	158,302	153,689	173,283
3 Inventories	447,030	389,356	494,328
4 Other current assets	474,770	682,890	1,760,687
Total current assets	1,120,939	1,308,895	2,504,947

UM School of Pharmacy
Circle K Studio | *San Francisco, USA*

Designed to resonate with an academic, scientific, and philanthropic audience, the publication appropriately presents its case in clear, understated, and respectful treatments of type and image. A quiet table of contents, set in a mixture of modern serif and crisp sans-serif capitals, continues the play of surface and space begun with the cover's equally quiet, yet strong, debossed typography. Its listings are set flush left on a wide column, in warm metallic silver ink that break the rich expanse of black that fills the page. Page numbers and the titles of editorial sections, along with a relevant quote supporting the report's title, *New Directions*, sparkle as white, reversed-out details. A large, lightly varnished arrow introduces a simple graphic metaphor that is used judiciously throughout. The report's quietness—a marked departure from other annuals whose intent is to celebrate and inspire—is justified in the dean's letter that immediately follows, describing a difficult academic year brought on by political, cul-

tural, and economic events that profoundly affected the school; despite these trials, the dean offers a message of perseverance and evolution. Sedate photographs in rich duotones of black and metallic silver move serenely across the spreads in the editorial sections thereafter. Each section is brief—one spread—marked by a one-word title, a selection of images shifting in scale, position, and proportion, and two primary blocks of text: an introductory paragraph that describes conceptual ideas, along with running copy that elaborates on these ideas as they relate specifically to the school. The arrow icon interacts with the text, separating thoughts and adding contrast to the delicate justified serif typography. A third section details financial information in a four-column grid that shows great care in its informational hierarchies and presentation.

1

3

4

2

5

1, 3

A rich, uncoated, red paper stock quietly administers the heavily debossed title and graphic signifier used throughout the report—an arrow. The school's academic insignia is printed in warm metallic silver ink. The contents (3) and interior are printed on a contrasting glossy white stock in black, warm silver, and red match inks.

2, 4

Stately editorial titles are carefully sized and spaced; they carry the same visual weight as the italic serif introductions, printed in red ink, that immediately follow them.

Text and images oppose each other formally. The text blocks are static; the images shift along horizontal and vertical intervals that create an upward motion from left to right. The light text elements contrast the photographs' density.

5

Tinted blocks help separate informational components in the financial section.

Van Lanschot
UNA (Amsterdam) Designers | *Amsterdam, Netherlands*

While the interior treatment of these funds reports is the same each time, the covers offer graphic experimentation that not only creates a beautiful series of images but also identifies each report. An initial letter is distilled to represent each fund in a given report—*G* for global equity, for example. The capital and lowercase forms of that letter appear together, divided across their axes and collaged among a set of rules, the texture of bank insignia, and other relevant visual elements. Overall, each fund report's cover is color coded and printed in several spot colors that include a metallic ink—texturally rich, yet subdued, as a result of printing on uncoated stock. A narrow unprinted area across the head margin carries the client's identifier and insignia. This head margin translates into the interior as a hangline for section heads and the baseline location of the folios.

Text and tabular data run in several configurations depending on complexity, articulating a precise ten-column grid based on the width of an eight-figure numeral, plus enough gutter space to separate it horizontally from another within a table. Text primarily occupies one column, defined by a grouping of these narrow columns, and all type is set in a distinctive, humanist serif with a large x-height and moderate contrast. The numerals are set with nonlining figures. Within the tables, different financial quarter's worth of information may be compared; that of the current quarter is called out through colored blocks or bands. The designers also block out important diagrams and graphs—and supplemental texts—with fields of color, reversing type out to white for legibility. The precise measurement of the grid is very flexible, able to accommodate a number of text and table contingencies, but uniform and direct, appealing to the targeted audience.

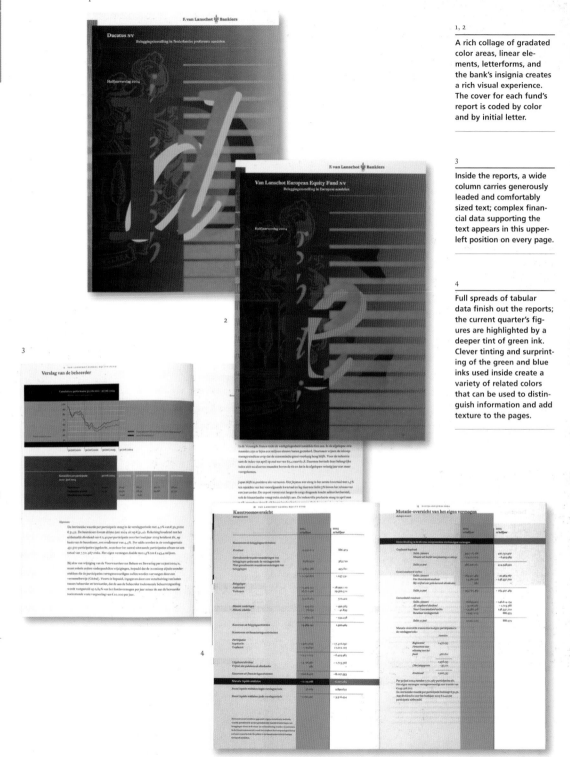

1, 2
A rich collage of gradated color areas, linear elements, letterforms, and the bank's insignia creates a rich visual experience. The cover for each fund's report is coded by color and by initial letter.

3
Inside the reports, a wide column carries generously leaded and comfortably sized text; complex financial data supporting the text appears in this upper-left position on every page.

4
Full spreads of tabular data finish out the reports; the current quarter's figures are highlighted by a deeper tint of green ink. Clever tinting and surprinting of the green and blue inks used inside create a variety of related colors that can be used to distinguish information and add texture to the pages.

PEN Canada
Soapbox Design Communications | Gary Beelik
Toronto, Canada

Saturated primary colors, aggressive conceptual illustrations, and clear, decisive typography all contribute to this annual report's clean, stylized presentation—oddly supporting and refuting the chilling information described in its pages. Much more than a conventional activity or financial update, the report is a document of human rights abuses worldwide being fought by PEN Canada, the Canadian branch of International PEN. The organization's goal is to secure freedom of expression for writers through media awareness, advocacy, and direct legal and political campaigns in aid of those whose lives and rights are in jeopardy. In this report, which details stories of such abuses (serial murders, imprisonment under false charges, and the like), documents from censored writers, essays about important cases, and statements of commitment alternate in a powerful rhythm with messages from the group's director, lists of prisoners freed, and lists of those still in danger. Individual texts are presented against blocks of color at various sizes, sometimes reversing out to white, sometimes surprinting black. The directness of the typography speaks to the group's pursuit of transparency and the power of freedom of expression at the same time it beautifully contrasts the foreboding, often shocking and grim realities of the content. Tremendous contrasts in scale activate the type, all set in Univers in only two weights throughout, pushing statements into the reader's space and pulling them back inward into the enormous format's expanse of space. Among the pages, fiercely expressive illustrations provide surreal representations of ideas such as censorship, imprisonment, and persecution, as well as hopeful images of freedom and empowerment.

1

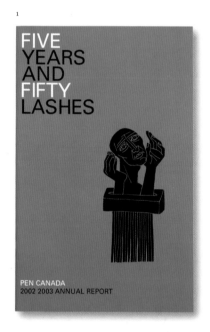

2

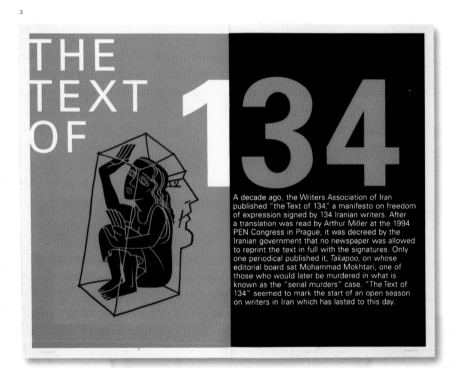

3

PEN'S CAMPAIGN TO CHALLENGE IMPUNITY WAS LAUNCHED IN NOVEMBER 2002 AT THE BIENNIAL MEETING OF THE WRITERS IN PRISON COMMITTEE OF INTERNATIONAL PEN IN SAN MIGUEL DE ALLENDE, MEXICO. PEN CANADA IS LEADING THE EFFORT, IN PARTNERSHIP WITH INTERNATIONAL PEN'S WRITERS IN PRISON

1

The large tabloid format creates an unmistakable presence for the report, alluding to the inescapable power of documents in exposing ideas. An all uppercase title alternates in black and white against a rich blue field that also displays one of the surreal illustrations by artist Luba Lukova: a forlorn figure being destroyed by a paper shredder.

2, 3

Changes from upper to mixed case, along with size changes, offer a direct, varied, and forceful set of contrasts among the type elements. In this detail (3), a direct statement is enhanced by all-uppercase setting that spans the width of the spread; the texture is also a welcome break from illustration-heavy pages.

4

DOUBLE
EDGED
SWORD

PEN believes that impunity in cases of violations of freedom of expression is a dangerous double-edged sword:
1. the killing of a writer or journalist is the first violation, also known as "censorship by killing;"
2. the second violation is the denial of access to the truth for the victim and family, and for society as a whole.

2, 4, 5

Stark color combinations—and enormous typographic headlines combined with Lukova's eminently human, hand-drawn images—create powerful stopping points for consideration. The colored fields, rectangular boxes, and linear type integrate visually with the language of the drawings, themselves bold combinations of mass and line.

4, 5

The illustrations range from the painful—clasped hands speared by a sword—to the inspirational—a yearning figure whose heart has taken root within.

6

Subtle graphic treatments convey concepts beyond those presented literally in text. On this spread, for example, an ominous field of black isolates a small blue square containing the table of contents—surrounding and dominating it. Color coding connects the blue square to the first headline, Impunity, giving the concept power and enhancing the sense of persecution directed toward the blue square.

6

IMPUNITY
GETTING AWAY WITH M

7

A wall of typographic texture gives evidence of widespread abuse, listing writers and activists killed by governments and terror groups. Red callouts indicate the countries where listed abuses took place.

7

CENSORSHIP
BY KILLING IMPUNITY WATCH

5

YOU
WILL
ANSWER
ONE
DAY

Octel
Ideas On Purpose | *New York City, USA*

30

For this 2003 annual report released by a chemical manufacturer, the periodic table of elements is used as a visual metaphor in need of little elaboration. The relatively small format—a little shorter than 8" (20.3 cm) square—is intimate and inviting; in the world of annual reports, it is remarkably understated, conveying anything but corporate excess. Typographic scale and the proportions of the space between elements are used to great effect. One neutral sans serif is used throughout, mostly in regular weight; apparent weight changes are the result of the type's scale. In a few instances, the bold weight is used for subheads. The idea of a dot—representative of chemical molecules and a nod to the

initial letter of the corporate name—provides an elegant counterpoint to the linear quality of the typography and the neutral geometry of the format.

The information in the report is broken into visually distinct segments. In the opening message spreads, conceptual ideas are distilled to an elemental symbol, the idea set below in the same weight; a narrow column of text elaborates on the given concept. In the last spread of the section, the "element" on the left is paired with a field of colored dots on the right that acts as a pause—and tie-in to the cover—before a summation in the next spread. This summation consists solely of type on a full-bleed

1

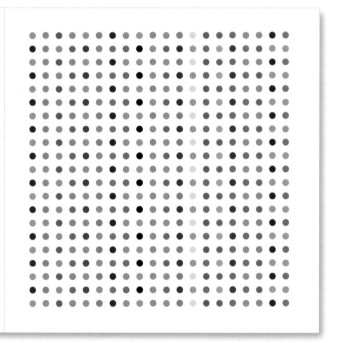

1–3

Spreads in the message segment follow a consistent layout. Space between the typographic elements becomes as important as the elements themselves. The spacing intervals are carefully considered, creating alignments and parceling out spaces in a way that echoes the square format. The asymmetrical organization of the typography creates movement and tension among positive and negative spaces.

07

Eq

Equilibrium

TEL + Specialty Chemicals

Balance is at the heart of our business strategy.

Our carefully calibrated business mix of Lead Alkyls (TEL) and Specialty Chemicals allows us to optimise our strategy for long-term shareholder value.

Fulfilling our mission of being a global, profitable, growing specialty chemicals company hinges on managing this equilibrium. So we maintain our sensible approach to spending.

While seeking the right acquisition opportunities, we have invested in integration, restructuring, and rightsizing; research and development; and organic growth. On one hand our Specialties business is growing steadily, and on the other we've achieved excellent cash generation in TEL.

At the same time, we have met our debt obligations, paid dividends, and continued with our share buyback program.

On balance, we're in balance.

2

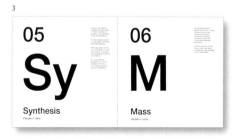

01

E

Energy

Ideas + People

02

B

Bonds

Customers + Satisfaction

3

05

Sy

Synthesis

People + Jobs

06

M

Mass

Global + Local

1, 5, 6

Colorful dots on the cover and within the pages allude gracefully to the idea of chemical elements without being overtly literal. In the last message spread before the summation, the dots form a grid that neutralizes their color to a certain degree and quiets the page down so that it doesn't steal thunder from the summation itself.

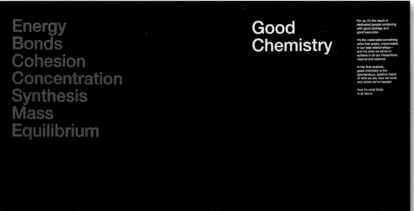

Energy
Bonds
Cohesion
Concentration
Synthesis
Mass
Equilibrium

Good
Chemistry

For us, it's the result of
dedicated people combining
with good strategy and
good execution.

It's the indefinable something
extra that arises, unprompted,
in our best relationships—
and it's what we strive to
achieve in all our interactions,
internal and external.

In the final analysis,
good chemistry is the
spontaneous, positive blend
of who we are, how we work,
and where we're headed.

And it's what Octel
is all about.

black spread, reversing out to white or deeply tinted. The second segment is a graphically treated list of the company's chemical products, each defined by a large colored dot; within the dot, the product's name and information reverse out to white in a hierarchic paragraph. A letter to the corporation's shareholders comprises the third segment, running in a four-column grid; the left-most column is left open. The final section is the financial report, which is produced in a single color on colored paper stock. The four-column grid in this section generally carries text over two columns, and tabular data is further subdivided as needed, based on the longest figures. Heavy rules break up the sections and provide a visual respite from the continuous text.

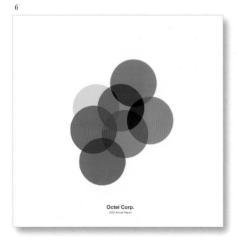

4

The message summation is a study in value and hierarchy. On the left-hand page, the tinted list of idea messages appears to recede in space, as its value is closer to black than to white. This allows the summation, Good Chemistry, to jump forward and take precedence in the hierarchy.

7–9

The financial section begins with a letter to the company's shareholders (7), continued on the same matte-coated white stock before switching (8) to an uncoated mint green stock. Four columns are clearly defined in the letter, while text and tabular financial data are run primarily over double-column widths (9).

Franklin Institute
Allemann, Almquist + Jones | *Philadelphia, USA*

31

Each of the two fiscal years represented in these annual reports for a science museum is given individual character and conceptual backdrops while carrying similar messages, visual language, and typographic detailing. Rich color palettes that encompass analogous groupings of color—greens, blues, violets and reds, oranges, and yellows—along with neutrals and surprise accents, help integrate a dynamic range of supplied promotional photographs of children, scientific images, historical documents and pictures, illustrative montage, icons, and symbols. The mixture of image content is one of the hallmarks of the institute's publications; its goal is to communicate the excitement and variety of learning and activities, as well as the cultural heritage and public importance of the museum. Strong asymmetrical compositions of realistic images and environments contain silhouetted figures, objects, and diagrams—sometimes with typographic callouts integrated illustratively into the abstract space—and add to the sense of wonder in the image and message sections of the reports. Although each annual explores a different aspect of

1, 2

Covers for the two fiscal years' reports are variations on a visual idea that involves children interacting with luminous abstractions that evoke wonder and science.

1–7

Color within the reports is rich and varied. Abstract, diagrammatic, and representational illustrations and photography are used in surprising combinations. Type callouts and graphic details are integrated as equal players with silhouetted images, as well as with shifting text columns and headlines. Futura, a geometric sans serif family with several weights, is used throughout, along with other type families associated with the client's overall identity—also developed by the reports' design team.

the institute's positioning, both are recognizable as being published by the same organization. Some of this similarity derives from systematic typographic structures, column structures, and typeface selection that both share. Both annuals differentiate overall sections through color adjustment among the spreads of a given section. The financial data in each is similarly treated, in tabular configurations on three-column structures, ample leading, and well-considered spacing in the figures.

6

The up-and-down arrangement of the columns are considered relative to the images and other details that occur within a given spread; every element interacts with every other element. The movement and interdependence not only is visual but also communicates the dynamic qualities of physics.

6

Historical documents and images are equally at home in the contemporary format, sometimes used as backdrops, integrated on the grid, or silhouetted.

7

Organizational diagrams related to the institute's programs and administration are treated graphically as important elements.

8

The financial sections follow similar structures and show thoughtful typographic detailing that clarifies tabular data, as well as coloring that unifies them with the more expressive sections of the reports.

7

8

32

Podravka
Bruketa & Žinić | *Zagreb, Croatia*

The theme "bon appétit" provides a fun, energetic context for this producer of food products—packaged soups and condiments, meat products, bottled water, and so on. With an emphasis on the "heart" of its employees, dramatic red type and image elements form a system of branded iconography that positions the success of the company and its products as the result of intense commitment to quality, enjoyment, and work ethic. The publication's booklike format—hardbound and sheathed in translucent vellum—along with silver foil papers, perforations, styled food images, and humorous photos of employees, deliver references to cooking, serving, interspersed with vivid typographic statements, thoughtfully styled financial data, and documentation of business development and performance. The sequential alternation of editorial, image, and financial content imparts a kind of cookbook of recipes for success—a variety of conceptual and managerial ingredients mixed together intuitively to create something special. Typography, accordingly, ranges from expanses of huge red sans-serif letterforms against clean white

pages to detailed text setting in contemporary serif, replete with careful hierarchic distinctions through weight and scale change, well-considered spacing around figures in tabular columns, and delicate dotted and solid rules that direct the readers through more complex information. The integration of wit, style, and expressive visual treatments with clear, sensible, editorial structure and typesetting speaks to the company's corporate culture of hard work and good living.

5

6

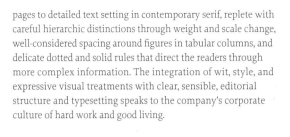

SOUR BEET WITH ROLLS

1 kg sour beet, 4 dg dry bacon, 4 cloves of garlic, 1 tablespoon flour, bay leaf, salt, grains of pepper, 1 Vegeta tablespoon. For trimming : 1 Cmok potato pasta mixture. Rinse sour beet if too sour and cook with bay leaf, grains of pepper and Vegeta. Finely chop dry bacon and garlic in a mixer or chop finely, add beet and leave to simmer until tender. Before done, add flour mixed with water and sparkle with salt if necessary. While cooking beet, prepare rolls from Cmok potato pasta according to the recipe on the packaging or take done from the freezer, cook before serving. Serve beet with rolls sparkled with butter-fried breadcrumbs.

DIONNAISE TURKEY

1.30 dg turkey breasts (1 piece), 1 tablespoon Dijon-mustard, 1 tablespoon grape mustard (mustard with ground mustard-seed), freshly ground black pepper, salt, 1 dl white wine or 0.5 dl vermouth, 3 dg butter, 3 dl cream, 2-3 apples, 2-3 pears, 0.5 dl oil, 1 Vegeta tablespoon. Marinate turkey: smear the meat with mustard and Vegeta mixture. Leave on room temperature for two hours. Put oil in baking pan, marinated turkey breasts, sparkle with pepper and bake on 180°C for 90 minutes During baking, occasionally water. before done baste with wine or vermouth. Warm butter in a pan, add peeled and sliced apples and pears, stew shortly, add cream, mustard collected from the meat surface, and dripping. Moderate temperature lower and cook the sauce for 5-10 minutes. If necessary sparkle with pepper and salt, and baste over cut meat. Serve warm with cooked noodle stripes, rice or corn soufflé.

1

The clothbound hard cover, wrapped in parchmentlike vellum imprinted with cooking icons, presents the report as a kind of cookbook.

2, 4, 6

Surprising spreads with huge red typography alternate with near-clinical, kitchen-clean spreads of white space and simple statements, as well as pages whose stock unexpectedly changes. The alternating mix of editorial, humorous, and financial content in various styles, featuring an assortment of production techniques, involves the audience in the company's business recipe for success.

3

In contrast to the expressive treatments of image and typography throughout the spreads, financial data is treated soberly, in sensible column structures detailed with rules and bullets for informational accessibility. Prose and tabular data are inset from the format edges with generous margins, focusing the attention of the reader when it's important for him or her to pay closer attention.

5

Just for fun, a series of theatrical photographs pose employees and executives in warm red scenarios. Clearly, the people running this company like to have fun in their work.

1

The catalog covers allow an opportunity for more expressive styling. Dynamic, ambiguous space and energetic composition, while contrasting the frontal, deliberately more reserved photographs within, still use actual employees as models. Linear rules and bitmap typefaces add a technological quality to the communication.

1

1–4

Bold colors, drawn from the world of sporting uniforms, enliven the pages and tie the silhouetted models to the various elements in the spreads.

20:04

SOCCER IS OUR WORLD. TEAMWEAR IS OUR LIFE

CHALLENGER TEAMWEAR
www.challengerteamwear.com

800.878.2167

Catalogs

Product and Service Offerings in Print, from Hardware and Art School Courses to Performance and Fashion

Challenger
Tracy Design | *Kansas City (MO), USA*

Product catalogs have the potential to be repetitive. Perhaps more than other kinds of publications, they must inspire their readership. In this catalog for sporting goods (specifically, soccer uniforms and equipment), the designer has capitalized on some of the visual energy associated with the subject—the varied, saturated colors of uniforms and the technological aspect of the equipment's manufacture—and wrapped the subject in a friendly, real-world concept. The models in the catalog are all company employees who play or coach the sport. By using real people instead of professional models or celebrity athletes, the designer can both manage the production budget and convey the idea of the sport being an accessible, inspiring activity that everyone can enjoy. Presenting the uniforms and soccer balls plainly on the people, or in their hands, gives the products an honest credibility. Within detailed product listings, images of specific products are silhouetted and presented against plain backgrounds so they can be easily relocated, changed, or deleted from edition to edition. Bold colors code the sections for easy reference. The list text itself is structured in a consistent, systematic application of case, weight, and size treatments that helps readers find size and material specifications, product numbers, and prices without difficulty.

2, 3
Straightforward shots of employees, posed simply with sporting gear, are fresh and direct, avoiding high-profile athletes and intimidating hard-bodied professional models who might distance the company and its products from its consumers.

2–4
The folios, heads, and call-outs are distinguished clearly for quick reference but also sensitively sized and weighted to let the product listing components draw the reader's attention. Within product listings, bold and cap settings set off informational components.

Elam
Designwork SrL | *Udine, Italy*

1

Juxtaposing quirky, semiabstract illustrations with serene, grid-based layouts, this catalog for a system of residential kitchen furnishings communicates the fun of cooking and entertaining while presenting the high-end merchandise clearly in contemporary settings. The bulk of the catalog is devoted to beautifully composed photographs of the manufacturer's kitchen systems in situ, shot with natural light from numerous angles. Close-in details and long shots show the kitchens in their home environments. The designers pace the detail and scenic images to alternate, creating a rhythm of scale change and complexity. Single-page images back up against flat fields of rich color, and inset images lay side by side across the column structure. Just as important in the sequencing is the relationship of shapes, angles, and colors from one image to the next, so that two photo-graphs displayed side by side in a spread integrate into a unified composition. Colored dividers, which carry marketing copy in a four-column grid, separate the individual product lines. All the type is set in a single size and weight of a very neutral sans serif. In contrast to the slick, contemporary presentation, simplified, flat-color line drawings of kitchen utensils, jars, pots and pans, and food items offer a humorous, friendly touch. The illustrations place objects in linear or flat translation—sometimes filled with a photographic wood or placemat texture—against abstract shapes that call to mind serving trays and other paraphernalia. The simplicity of the drawings complements the austerity of the typography, lending additional style without competing for attention with the rich, luminous photographic images representing the products.

2

1

The cover (1) begins the catalog with one of the illustrations that appear within the pages (right). The simplified spoon form is filled with a photographic wood texture. Within the square format, the designers have decisively arranged the spoon against other forms—rounded-corner rectilinear shapes that might be placemats or stove burners—in a complex arrangement that creates a sense of movement around the various contours. Like the photographs, the proportions of shapes, the weights of linear elements, and the negative spaces between them have been resolved to a high degree to create harmonic compositions with tension, openness, and contrast between linear and flat forms.

3

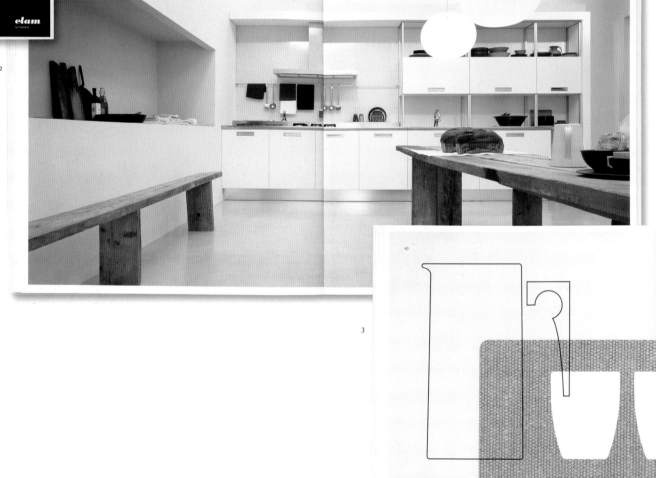

Bold, simple images adjoin more complex, spatial ones to unify compositions in a spread and to create movement through related forms across pages.

5

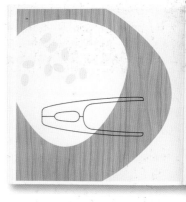

4

6

A smart, simple detail—the refraction of light through liquid that appears to bend the spoon in the glass—lends intelligence and wit to the illustrations.

7

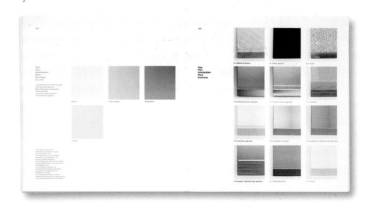

7

Technical specifications and an exhibit of accessories, finishes, and materials are relegated to the back section. Here, the four-column grid is used to clarify informational sets, with relevant subjects running in the leftmost column as indicators for supporting information or square inset examples arranged in the remaining three grid columns.

J.Crew
J.Crew Creative Services | Colleen Stokes, CD;
Lillian Hough, designer | *New York City, USA*

35

Along with its stores and ecommerce website, American fashion retailer J.Crew relies on its stream of catalogs to drive sales of its classic clothing. Major seasonal books—spring, summer, fall, and winter or holiday, which introduce complete lines of clothing—are supplemented throughout the year, averaging ten to twelve separate publications. In keeping with J.Crew's status a purveyor of comfortable, mostly casual, American fashion, its in-house design team approaches the layout of the catalog from several vantage points: the functional aspect of showing different apparel lines in all available colors, systematically supported by descriptive and pricing information so that the catalog can be used to order; the organization of apparel into story sections that are sequenced according to marketing objectives; and visual styling (in terms of model selection, environments, color schemes, and typography) to convey not only those messages specific to seasonal contexts but also those that communicate the essence of the brand and its position versus competitors. The latter aspect dictates a great deal of the design sensibilities that are leveraged in presenting the clothing: classic, unpretentious typography, sensible layouts that show the clothes clearly, and lifestyle-based imagery and color that reflect American attitudes about style, comfort, and cultural experience. In terms

1

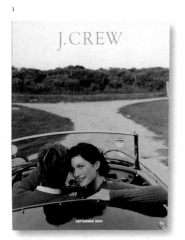

2

2, 3, 8

Apparel lines are promoted in stories, sequences of photographs that are related through the style of the items shown, the models wearing them, locations, and background colors or prop details. Each story begins with an opener that follows a similar structure—a full-bleed image opposite an expository arrangement of images, accompanied by a headline and introductory deck.

3

1–4

Models with diverse kinds of attainable beauty are selected to resonate with the aspirations of the customer; they are directed toward unforced, naturalistic poses that involve interaction with each other in typical weekend, vacation, or sporting activities. Environmental context plays an important role in establishing the clothing's position relative to the lifestyle; in this cover and selected spreads, the landscape and interior setting convey the easy, rugged, and stylish spirit of American life.

of function, the catalog is a machine of alternate grid structures that permit a wide variety of presentation, from grids of single items laid down on colored backgrounds, to on-figure shots of models in a studio setting, to photos of typical customers enjoying their J.Crew apparel as part of their daily lives in typical American locales. Functional strategies, such as stacks of fabric swatches and detailed product cataloging text, allow potential buyers to see available colors, understand specifics about garment construction or styling, and buy directly from the catalog.

4

5

6

7

8

2–8

Typography is limited to two families—a sharp, slightly condensed contemporary serif and a family of sans-serif gothic. The sans serif alone is used for all informational type—captions, color swatch names, sizing, and pricing. Promotional headlines and decks are set in the serif.

4–8

Garments are displayed in a system of presentations: the location shot on figure; the studio on figure; the single-item or "schmear" laydown, silhouetted against white or a color, or shot combined with accessories or props. Laydowns may appear in a number of grid configurations, accompanied by descriptive text, sizing, and pricing information: four-, six-, or nine-up on a given page.

Accompanying an exhibition commemorating the Dutch Municipal Transit and Waterways Agency's seventy-fifth year, this catalog presents information in a rich, layered experience that communicates its achievements and public role through time.

Historical and contemporary photographs are presented in freeform arrangements that contrast a consistent, academic, hierarchic two-column grid structure. The images, in duotones, tritones, and colorized halftones—as well as full-color—overlay one another, fade at their edges, and are superimposed with typographic elements, creating a predominantly horizontal motion that recalls our linear conception of time. This horizontal emphasis is countered by the text's vertical motion and the stark juncture between the two columns—one narrow (to the left) and one wide. The narrow column carries image captions and callouts; the wide one, primary text.

The catalog's typographic treatments are simple and distinct. Primary text is set in a relatively large-size serif, with ample leading to accommodate footnotes. Paragraph entry lines are set in a medium-weight sans serif and underlined, providing clear contrast. The same sans serif is used for captions and notes, as well as section headlines and introductory decks. A dot-matrix display face, used for section numbers at an extreme scale, titling on the covers and front matter, and selected expressive callouts, lends additional textural contrast and conveys the technological focus of the municipal agency's activities in monitoring traffic, water quality, and other public environmental aspects.

1

2

3

1, 2

While most of the type throughout is set in a neutral sans serif, details like numerals and some callouts are set in a dot-matrix typeface that lends a technological edge to the layouts. Vertically oriented section titles repeat the vertical motion of the narrow left-hand column that carries captions and other supporting text.

2

The simplicity of the text arrangement—one narrow column, one wide—is contrasted by the section opening image composites on the left pages, and by unusual treatments in the text itself. Here, for example, subheads are run inline with text but underlined and shifted above the baseline on which the first line sits.

2, 3

Text with different functions is set in different colors. The captions, for example, are set in a deep blue; their image numbers, in red, link the images to the running text, where the numbers appear as superscripts. Section titles and subheads are set in an ochre color.

CA Design '03
Chen Design Associates | San Francisco, USA

Neutral doesn't necessarily mean dull. Sometimes, neutrality—or the appearance of it—can be very intriguing, as in the case of this publication for an exhibit of current design practice in California. Aside from an opening segment and sparse end matter, the entire book is devoted to showcasing design work in five distinct areas: consumer products, graphic design, fashion, furniture, and transportation, which are represented by small icons that indicate the practice area of a particular project. Readers will immediately be struck by the book's fluid pacing, open and asymmetrical arrangements, and spatial layouts of material.

An apparent system of tick marks and linear grid references deceptively leads the design-savvy reader to believe that there is some regulating system when, in fact, there is none: the elements float, unattached to any structure. While there are outer margins and some relatively similar decisions about placement on occasion, every element in every spread—except for the folios—is placed intuitively where it needs to be placed. The designer makes visual connections among edges, angles, scale changes, groupings, verticality and lateral motion, but nowhere does a hangline remain consistent—nor alignment logic, nor column widths of paragraphs, nor location of icons, and so on. Balancing this randomness is a cool, effortless minimalism in the typography.

Only one sans serif face is used, and it is always the same size, weight, and set on the same leading. Paragraphs of running text are set justified, but everything else is set asymmetrically. Subtle color distinctions in text components clarify meaning. The result is an organic compositional journey that subversively transforms the neutral into something highly unusual.

1, 2, 4
Although some elements do align with each other, they never do so twice in the same way. Each relationship between elements on a spread—and between spreads—is unique, determined by the designer's own sensibility as to how the images should relate to each other to create a visual rhythm.

3
Only a color change between typographic components distinguishes them. This color difference is subtle, but sensitively controlled. The two-line firm and city notation is the darkest; the designers' or studios' names are the only type printed in black.

4
The dialogue between neutral and stylized continues in the way fashions are shown. To show drape, garments were photographed on mannequins, rather than people; the mannequins were then silhouetted, making them as neutral as possible. However, the designers took great care to ensure that no two mannequins were in the same position.

Cetinje Biennial
Arkzin | Déjan Krsic | *Zagreb, Croatia*

38

It is challenging to design exhibition publications that complement the exhibited work. One approach is to create a neutral field that essentially disappears around the artwork; another is to derive abstract, color-based, and typographic treatments from the art and let them interact with the subject. In the case of this exhibition catalog, the first published for a growing biennial exhibition in Croatia, the variety of work and text—in terms of media and sources—excluded the latter option; conversely, promoting the budding festival and exhibition energetically meant devising a unique visual presentation without upstaging the content. The result is a catalog with a strong, identifiable presence that nonetheless lets the art, along with contributed essays and artist profiles, speak just as forcefully. Produced only in two colors—black and red—the catalog effectively characterizes the visual legacy of the Balkan region: a mixture of potent sans-serif and serif typefaces, heavy rules, bullets, and dramatic composition give personality to the identity of the biennial. A five-column grid organizes content of wildly different kinds in a variety of presentations—two-column arrangements with captions; single, wide columns of text and large

2–4

A selection of contents and informational pages from the catalog shows the dramatic mixture of typefaces, heavy rules, and aggressive composition that characterizes the catalog. The designer plays with the grid here; type is permitted to bleed off the format edge; and color breaks call found words out of the titling.

1

2

3

4

1

The designer gave the catalog a title based on a Turkish artwork featuring the phrase "Love it or leave it." Transformed typographically with a condensed sans serif in all-cap setting and broken in red and black, the phrase becomes an identifier for the spirit of the biennial.

2–5

Aggressive display faces appear in titling and are used for the folios, transforming them from simple markers to active visual elements.

5

The Things We Always Wanted To Talk About workshop with
students from **art academies of Tirana, Cetinje, Munich, and Kassel** ●

Shkodra | **Albania** | **21-26/08** ● **Unpredictable work situation on site ● Prejudice ● Visions of one another ● Self-organization as an artist ● Artistic presentation to the outside ● Different location ● Building of networks ● Developing publicity ● Strategies ● Tactics ● How do you get money? ● Different educational systems ● Motivation ● Different media ● Support systems ●** MUNICH [prof. Olaf Metzel] Claudia DJABBARI |
Christian ENGELMANN | Anna FRIEDEL | Isabel HAASE | Franka KAßNER | Alexander LANER | Carsten RECKSIK | Tim WOLFF ● CETINJE [prof. Branislav Sekulić + prof. Pavle Pejović + prof. Mileta Grozdnić + prof. Anka Burić] Anka GARDAŠEVIĆ | Boris ABRAMOVIĆ | Ivana PEJOVIĆ | Miodrag ILIC | Saša VUKOTIĆ ● TIRANA [prof. Edi Hila] Adela DEMETJA | Fatmir JUKA | Irgin SENA | Syhabit SHKRELI | Violana MURATAJ ● KASSEL [prof. Björn Melhus] Aladin Bugi COROVIC | Daniel MASSOW | Franziska CORDES | Jutta HERMANN | Marco di CARIO | Markus BERTUCH | Oliver SCHARFBIER

30

callouts; listings of contributors; displays of artwork and artist profiles; as well as essays, interviews, and panel discussions. Sometimes, the grid is violated in favor of a particular kind of presentation, particularly in the context of more informational content, as in the table of contents and artist profiles. Still, the use of typographic treatments and color breaks is highly systematic—heads, subheads, captions, and notations follow consistent and detailed logic—and the varied arrangement on the underlying structure doesn't seem to sacrifice the overall unity. Rather, the visual style of the publication is quite recognizable and, given the range of content, appropriately dissimilar. Strong contrast, spatial breaks, and typographic confidence give the biennial a vibrant identity.

6

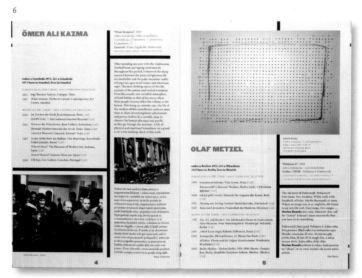

7

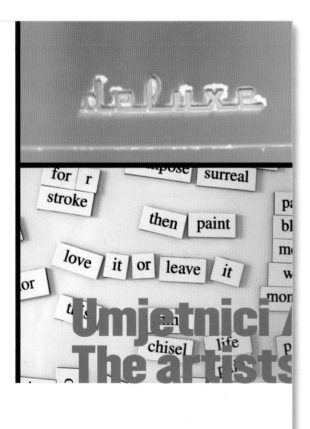

31

5

In this spread, the seeming disappearance of the five-column grid is a trick of the typographic arrangement; several column-widths are combined into one, with a wider left margin, to run a list of bulleted questions being considered in the text. The two-column presentation is common throughout for running text.

6, 7

A systematic logic is applied to informational material throughout the catalog. In this particular section, biographic information is set in a bold serif. Exhibition histories, prefaced by all-cap lines of regular serif, use a tabbed format, with hierarchical subdivisions clarified by posture changes. The titles of works shown in the profile, also in the serif face, run in red ink. Gallery locations are set in an alternate sans serif with quirkier details. Finally, captions appear in one sans serif at a smaller size, with weight change and vertical rules demarcating informational breaks.

Otis College of Art+Design
Studio Blue | Cheryl Towler-Weese | *Chicago, USA*

39

Each semester, Otis College of Art + Design in Pasadena, California, publishes a course catalog targeted to prospective students. The books are organized into major sections: front matter, used for conceptual messages that set the visual and editorial tone of respective editions; a section with information about the academic year, housing, and student life; a series of subsections detailing the various disciplines and course curricula; and a section with application and tuition forms. Among sections in a particular edition, strikingly different visual and structural treatments have been created to weave recurring information seamlessly into layouts that can vary in each edition; essentially, a kit of parts that can be reconfigured to reuse existing images while making space for new ones as semesters progress. Within a single section—the departmental descriptions and course offerings, for example—the structure may be simple: a block of color with paragraphs reading horizontally and callouts within text effected through changes in type style and color. In other sections featuring student work in various disciplines, the breaking of images in vertical bars, grids of images, and blocks of color create more complex compositions that are experiential in focus.

1

3

2

4

1, 4, 5

Stylized typefaces with scriptlike ligatures and linear geometric decoration provide enough edginess to appeal to prospective students looking for a cool "art school experience," but don't alienate readers by making information inaccessible.

1, 3, 5, 6

The *O* reference of the covers appears inside in different incarnations from edition to edition, alternately used as a background for diagrams, in photographs with students, or layered in as a texture that connects it to the content of a particular section.

2, 4

Numerous typographic variations appear among editions. The designers have created a kit of parts, so to speak—a set of stylistic and structural ideas from which they can draw as needed. Here, two kinds of vertical type arrangements are shown. One is used as an overall graphic (2), while the other is integrated into a photograph to repeat the vertical rhythm of the dress forms.

Alternating between the various type and image structures creates a kinetic pacing that is flexible and constantly fresh. While individual spreads may change, the system affords an overall unity among editions. The front matter, however, changes radically each time—in both its content and visual treatment.

Because the catalog represents the vision and creativity of an educational institution devoted to the study of art and design, the designers are permitted broad latitude in experimenting with typographic structure and detail, using unconventional, highly stylized typefaces, mixtures of grid-based and organic structures, abstract geometric and organic elements, and bold color combinations to convey the subject as dynamically as possible. Interestingly, informational clarity is never compromised despite the extremes of composition and typographic styling; careful attention is paid to creating recognizable and accessible arrangements of information that repeat in each section and are spatially and stylistically separated from the remainder of the content. These arrangements are used consistently so that readers are able to find them and acquire important information when needed.

1, 6

The cover of this particular edition can be removed and unfolded to create a poster of abstract paintlike forms. This visual language appears throughout the edition along with standard treatments.

7

Each section with academic information repeats a recognizable structure. Course descriptions appear in a column structure, set in colored blocks. Subheads are called out with a change of typeface and color. The wide head and foot margins are used to list important departmental information.

5

6

7

Colour Cosmetica
Voice Design | *Adelaide, Australia*

40

Eschewing expectations of full-color, glossy, stylized presentation, the designers of this course catalog for an educational institution that trains makeup artists, designers, photographers, and hairstylists approached the publication with the goal of clearly differentiating the school from its competition. Though glamorous color photography does play a role in the layouts, it is used to support the text and add spatial depth rather than to be flashy and glamorous for its own sake. Instead, the institute is given a visual persona that elevates the beauty and fashion professions—and their study—to the level of art. Black-and-white compositions of marks varying in complexity wrap the cover—predominantly white—and separate major sections inside the catalog. The marks appear to be composed from snippets of sketches, type elements, hair, grease pencil, or other detritus left over from the process of studying or designing. The program description pages are markedly more straightforward, contrasting the section dividers' expressive and evocative positioning with informative, structured listings of course material, facilities, faculty, and the like. Text is situated on the right-hand page, while a gridlike series of geometric photo arrangements adds color and interest. These images are cropped and combined in a mix of vertical and horizontal rectangles, squarish blocks of varying proportions—but

1

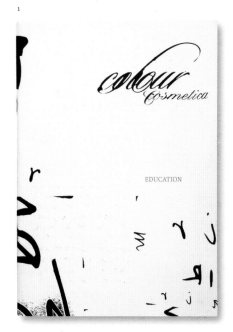

2

1–3

Black-and-white compositions powerfully redirect the perception of the school away from the expected toward a highly refined sense of the program as artistic training. Much of this communication results from the abstract qualities of the recognizable snippets that form the compositions, as well as their spontaneous, almost painterly, distribution around the format.

2, 3

Black-and-white divider spreads separate each section of the course catalog.

all adhering to a modular understructure independent of the type grid. Though they introduce a sense of the industry with high-contrast lighting, extreme close-ups of made-up faces, and dramatically colored hair, they do not compete with the information. At the same time, they subtly restate the cut-up, work-in-progress abstraction of the black-and-white compositions in a manner that integrates typographic geometry with the guiding visual concept.

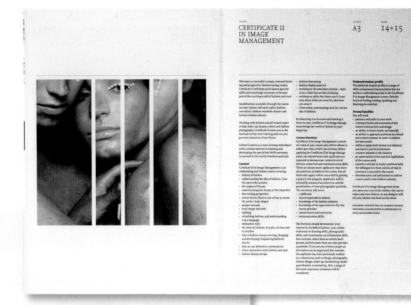

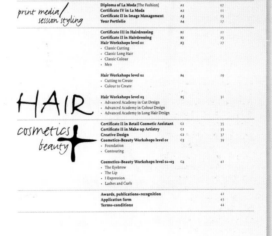

4

The sober arrangement of course information, in contrast to the organic power of the conceptual artwork, establishes credibility for the school as an institution of higher learning that can train professionals who happen to be artists.

4, 5

The photographic arrangements offer a third visual texture to the catalog, after the expressive artwork and grid-structured typography—color, depth, light, and movement—but is formally related to both art and type. It is expressive and cut apart like the cover artwork, but its croppings are geometric and defined on a modular system, as is the type.

SECTION B

Belden Fittings
Hutchinson Associates | *Chicago, USA*

41

The hallmark of successful mechanical engineering is repeatable, reliable performance; the designers of this catalog have communicated the client's commitment to this standard via accessible organization and tremendous attention to informational detailing in both image and typography. Every page—whether it's a section divider, specification page, or the cover itself—presents its information on the same hierarchic two-column grid. Two columns—one narrow, one wide—separate primary information from secondary elaboration in an asymmetrical sequence left to right. The grid itself repeats asymmetrically from left page to right page. Subject and relevant callout information appear in the narrow, left-hand column; supporting information follows in the wider, right-hand column. A system of horizontal breaks separates material top to bottom within the two columns: a narrow band at the top carries the individual product name and running head, along with the folio; a wider band carries callouts and supporting text; the middle area, wider still, presents images and diagrams; the largest division presents tabular information. Within these major page divisions, parts may be rearranged, added to, or altered to accommodate differing types of information. A network of structural rules of differing thicknesses—some solid, some dotted—in black or a colored ink, clarify the informational divisions, speaking to the precision and systematic nature of the material. The catalog is, in essence, a machine for getting product information quickly and in great detail. One sans-serif type family, in roman, italic, and in two weights, keeps the focus on accessibility and avoids competition with the crisp silhouetted product photography and exquisite engineering diagrams.

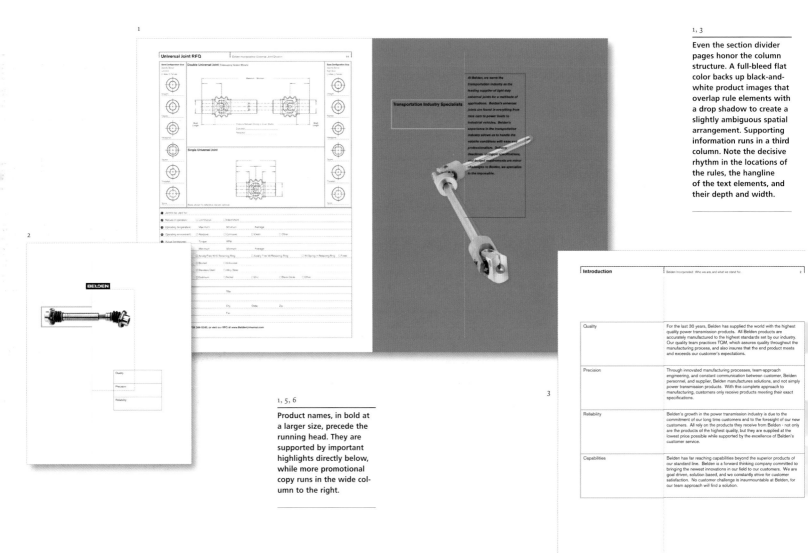

1, 3

Even the section divider pages honor the column structure. A full-bleed flat color backs up black-and-white product images that overlap rule elements with a drop shadow to create a slightly ambiguous spatial arrangement. Supporting information runs in a third column. Note the decisive rhythm in the locations of the rules, the hangline of the text elements, and their depth and width.

1, 5, 6

Product names, in bold at a larger size, precede the running head. They are supported by important highlights directly below, while more promotional copy runs in the wide column to the right.

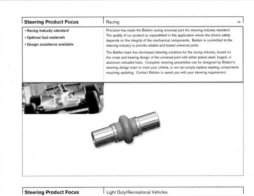

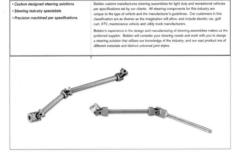

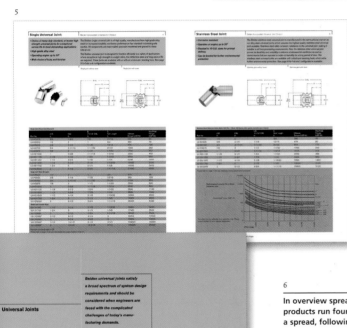

4

The table of contents presents a clear organization for each major product section, indicated by bold type, in a matrix of colored rules. Opposite the contents, a series of crisp photographs is accompanied by customer testimonials—one of the few technically unrelated items of copy in the catalog.

5

Informational tables are laid out with precision, the alignments of the columns reflecting the number of informational compartments needed and the space required to separate them adequately. Tinted bands of alternating darkness help link information for related specifications on the horizontal axis. Diagrams, much like the supporting text (and similarly linear in presentation), follow in the right.

6

In overview spreads, products run four up on a spread, following the same compartmentalized structure as the detail pages but doubled up on a single page. Heavier colored-rule boxes draw attention to the text. Images, as elsewhere, always occur in the left-hand column.

Takashimaya 10
Design: MW | Allison Williams, JP Williams |
New York City, USA

This catalog is the tenth retail catalog designed by the same studio for Japanese department store Takashimaya. Their long-standing working relationship has yielded a publication notable for its saturated and esoterically styled photography, rich colors and paper stocks, and jewellike minimal typography. The catalog is itself a high-end product, designed to be as much object as communication; clients are drawn to the store for its aesthetic inimitability. The first clue to this publication-as-object approach is the staggered interfold of the format—a Z-shaped base spine with two sets of signatures bound in opposing directions—in which the cover flap and pages end short to reveal contrasting

layers of color, texture, and image. Added to this already intricate binding are gatefold pages and matte-coated flysheets with a slightly slippery surface; these pages list product information and prices. The text prints a deep metallic on a smoky, desaturated violet background. A lightweight, slightly extended sans serif is set all uppercase in a justified column beginning a third or so below the top edge of the format. Details such as slashes, vertical rules, and other linear elements separate item names from descriptions and prices; the attention to letter- and wordspacing, column width, leading, and the attributes of punctuation results in finely tuned typography that becomes

1

1

A near zenlike—though thoroughly modern—simplicity of approach sets the store's name, alone, on the cover, countered by the hint of complexity offered by the stepped binding that peeks out from the sides. The smoky violet is characteristic of the color feeling throughout the catalog.

2

as much a luxury as the images. The photographs are mostly devoid of models (save one or two full-gatefold bleed occurrences that showcase jewelry), instead showcasing sensitively arranged tableaux of the products. Textures, forms, and color schemes among the objects in the photographs are considered and arranged to create interesting juxtapositions that enhance the individual qualities. Lighting is highly controlled to impart a dreamy, reverent—even spiritual—glow to the scenes. The quality of their reproduction is outstanding, all the more remarkable given that they are printed on an uncoated paper stock.

2–4

Product imagery dominates the catalog, arranged in artful compositions that are still and contemplative, yet decadent with color and texture. Curved forms and angles engage in dialogue with one another; glossy textures contrast rough, earthy ones.

3

The stark, machinelike typography of the body copy and product descriptions—all one sans-serif face, in one weight—offers minute typographic detailing but minimal interference with the presentation of images. Linear details enrich the text's understated whisper and clarify informational distinctions within the running copy. Note the absence of rivers and hyphens in the justified paragraphs.

3

4

1, 2

The stepped pages— longer for photographic spreads, shorter for pricing flysheets—as well as the binding, insist on unhurried exploration, revealing intriguing color combinations that change with the turn of a page.

1

2

1, 2

A large area of the front page is devoted to imagery; the appearance of illustration on the front page is a refreshing departure from convention.

The masthead is drawn in a quirky, condensed slab serif—reminiscent of old wood types—that lends a friendly, community-focused feeling to the paper and contributes to its accessible quality.

The left-hand column offers third-level story starts and pagination links to guide readers. At the top of the column, a personality of local interest and a pull-quote are featured. A minimum of story starts—treated systematically—is a recognizable navigation strategy that prevents readers from becoming overwhelmed.

Newspapers

Dailies, Weeklies, Tabloids, and Supplements

Postimees

Postimees In-House Design I Vahure Kalmre
Tartu, Estonia

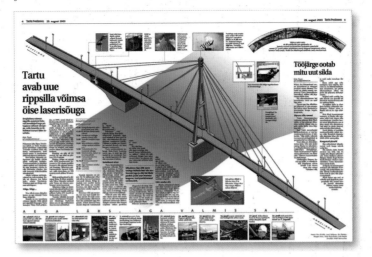

Imagery plays a tremendous role in the layout of the paper, even within interior spreads. Most of the photography used is color rather than black and white. In supplement pages, the images leave the boundaries of the grid. Here, an enormous silhouetted image interacts with text (5) and, in another example (6), the image forms a backdrop to the text structure and insets.

This Estonian newspaper makes use of a great deal of image and a navigable presentation. Like many papers, it is structured on a much more precise grid than is usually needed—twelve columns, even though most of the information on a given page will be arranged in five or six. An overall approach of simplicity, however, makes this paper easy to sort through, providing an opportunity to include very large images that enliven the pages.

This approach is immediately discernible on the front page, where three to four column widths are given over to imagery (these are sometimes illustrative, in a notable difference from most newspapers) that often spans the full height of the page from masthead to foot margin. The image area may include headline and lead info as well, directing the reader to a specific jump page to follow the story. A narrow column at left on the front page carries a commonly used device—a listing of content callouts for interior sections and supplements. To the right of the lead story image area, three to five secondary headlines and decks, accompanied by photographs, direct the reader to the major stories of the day.

Hard news stories and supplements share equally in presenting a wealth of color imagery. In the former, pictorial matter adheres more conventionally to the grid in rectangular insets; in the latter, the designers are granted some leeway in actively engaging imagery with the text—silhouetting dramatic shapes or floating type and inset images on top of full-bleed photographs. Two type families—a moderately condensed serif with slightly modulated strokes and varied contrast, paired with a family of sans serifs that is based loosely on a serif type—predominate. The serif is generally used for text and large headlines, while the sans serif is used for secondary headlines and supporting text, as in the left-hand column of the front page.

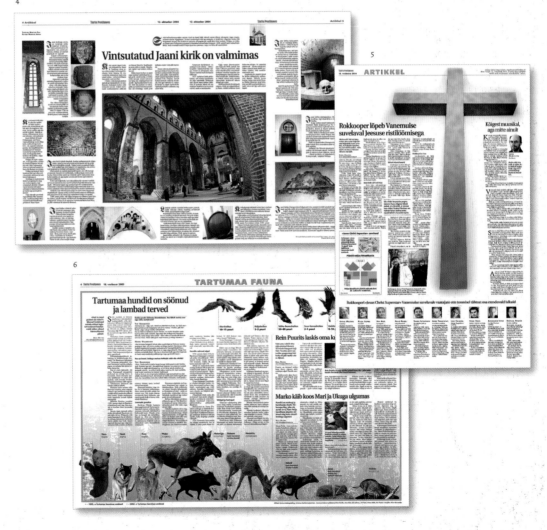

The Seattle Times

Jeff Neumann | *Denver (CO), USA*

This recent redesign of the *Seattle Times* combines a more precise and varied grid structure with a complex mix of typefaces, color treatments, and magazine influences to bring a dynamic, textural, and expressive quality to what is often a gray, uninteresting wall of informational text in conventional newspaper layout.

Without sacrificing legibility, navigational clarity, or the flexibility needed to produce editions with ever-evolving content rapidly, the *Times* design takes cues from other newspapers that have shifted toward more engaging, illustrative, and friendlier presentations of news. A tight twelve-column grid divided into twenty-two modular rows is used to structure articles on a number of compound column configurations: one, two, three, four, five, and six. Distinct column configurations—for example,

three- and four-column structures—may appear side by side on the same page, even contiguously in a given row-set, so long as their configuration adds up to the full twelve columns wide. Aside from creating subsystems for informational components that repeat each edition—such as the Newsline content flag at the left of the front page—the variety of text widths clearly separates stories and lends a dynamic tension among spaces that engages the eye and helps navigate the content. The use of several type families adds to this complexity. A high-contrast serif carries primary articles and their accompanying heads, decks, and subheads. Secondary content alternates systematically between a slightly condensed, tightly set sans-serif family and a similarly condensed slab serif, usually set in bolder weights for

1

2

3

1–3

The mastheads for major sections, such as Sports, use an all-uppercase setting of an inline serif with a great deal of contrast. This treatment derives from the inline detail of the *S* in the front page masthead, without requiring individual blackletter drawings of each masthead—drawings that would likely be time consuming to produce, would take up a great deal of space, and might compete with the primary masthead.

4

1, 2
Magazine-like headlines—here, the use of large-scale sans serif type in staggered-width lines and a tight vertical setting—help distinguish softer news sections from hard news.

4
Clarity is no deterrent to stylish, accessible presentation. The sizes, weights, and width proportions of the type are rigorously controlled for maximum visual effect. A simple weight change within enclosed decks add detail without distracting from higher elements in the hierarchy.

contrast. Sometimes, the sans serif makes an appearance as a deck within the domain of a serif-set article, adding further contrast.

Graphic devices—such as tinted zones, callouts, sidebar boxes, colored subheads, and magazine-like feature-article titling set in a large scale—help invigorate the grid and give distinct character to subsections, such as the Sports pages or the Entertainment and Dining section. These pages also exhibit a characteristic unusual in newspapers: the introduction of white space among columns, further distinguishing these sections from the hardcore news reportage and bringing a more magazine-like feel to the layouts. A host of typographic nuances, such as vertical slashes, bullets, indents, rules, and varied case/weight settings, helps carry the energy of the pages into the smallest details of the typesetting.

5, 6

The front page of the paper is a study in variations—in column width, text size and style, linear detail, color, and space. All told, there are more than ten different, unrelated compartments of information organized for easy navigation: a headline story and three secondary stories, a Newsline listing to the left, and leads for four major sections above the masthead. Part of the clarity of the organization comes from the different column widths that are created from the precise underlying grid: varying the column widths among stories makes them appear optically different. Type style, size, and weight also help differentiate material.

5

The masthead is set in a bold blackletter style that has been altered to improve legibility. The x-height of the lowercase letters has been enlarged, opening the counters and allowing their strokes to be thickened and simplified. An inline detail along the spine of the *S* introduces texture and calls out the initial letter of the city name.

The Seattle Times — front page

Sports >
GARCIA SHACKY, BUT MS WIN 3-1

Food >
CHICKENS HOME ON THE RANGE

NWLife >
DEPRESSION IN YOUNG KIDS

Business >
TELEMARKETERS STILL CALLING

The Seattle Times

METRO EDITION

WEDNESDAY
AUGUST 13, 2003

25¢ King, Pierce, Snohomish Counties and Bainbridge Island · 50¢ Island, Kitsap and Thurston Counties 75¢ Elsewhere

INDEPENDENT AND LOCALLY OWNED SINCE 1896 · seattletimes.com

2 Pakistanis arrested at Sea-Tac; one man's name on terror list

BY MIKE CARTER AND CHERYL PHILLIPS
Seattle Times staff reporters

MISSILE-SALE PLOT FBI arrests Briton > 10
BAGGAGE SCREENING Overhaul at Sea-Tac > Local 1

Windows worm hits PCs worldwide

MICROSOFT TARGETED

Viruslike program snarls businesses, slows internet

BY KIM PETERSON
Seattle Times reporter

If you think your PC has been attacked:

MORE WAYS to deworm your PC > 9

Newsline
A quick look at today's news

Liberian rebels: Say they'll withdraw from capital by tomorrow > 3

Suicide attacks: Palestinian teens' attacks slow Mideast peace prospects > 3

Organ donors: Living donors rather than cadavers now the main source for organ transplants. But risks not always revealed > Closeup, 3

Herbal supplement: One study shows cholesterol raised rather than lowered > A 4

Raymond deaths: Police looking into roles of husband and wife in deaths of three friends > Local 1

Sen. Paul Roach: Claim filed says she doesn't live at Enumclaw address and therefore is not eligible to run for King County seat > Local 1

Seattle Storm: San Antonio snapped Storm's 8-game home winning streak, 87-77 > Sports 1

Telemarketers: Do Not Call Registry with 30 million numbers still has some loopholes > Business 1

McCormick & Schmick is hot: Portland restaurant grossed $11 million last year > Business 1

Jobless rate drops: going from 7.8 to 7.5 percent in July doesn't mean recovery, experts say > Business 1

Depressed kids: Doctors diagnosing mental illness at younger and younger ages > NWLife 1

> Breaking News
seattletimes.com

Today's Weather
Mostly sunny after morning patchy clouds. High 74, Low 49. > BEHIND LOCAL

Index
Comics > NWLIFE 6,7
Crosswords > NWLIFE 7
Dear Abby > NWLIFE 8
Deaths/Funerals > LOCAL 4
Editorials > LOCAL 6
Lottery > PAGE 2
Movie Listings > NWLIFE 3
Sports on the Air > SPORTS 11
Television > NWLIFE 8

SARS crisis over, Asian adoptions resume

DEAN RUTZ / THE SEATTLE TIMES

After months of waiting for China to grant them permission to travel there to adopt their baby, Vivian Rose-and-after waiting even longer when travel was halted during the SARS outbreak-Beth Ziebell-Cram and Christopher Cram returned to Mount Vernon with a baby girl. Dozens of other families have shared the same ordeal. > CHINA ADOPTION, LOCAL 1

Families worry that quick tour turning to long-term occupation

Troops told to expect at least a year in Iraq

BY NIKO PRICE
The Associated Press

SCOTT NELSON / GETTY IMAGES

Pfc. Cesar Mujica and other soldiers of the Army's 4th Infantry Division have been told they will be rotated home from Iraq around April. > SOLDIERS, 11

8,000 doctors back federal health system

OPPONENTS DISMISS REFORM AS TOO RADICAL

Plan would abolish insurance companies and for-profit hospitals

BY KYUNG M. SONG
Seattle Times staff reporter

Healthtoday

ORGAN DONORS: Living donors often not tole about risks > Closeup 3

"BOUTIQUE" MEDICINE Doctors and patients praise flat-rate system > Local 1

DEPRESSED KIDS Mental illness diagnosed at younger ages > NWLife 1

> HEALTH PLAN, 12

> The Back Page

PRACTICAL GARDNER
Growing citrus here in apple land
Behind NWLIFE

> WINE
> Cave B winery
> Cooking with wine
> Wine Q&A
Behind FOOD

294 King, Pierce, Snohomish Counties and Bainbridge Island · 50¢ Island, Kitsap and Thurston Counties · 75¢ Elsewhere

Copyright 2003
Seattle Times Company

REACH THE EDITORS: David Boardman/Managing editor 206-464-8278 dboardman@seattletimes.com | Mike Stanton/Front Page editor 206-464-8284 mstanton@seattletimes.com | Suki Dardarian/Local and Sunday 206-464-8284 sdardarian@seattletimes.com

---

LOCAL News — section front

The Seattle Times

LOCALNews

Opinion pages
It's about time DSHS ensures employees, clients free from sex harassment > EDITORIALS, 6

Roach residency challenged

CLAIM FILED SAYS 9TH DISTRICT CANDIDATE DOESN'T LIVE AT ENUMCLAW ADDRESS

Senator moved in with friends, pays rent, even though husband lives in Sumner

IT'S CLEAR: YOU LOVE ME NOT

Nicole Brodeur

Wife's role in deaths scrutinized

WITNESSES SAY WIFE ATTRACTED THE VULNERABLE

Prosecutors prepare charges in 3 deaths, looking into fourth

Precious delivery from China

Patience, persistence pay off for Mount Vernon adoptive family

Baggage screening to get overhaul at Sea-Tac

$140 MILLION NOT FROM PROPERTY TAXES

Plan includes new building, bomb-detection machines

In this section >

—REDMOND CONDOS: Hundreds swing hammers in Habitat for Humanity project >

—BOUTIQUE MEDICINE: Patients, doctors praise system >

NORTHWEST WEDNESDAY >
SUNRISE & SUNSET >

Publication Design Workbook | Publications in Action

Vecernji List
Mirko Ilic Studio | *New York City, USA*

The driving structural conceit behind the prototype redesign of this Croatian news daily is the placement of the masthead vertically along the paper's spine. This position not only creates the largest possible masthead of any newspaper but also responds to the fact of papers stacked at newsstands on the street. In a pile, the repetition of the colorful spines in an edition creates a highly visible and recognizable branding presence among other papers. The verticality of the masthead influences the articulation of the paper's six-column grid, inspiring an approach that creates channels of pictorial and text content with a pronounced effect on the way stories and images run together. Broken by strong median flowlines at intervals of halves and quarters, stories may fill the six columns left to right within the fractional section; the columns within one of these sections may arbitrarily be reduced in number to create visual difference from the other. Overall, the quarter and half divisions make for clear storybreaks, especially when they jump from lead page to another. Often, the jump follows in the same relative location on the new page;

1

2

1, 2

The vertical rhythm of the column structure—and more simple horizontal intervals—creates an easily navigable and flexible structure for images and text. On the front pages shown here, a grouping of columns creates a wide vertical channel for top featured stories and large images, with additional channels for secondary stories and leads to other sections.

3

A comparison of *Vecernji List*'s presence against competing papers makes a clear case for the designer's idea of running the masthead along the paper's spine. In the mass of busy, textured tabloids, the red stripe is a standout even on its own— let alone when the papers are stacked.

even when it doesn't, the simplicity of the page divisions aids continuity. Alongside a primarily sans serif typographic presentation (with a serif used for subordinate material), a set of geometric icons directs readers to the entry points of articles and other pertinent details, such as the story location. A system of bright, easily differentiated colors customizes the various supplemental editions, such as film and automotive sections. Within the hard news sections, corresponding bars of color head teasers that link to the supplements.

6
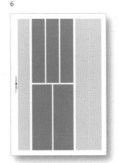

7

8
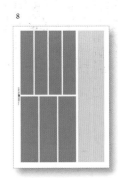

3

4

5

Ivana Banfić

DVOBOJ: SANDRA BAGARIĆ I SANJA DOLEŽAL

Sandra stasom, Sanja glasom
Medicinski zanimljiv i svakako će pomoći pri daljnjim istraživanjima u liječenju bolesti jetre nastojanjem da se, gdje je god to moguće, izbjegne presadivanje medicinski zanimljiv i svakako će pomoći pri daljnjim istraživanjima u liječenju bolesti jetre nastojanjem da se▸ 28

4, 5

The Screen section (4), covering film and television entertainment, uses a similar masthead structure and one of the supplementary colors from the color coding system. The simple half-based flowlines and vertical channels are visible here as well.

6–8

Strong, multichannel vertical movement helps separate single stories—and groupings of smaller ones, as seen in these grid diagrams from the paper's style guide. Horizontal subdivisions are fewer and based on halves, massing information within the vertical channels into even clearer groupings.

SJM Television
San Jose Mercury News | Stephanie Grace Lim
San Jose (CA), USA

Under the constraints of tight deadlines and quality limitations imposed by paper stock and press work, this series of illustrative covers for a newspaper's supplemental television schedule uses hard-edged vector drawings and simplified, high-contrast photographic elements. Avoiding potential quality issues in reproducing color photographic halftones on newsprint, each cover presents a typographic or simplified line-work illustration, representing one featured program for a given week. The illustrations often use only black and a single accent color. In combination with a consistent masthead and secondary titling type, the result is a quick visual statement that engages readers in an uncomplicated, fun, and immediate way.

1

2

3

4

1, 2

Typographic illustration is the most commonly used imagery for the covers of this newspaper supplement. In these two covers, type is used dramatically in a large-scale texture (1) or as a substitution for part of a diagram-like illustration (2): a supporting deck replaces the body of the stick-figure child.

3

A simplified graphic translation of a face presents the same immediacy in engaging readers as does a typographic solution.

X-TRA / X-TRA FF
CODEsign | *Leonardo Sonnoli* | *Rimini, Italy*

47

Simple, posterlike cover systems for these related publications make bold use of space and typography. For *X-TRA FF*, the issue number dominates the central area of the tabloid sheet. Its stark, uniform bold weight is mediated by an image of classical sculpture or antique sports figures. The photographic images are formally congruent with the gigantic numerals in the simplicity of their contours, while adding detail and texture with their valued tonal range. On the covers of *X-TRA*, ingenious color drawings of the masthead letters—X, T, R, A—are arranged in quadrants and other geometric relationships, adding bold color and an abstract presentation that constantly changes.

The masthead itself is spread across the upper quarter of the front page in an uppercase setting of a medium-weight sans serif. Volume and issue number, date, and content callouts are arranged still further above, flushing left against column divisions defined by the grid inside the papers.

The interior spreads follow a straightforward four-column grid and display text in one sans-serif face at various sizes; occasionally, a colored ink is used as an accent.

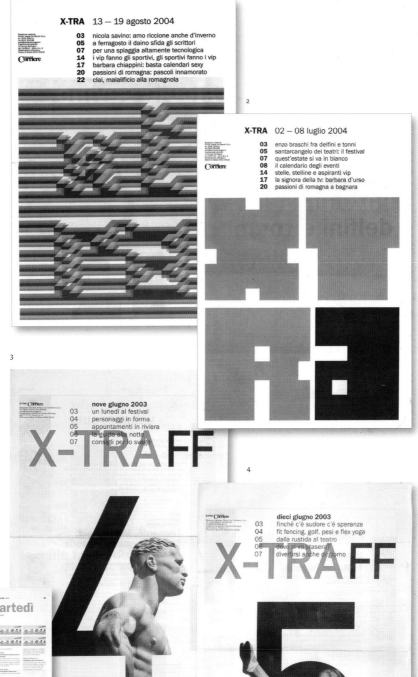

1, 2

Vividly colored lockups of the masthead letters results in an ever-changing cover image. These experiments range in complexity from abstract surprints of line in different inks (1) to simple, geometric translations of the four letters (2)

3, 4

Stark combinations of letterform and figure evoke European athletic posters of the early twentieth century. Photographs of real figures (3) and sculptures (4) are interchanged as needed, depending on what image best interacts with the issue number.

5

A sample interior spread shows the four-column grid and use of an accent color to enliven the straightforward layout.

Slobodna Dalmacija
Arkzin | Déjan Krsic | Zagreb, Croatia
Mirko Ilic Studio | Mirko Ilic | New York City, USA

48

One aspect of this Croatian newspaper that strikes viewers immediately is the deep blue color of the ink. In the paper's recent redesign, which took place during a difficult transition into privatization, the designers turned financial and technical hardships to their advantage, creating a new look that referenced the paper's history—the blue ink being a holdover from the 1950s and a single-color press that necessitated that each section be produced in its own color.

1–7

The deep blue ink creates an immediate impression of difference between this and other newspapers; it is rich and colorful in text, but strong enough (and somewhat desaturated when it is tinted) to carry halftones. Occasional details in red ink are a dramatic surprise.

1

4

3

Along with the introduction of as-yet-unpublished newspaper serifs and gothic faces, supplied by Hoefler and Frere-Jones of New York City, the designers further evolved the old-fashioned qualities of the paper to differentiate it from its better-financed competition. The deep blue ink becomes noticeable in the large-scale feature headlines and story subtitling, set in a mixture of condensed and rounder, geometric sans serifs. Heavy rules reference early twentieth-century propaganda publications, complementing the bold gothic headlines and breaking up the texture of the pages. Thinner rules continue the logic as separators for picture captions. Serif type runs in justified columns, while the sans serif is set flush left/ragged right. The geometric sans serif is generally used for feature story decks and callout lines above titles; the serif is sometimes used at large sizes for headlines in specialized sections and in supplements. Mixing three-, four-, five-, and six-column configurations provides dramatic separation between story blocks, with different column structures flowing above or below each other within similar overall widths—a four-column feature story in the upper section of a page, for example, fits the same width as three columns in a secondary article below.

1–7

Gotham and Champion, faces provided by Hoefler and Frere-Jones, complement each other in their boldness but provide different rhythms for heads, decks, subheads, and captions. The Champion is rather condensed, whereas the Gotham is much rounder and geometric in its drawing. Heads running all uppercase, as well in mixed case, provide added contrast and flexibility.

3–5

Supplements and softer news sections make use of the serif face at a large scale that is nonetheless elegant and clearly different from the rapid-fire presentation of the hard news section. Images halftoned in the blue ink take on an unusual character but retain their strength.

1–7

Bold horizontal rules separate unrelated articles, breaking up the wall of text with dramatic contrast.

Directory of Contributors

AdamsMorioka, Inc.
8484 Wilshire Boulevard, Suite 600
Beverly Hills, CA 90211 USA
www.adamsmorioka.com
17 | 24 | 57 | 59

Allemann, Almquist + Jones
124 North Third Street
Philadelphia, PA 19106 USA
www.aajdesign.com
54 | 67 | 191 | 206–207

And Partners, NY
156 Fifth Avenue, No. 1234
New York, NY 10010 USA
www.andpartnersny.com
67 | 85 | 110–113 | 196–197

Arkzin
c/o WHW
Baruna Trenka 4
HR-10000 Zagreb, Croatia
dejan_krsic@zg.htnet.hr
218–219 | 236–237

Blue River Design
The Foundry, Forty Banks
Newcastle-upon-Tyne, NE1 3PA UK
www.blueriver.co.uk
178

Bruketa & Zinic
Zavrtnica 17
10000 Zagreb, Croatia
www.bruketa-zinic.com
198–199 | 208–209

C. Harvey Graphic Design
415 West 23rd Street, Suite 4A
New York, NY 10011 USA
www.charvey.com
64 | 172–173

Chen Design Associates
589 Howard Street, 4th Floor
San Francisco, CA 94105 USA
www.chendesign.com
217

Circle K Studio
300 Brannan Street, Suite 308
San Francisco, CA 94107 USA
www.circlekstudio.com
21 | 63 | 200

CODEsign
Via Giordano Bruno 51
47900 Rimini, Italy
leonardosonnoli@libero.it
56 | 81 | 235

Conquest Design, Inc.
226 Massachusetts Avenue, Suite 2A
Arlington, MA 02474 USA
www.conquestdesign.com
57 | 188–189

Creuna Design
Stranden 3A
NO-0250 Oslo, Norway
www.creunadesign.no
56 | 66 | 67 | 144–149

Design: MW
149 Wooster Street
New York, NY 10012 USA
www.designmw.com
18 | 226–227

Designwork SrL
Via Gaeta 88
33100 Udine, Italy
www.designwork.it
23 | 25 | 51 | 73 | 128–133 |
162–163 | 212–213

Eggers + Diaper
Heckmannuferstrasse 6A
10997 Berlin, Germany
www.eggers-diaper.com
18 | 168–169 | 180–181

Empresa Editora el Comercio SA
Jiron Miró Quesada, No. 300
Lima, Peru
www.comercio.com.pe
152–153 | 194–195

Ewing Creative, Inc.
P.O. Box 219
Manchester, WA 98353 USA
www.ewingcreative.com
87 [Masthead Close-Up sidebar]

Faydherbe/DeVringer
2E Schuytstraat 76
The Hague, Netherlands
www.ben-wout.nl
26 | 40 | 51 | 83 | 116–121

Flat
391 Broadway, 3rd Floor
New York, NY 10013 USA
www.flat.com
24 | 71 | 164–165

Gorska Design
1277 8th Avenue, No. 105
San Francisco, CA 94122 USA
www.gorska.com
19 | 48 | 134–137

Graph Co., Ltd.
228 Moutani-Cho Kasai-Shi
Hyogo, Japan
www.moshi-moshi.jp
96–103

Hutchinson Associates, Inc.
1147 West Ohio Street, No. 305
Chicago, IL 60622 USA
www.hutchinson.com
21 | 67 | 224–225

Ideas On Purpose
27 West 20th Street, Suite 1001
New York, NY 10011 USA
www.ideasonpurpose.com
22 | 51 | 204–205

Inpraxis, Konzept + Gestaltung
Nigerstrasse 4
81675 Munich, Germany
www.inpraxis.com
160–161

Interkool
Schulterblatt 14
20357 Hamburg, Germany
www.interkool.com
77

J.Crew
770 Broadway, 12th Floor
New York, NY 10003 USA
www.jcrew.com
14–15 | 19 | 81 | 214–215

Kendall Ross
1904 Third Avenue, Suite 1005
Seattle, WA 98101 USA
www.kendallross.com
192–193

La Voz de Galicia
Avenida de la Prensa 84-85
15142 Arteixo, A Coruña, Spain
www.lavozdegalicia.es
47 | 104–109

Mirko Ilić Corp.
207 East 32nd Street
New York, NY 10016 USA
www.mirkoilic.com
232–233 | 236–237

Jeff Neumann
7124 West Weaver Place
Littleon, CO 80123 USA
jneumann@denverpost.com
21 | 25 | 31 | 33 | 79 | 230–231

OrangeSeed Design
800 Washington Avenue N., Suite 461
Minneapolis, MN 55401 USA
www.orangeseed.com
71 | 75 | 184–185

Postimees
Gildi 1, Tartu 50095
Estonia
www.postimees.ee
228–229

Premier Media Group
4924 109th Street SW, Suite A
Lakewood, WA 98499 USA
www.premiermedia.net
59 | 63 | 154–155

Ruder Finn Design
301 East 57th Street
New York, NY 10022 USA
www.ruderfinn.com
29 | 67 | 71 | 83 | 122–127 | 156–157

Rule29
821 Kindberg Court
Elburn, IL 60119 USA
www.rule29.com
179

Sägenvier Designkommunikation
Sägerstrasse 4
A-6850 Dornbirn, Austria
www.saegenvier.at
182–183

Scott King
35 Baker's Hill
London E5 9HL UK
Scott.king2001@virgin.net
158–159

Slatoff & Cohen
357 West 22nd Street, No. 4
New York, NY 10011 USA
tamarcohen@nyc.rr.com
71

**Soapbox Design
Communications**
187 King Street East, 3rd Floor
Toronto, Ontario
M5A 1J5 Canada
www.soapboxdesign.com
22 | 40 | 63 | 190 | 202–203

Stephanie Grace Lim
The *San Jose Mercury News*
750 Ridder Park Drive
San Jose, CA 95190 USA
slim@mercurynews.com
234

Stereotype Design
39 Jane Street, No. 4A
New York, NY 10014 USA
www.stereotype-design.com
190

STIM Visual Communication
436 West 22nd Street, No. 4C
New York, NY 10011 USA
www.design-stim.com
63

Strichpunkt
Schönleinstrasse 8A
70184 Stuttgart, Germany
www.strichpunkt-design.de
28 | 138–143

Studio Blue
800 West Huron, Suite 3N
Chicago, IL 60622 USA
www.studioblueinc.com
16 | 33 | 56 | 80 | 220–221

Studio Calavaria
3929 SW Council Crest Drive
Portland, OR 97239 USA
www.calavaria.com
23 | 30

Studio di Progettazione Grafica
Ca' d'Bariff
6675 Cevio, Switzerland
soberholzer@swissonline.ch
70 | 90–95 | 174–175

Tracy Design
118 Southwest Boulevard, Suite 200
Kansas City, MO 64108 USA
www.tracydesign.com
210–211

U9 Visuelle Allianz
Fichtestrasse 15A
D-63071 Offenbach am Main
Germany
www.u9.net
53 | 73 | 170–171

UNA (Amsterdam) Designers
Korte Papaverweg 7A
Amsterdam, Netherlands
www.unadesigners.nl
41 | 57 | 166–167 | 186–187 | 201

Voice Design
217 Gilbert Street
Adelaide SA 5000, Australia
www.voicedesign.net
222–223

Worksight
46 Great Jones Street
New York, NY 10012 USA
www.worksight.com
33 | 176–177

BIBLIOGRAPHY AND RECOMMENDED READING

Arnheim, Rudolf. *Visual Thinking.*
Berkeley and Los Angeles, California: University of
California Press, 1969 (renewed 1997 by the University
of California Regents).

Bosshard, Hans Rudolf. *The Typographic Grid.*
Sulgen/Zurich, Switzerland: Niggli AG, 2000.

Bringhurst, Robert.
The Elements of Typographic Style, Version 2.4.
Vancouver, Canada: Hartley & Marks, 2001.

Burnett, Ron. *How Images Think.*
Cambridge, Massachusetts and London, England:
The MIT Press, 2004.

Dair, Carl. *Design with Type.*
Toronto, Canada: University of Toronto Press, 1992.

Harrower, Tim. *Newspaper Designer's Handbook.*
New York: McGraw-Hill Humanities, 2001.

Jury, David. *About Face.*
Mies, Switzerland: RotoVision SA, 2002.

King, Stacey. *Magazine Design That Works.*
Gloucester, Massachusetts: Rockport Publishers, 2001.

Leslie, Jeremy. *MagCulture: New Magazine Design.*
New York: Harper Design, 2003.

Meggs, Philip B.
A History of Graphic Design, Third Edition.
New York: John Wiley & Sons, Inc., 1998.

Samara, Timothy. *Making and Breaking the Grid.*
Gloucester, Massachusetts: Rockport Publishers, 2001.
Typography Workbook. Gloucester, Massachusetts:
Rockport Publishers, 2003.

Acknowledgments

This book, like my previous two, is the result of a great deal of collaboration—mainly in terms of the contributions from a lot of very busy people that help illustrate the ideas within and provide a sampling of the ongoing evolution of the graphic design field. My thanks to all the designers who took time from their often hectic schedules to send me material. In particular, I would like to thank the participants in the case studies who, in addition to their work, provided me with their insight into their individual creative processes. Last, but by no means least, the team at Rockport—Kristin, Rochelle, Kristy, and Regina—deserves my gratitude once again for their patience, persistence, and hard work in helping to get this project from proposal to shelf, despite unexpected tribulations along the way.

This book is dedicated to Sean (also known as Beebee), my parents, my friends, Kissy-Squirrel, and all my students around New York.

About the Author Timothy Samara is a graphic designer and educator based in New York City, where he divides his time between teaching at the School of Visual Arts, NYU, Fashion Institute of Technology, Parsons School of Design, and Purchase College; and writing, lecturing, and consulting through STIM Visual Communication. His design work focuses on brand development and information design for corporate and nonprofit clients, in projects spanning print, environmental, and digital media. He has taught and lectured at U·Arts, Philadelphia; Newhouse School of Communications, Syracuse University; Western Michigan University; Rensselaer Polytechnic Intitute; SUNY Fredonia; Mohawk Valley Community College, Rochester; and Alfred University, Alfred, New York. He is the author of *Making and Breaking the Grid* (2001) and *Typography Workbook* (2004), both from Rockport. His fourth publishing project, *Type Style Finder*, is available in early 2006. Samara graduated a Trustee Scholar from the U·Arts, Philadelphia, in 1990 with a BFA in Graphic Design. He lives in New York's Chelsea district with his partner of five years.